Heroes and Landmarks of British Military Aviation

To Mum and Dad, with love, always

Heroes and Landmarks of British Military Aviation

From Airships to the Jet Age

Richard Edwards & Peter J Edwards

Pen & Sword
AVIATION

First published in Great Britain in 2012 by
Pen & Sword Aviation
an imprint of
Pen & Sword Books Ltd
47 Church Street
Barnsley
South Yorkshire
S70 2AS

ISBN 978-1-84884-645-6

Typeset in 11pt Ehrhardt by
Mac Style, Beverley, E. Yorkshire

Printed and bound in t e UK by CPI Group (UK) Ltd, Croydon, CR0 4YY

Pen & Sword Books Ltd incorporates the Imprints of Pen & Sword Aviation,
Pen & Sword Family History, Pen & Sword Maritime, Pen & Sword Military,
Pen & Sword Discovery, Wharncliffe Local History, Wharncliffe True Crime,
Wharncliffe Transport, Pen & Sword Select,
Pen & Sword Military Classics, Leo Cooper, The Praetorian Press, Remember
When, Seaforth Publishing and Frontline Publishing.

For a complete list of Pen & Sword titles please contact
PEN & SWORD BOOKS LIMITED
47 Church Street, Barnsley, South Yorkshire, S70 2AS England
E-mail: enquiries@pen-and-sword.co.uk
Website: www.pen-and-sword.co.uk

Contents

List of Maps

Chapter 1

Ernest Willows and the Airship over the Channel

The airship designer and aviation pioneer Captain Ernest Thompson Willows is mostly forgotten today, despite being the first person to fly across the English Channel from England to France in a heavier-than-air craft. His work and inventions went on to have an impact on military and civil aviation that has lasted to this day. Willows invented a method of powering a hot air balloon with two movable propellers that meant that for the first time dirigibles could be steered whilst in flight. Willows' pioneering invention opened the way in Britain for the development of the airship and a fledgling aviation industry. Not surprisingly, he was the first person in the UK to hold an airship licence, being awarded Airship Pilot's Licence Number 1 by the Royal Aero Club.

Willows was born to Joseph and Eva Willows on 11 July 1886 at a house in Newport Road in Cardiff, South Wales. His father was a wealthy dentist and sent Willows to Clifton College, an independent public school in the Clifton area of Bristol. He left school at the age of fifteen to follow in his father's footsteps and began training as a dentist, but his passion for aviation was a constant distraction. His aim was to develop a rigid framed dirigible that could be powered with a small engine and steered by the crew, thus enabling it to fly freely. With the backing of his father he gave up his dentistry training and began developing designs for his own craft, despite the lack of any formal engineering training or significant financial investment.

In 1905, two years after the Wright brothers made their pioneering flight, he completed the construction of his first airship, the *Willows I*, at Pengam Moors, two miles south east of Cardiff. He was just 19 years old. The airship was 74 feet long, 18 feet in diameter, had a silk envelope and a small gondola suspended below. The *Willows I* was powered by a 9hp Peugeot motorcycle engine that drove two propellers that were used to steer the craft. The site was later to become a private aerodrome, then Cardiff Municipal Airport and between June 1938 and January 1946 it was the site of RAF Pengam Moors. The *Willows I* took to the air for the first time on 5 August 1905 from East Moors and flew for an astonishing eighty-five minutes. Willows made a further five flights in the airship before he completed his second craft, the *Willows II*, which took-off on its maiden flight on 26 November 1909. The *Willows II* had a capacity of 20,000 cubic feet and was powered by a 35hp JAP engine. A series of high-profile flights in the *Willows II* helped to cement his position in aviation history as the father of modern airship development. On 4 June 1910 he gained a great deal of publicity when he landed the *Willows II* outside the City Hall in Cardiff, to the delight of the cheering crowds that had gathered to watch the spectacle. The flight over Cardiff was an attempt to win a £50 prize for the first person to fly over the city and an opportunity for Willows to maximize the publicity of his flights in order to try to attract valuable sponsorship to help him finance the development of his airships.

On 11 July he flew the *Willows II* from Cheltenham to Cardiff in just four hours. Then in August he flew the airship from Cardiff to London and broke three important records. The journey was the longest cross-country flight at that time, a total of 122 miles; it lasted 10 hours, the longest that anyone had ever been airborne and the route that he took meant that he became the first person to fly across the Bristol Channel. During the flight to London he had to descend to around 12 feet and use a megaphone to ask astonished passers-by for directions. In the end he made it by simply following the railway lines that he could clearly see below him, then along the route of the River Thames and over St Paul's Cathedral.

By 1910 Willows had built a name for himself as an airship designer and was determined to prove the viability of the airship for long-distance flights. He had heard that a prize of £2,000 was being offered for the first person to fly from Paris to London. In order to make an attempt on the prize and to gain valuable publicity he decided to undertake a flight from London and across the English Channel to Paris. He had already been working on a number of design improvements to the *Willows II* and so set about rebuilding the airship. The *Willows III* had a capacity of 33,000 cubic feet, was 110 feet long and had a maximum diameter of 24 feet. The airship was named *City of Cardiff* and it made its maiden flight on 29 October 1910.

On 11 November 1910 Willows took off from London and set off for Paris with his mechanic Frank Godden in the *Willows III* and in doing so became the first person to fly across the English Channel from England to France. The flight was not without incident. On around a dozen occasions during the flight Willows descended to around 12 feet and shouted to passers-by with a megaphone for directions. He had to climb out onto the envelope in the dark to make repairs. Petrol froze in the engine and during the night Godden dropped the maps over the side. The problem with the airship's envelope persisted and they were forced to land at two o'clock in the morning at Corbehem near Douai in the Nord-Pas-de-Calais region of France. French aviator Louis Breguet, who in 1919 founded the Compagnie des Messageries Aériennes, which would eventually become Air France, lived nearby. With his assistance Willows was able to repair his airship and continued his flight, arriving ceremoniously in Paris on 28 December 1910. He celebrated the new year a few days after his arrival by making a series of dramatic flights around the Eiffel Tower to demonstrate the manoeuvrability of the *Willows III* and his pioneering design. In January 1911 he returned to Cardiff with his airship by road and sea.

Willows believed that airships would prove to be much more practical as a means of travel than aircraft and in the years before the First World War had sold two airships to the War Office. In 1912 Willows established ET Willows Limited at 24–32 Villa Road in Hansworth, Birmingham. He offered stock dirigibles for sale, which according to one of his newspaper adverts included the 'City of Cardiff' Type to carry 4, £900 complete' and the 'New Light 2-Passenger Model, £370 complete'. The *Willows IV* was built in Birmingham and first flew in 1912. It became His Majesty's Naval Airship No. 2, when it was sold to the Admiralty for £1,050. The *Willows IV* had a capacity of 20,000 feet, was 90 feet long and had a maximum diameter of 20 feet. It was powered by a 35hp Anzani engine, which drove two four-bladed propellers that gave the airship a maximum speed of 50mph. A two-seater gondola was suspended below the airship, which was later adapted to allow for a third person. He used the proceeds from the sale to establish a spherical gas balloon school at Welsh Harp at Hendon. The following year he completed the four-seater *Willows V*, which flew for the first time on 27 November 1913 and was subsequently used for taking paying passengers on joy rides over London. The *Willows V* had a rubberized fabric covering and capacity for four people in the gondola.

During the First World War Willows built barrage balloons in Westgate Street, Cardiff. He is credited with having developed a barrage balloon that could reach an altitude of 10,000 feet, where other balloons at the time could only reach a maximum of 4,000 feet. In 1916 he joined the Royal Flying Corps at the rank of Captain. After the War he continued with ballooning but his pioneering achievements made him very little money. In October 1921 he was living in a run-down house-boat on the River Thames in London. He made a modest living making tethered balloon flights for paying passengers at fairs and attractions around the country. By this time Willows had begun to fade into obscurity and be forgotten, whilst others continued to achieve new records. In 1926 the Norwegian explorer Roald Amundsen, along with fifteen other men, was the first to fly over the North Pole in the airship *Norge* that was designed by the aeronautical engineer Umberto Nobile. Amundsen had led the first expedition to reach the South Pole and was the first person to reach both the North and the South Poles. The *Norge* flight included Lincoln Ellsworth, Hjalmar Riiser-Larsen, Oscar Wisting and an Italian aircrew captained by Nobile. They departed from Spitzbergen on 11 May 1926 and landed in Alaska two days later.

Willows died on 26 August 1926 at the age of forty-two. He had taken four passengers on a joy-flight in a tethered balloon at a flower show at Hoo Park in Kempston, Bedford, when the balloon's net covering began to tear. Very quickly the basket broke free and plummeted to the ground, killing all inside. Willow's grave is now overgrown and difficult to find in Cathays Cemetery in Cardiff, but thankfully Willows and his achievements are still remembered in Wales today. The Cardiff branch of the Royal Aeronautical Society inaugurated the annual Ernest Willows Lecture as part of the Centenary of Powered Flight celebrations and a special commemorative clock has been erected at Mermaid Quay, overlooking Cardiff Bay. The clock features a number of airships that orbit the clock face with a plaque located below that reads:

The Clock Tower. The dramatic clock above celebrates the life and achievements of local aeronautical pioneer Captain Ernest Willows (1886–1926). Captain Willows became the first man to cross the Bristol Channel in a powered aircraft, when he flew his airship from Cardiff to London in 1910. The clock's two faces incorporate kinetic elements, which illustrate key themes and events from Captain Willows' life.

A fitting tribute to a man who has faded from the consciousness of aviation history and deserves greater recognition for his role as an aviation pioneer.

The First into the Skies
The race to be the first to fly across the English Channel was given an impetus by Alfred Harmsworth, 1st Viscount Northcliffe, proprietor of the *Daily Mail* newspaper in London, who in 1907 began to offer substantial prizes for achievements in aviation. He offered a prize of £1,000 in 1908 for the first person to cross the English Channel in a heavier-than-air craft. French aviator Louis Blériot achieved this feat a year before Willows' airship flight. Blériot took off from Les Baraques in northern France on 25 July 1909 and covered twenty-two miles before he crash-landed near Dover.

However, neither Blériot nor Willows were the first to actually fly across the English Channel in any direction. This achievement and the real birth of today's airships began 124 years earlier on 7 January 1785 when French inventor and balloonist Jean-Pierre Blanchard, with American Dr John Jeffries, flew a hydrogen balloon from Dover Castle to Guînes, six miles from Calais. The flight took two and a half hours and earned Blanchard a significant pension from Louis XVI. Later the same year, on 15 June 1785, Jean-François Pilâtre de Rozier made an ill-fated attempt to cross the English Channel from France to England and was killed when his balloon crashed.

On 6 July 1784 a fish-shaped airship rose into the air amid the cheering huzzahs of a Parisian crowd. This airship, 52 feet long, 32 feet in diameter and with a cubic capacity of 30,000 cubic feet, had been manufactured by the Robert brothers of

Paris during the previous four months. His Grace the Duke of Chartres was in command; he had raised his hat to the crowd, stamped inside the car and given his instructions for the ascent. At first all went well as the airship had majestically floated away and risen higher, rowed by air oars 6 feet in diameter and operated by the occupants of the car. Despite using the principles calculated during the same year by General Meusnier of the French Army Corps of Engineers, various aerodynamic problems had not been solved. The airship continued to rise as the hydrogen gas in the envelope expanded until the vessel was almost in a state of bursting. At this stage the crew became distressed. His Grace the Duke of Chartres took command of the situation and pierced the expanded envelope with his walking stick, thereby releasing some of the gas so that an orderly and dignified descent was made. This was the first flight of any airship and it had been comparatively successful despite the shortcomings of the then known technology. Modifications were made and a further flight took place two months later.

The first successful flight by any airship driven under motor power was made by French engineer Henri Jacques Gifford in 1852. This airship had a capacity of 70,500 cubic feet, a length of 144 feet and a diameter of 40 feet. The vessel was powered by a steam engine rated at 3hp and propelled by two-bladed propellers 10 feet in diameter. On 24 September 1852 Gifford flew his airship from the Hippodrome in Paris to Trappes, a commune in the Yvelines department in the Île-de-France in north-central France. The flight was over a distance of 17 miles at a maximum speed of 5mph and the airship was steered by means of a sail. The main problem associated with flying during the eighteenth and nineteenth centuries had been the failure to discover a suitable power unit and it was not until 1860 that a heavy oil engine was built by Etienne Lenoir suitable for aerial navigation. Twelve years later Austrian Paul Hanlein built an airship with a capacity of 85,005 cubic feet, a length of 165 feet and a diameter of 36 feet that was powered by a four-cylinder gas engine rated at 2.8hp.

On 2 July 1900 Count von Zeppelin launched his first rigid airship from her shed at Lake Constance off Manzell near Friedrichshafen in Germany overlooking the Swiss border. The airship had a capacity of 399,000 cubic feet, a length of 418 feet and a diameter of 38 feet. She was pencil shaped, with sixteen aluminium transverse frames set at right angles to the direction of travel. Wire stays braced the metal transverse frames and girders connected each frame along the length of the vessel. This airship had been the work of a company formed in 1898 with a capital of 1 million marks, of which 300,000 marks had been subscribed from public funds. It was obvious that airship flying in Germany was becoming a reality and that a certain section of the German public took a great interest in its development.

British Airship Developments
Shortly after the Zeppelin flights Ernest Willows commenced his construction of airships at Cardiff in 1905. By comparison the much smaller *Willows I* had a

cubic capacity of 12,000 cubic feet, a length of 74 feet and a diameter of 18 feet. She was powered by a 9hp Peugeot engine and was fitted with propellers at each end of her keel. At this time the British government formed a strong interest in airship construction and development work was started by the Royal Engineers who had been manufacturing observation balloons in a small workshop at Aldershot. They brought their knowhow to South Farnborough in 1906 where an airship shed 160 feet in length and 72 feet in height was constructed and a large electrolysis plant for generating hydrogen gas was built near the hangar.

On 10 September 1907 Colonel John Capper RE completed the first British government-built airship. She had a cubic capacity of 55,000 cubic feet, was 122 feet long, with a diameter of 26 feet and was powered by a French Antoinette 50hp engine, which gave a top speed of 16mph. Unlike the German Zeppelin the British airship was a non-rigid, round-ended vessel. Her envelope was one large gas bag without any internal structure. Only the pressure of the gas kept the airship in shape. Beneath the envelope the control car was suspended by means of netting around the balloon. On 5 October 1907 this airship, now named the *Nulli Secundus* (second to none), made a long-range flight to London. With Colonel Capper in command and crewed by Captain King RE and Mr Cody, the airship flew to the capital where it circled St Paul's Cathedral and manoeuvred over Buckingham Palace. Meanwhile, development work by the small group of Army engineers continued apace with the building of the airship *Baby* by May in 1909. This airship had a capacity of 24,000 cubic feet, a length of 81 feet and a diameter of 24 feet. Once again the airship was a non-rigid design in which the envelope was blown up in the manner of a balloon. The airship was powered by a 25hp radial air-cooled REP engine, which had been salvaged from the second Dunne aeroplane previously manufactured at Farnborough. A maximum speed of 20mph was established but stability problems had been experienced with the envelope. Army engineers then decided to enlarge the envelope and having been re-launched the airship was christened HM Airship *Beta*.

During May 1910 the craft reappeared as a semi-rigid airship in which the ends of the envelope had been pointed and the cubic capacity increased to 35,000 cubic feet. A trial flight was made under the command of Captain King with Captain Carden and Lieutenant Westland as crew, during which a maximum speed of 22mph was achieved, later the craft was able to reach 35mph.

On 21 July 1908 Admiral Sir Reginald Bacon, who had observed the first international air races to France at Rheims, decided to forward a paper on the subject to Their Lordships of the Admiralty, which contained three main proposals. First that a Naval Air Assistant should be added to the Naval Staff at the Admiralty, second that the War Office should be asked if their superintendent of the Balloon Factory at Farnborough could be consulted by the Admiralty, and third that a rigid airship should be built for the Navy by a consortium of Vickers Limited and Maxims Limited. This paper found its way to the First Sea Lord, Admiral Lord Fisher, who was favourably impressed and the proposals were accepted by the Admiralty. It was submitted to the Committee of Imperial Defence for approval. The Committee agreed six months later and in the Naval Estimates for 1909 and 1910 an estimate of £35,000 was included to cover the construction of this airship. Naval airship number one was known as the *R1* because it contained a rigid frame and was sometimes known colloquially as the *Mayfly*. Construction commenced at the Vickers yard at Barrow-in-Furness with naval liaison under the direction of Captain Murray Sueter RN.

During 1908 the Navy, in co-operation with the Cabinet, had set up the Rigid Airship Construction Organization. The Prime Minister and Cabinet were directly in touch with the Committee of Imperial Defence under whom the Admiralty were operating. An Advisory Committee of Aeronautics had been established within the Admiralty organization consisting of ten members under Lord Rayleigh as President, which through the offices of an Inspecting Captain RN of Airships maintained liaison with Short Brothers, Vickers Limited and the Wolseley Engine Company. The committee comprised not only naval officers interested in flying but also members of the manufacturing industry who had a direct interest in airship construction.

The year 1909 was memorable for three major events that took place. In Germany the Zeppelin Airship Construction Company formed the Deutsche Luftschiffahrts AG for the purpose of transport operations. The company built hangars at Frankfurt, the finance capital of Germany, as well as Baden-Baden and Düsseldorf. During the next four years this company was to pioneer the first ever major airship passenger service and to its credit never lost the life of a single passenger due to an accident of any description. In France the Astra-Torres Airship Company formed a similar transportation organization called Compagnie Générale Transaérienne in association with Maison Clement Bayard and Société Zodiac. This passenger service had carried nearly 3,000 passengers within a short time of commencing the operation. In the United Kingdom the airship, which Admiral Sir Reginald Bacon had first suggested the previous July, was laid down and built by Vickers Sons and Maxims Limited at Barrow-in-Furness. The *R1* was a rigid airship that was 512 feet long, 48 feet in diameter, had a capacity of approximately 640,000 cubic feet and was manufactured in the metal duralumin. Power was obtained from two Wolseley motors of 180hp each.

With the Royal Navy now fully committed to the development of airships and the rapid progress being made by the Royal Engineers at South Farnborough, the development of British airships continued during the next two years by means of increasing the size of already existing vessels. Test flights were undertaken from time to time and in 1910 Captain HPT Lefroy, who in October 1909 had been put in charge of all wireless experimental work with the Army, manufactured a wireless telegraphy set at Farnborough for use on airships and aeroplanes. The Secretary of State for War, Richard Haldane, was so impressed with the development work that was being undertaken that an official inspection was arranged during November 1910 and the *Beta* was selected for a test flight. It was piloted by Captain Broke-Smith RE and Haldane became the first Secretary of State for War in any European country to fly. The wireless telegraphy experiments of 1910 were continued late into 1911 and proved highly successful with receptions of up to thirty miles distance. During this year the *R1* broke her back whilst being taken out of her floating hangar. The Admiralty, which had already spent £35,000, promptly disbanded the newly created Air Department and bluntly refused to throw further good money after bad. Airship development was subsequently vetoed by the Admiralty for the next two years.

In the years prior to the First World War airship enthusiasts of the Navy and the Army continued to press for further research, development and manufacture. Captain Murray Sueter and Lieutenant Colonel Mervyn T O'Gorman were sent by the Committee of Imperial Defence on a clandestine visit to Germany disguised as visiting Americans to observe German airship operations. With American accents and claiming a lack of knowledge of the German language they were able to take a series of trips in the passenger Zeppelins. Careful note was made of the method of operation, the crewing of these vessels, the training of service crews and other general information relating to the design. On returning to London the Committee were highly impressed with these and other operations, which had prised open many of the secrets of the Zeppelin's successes. As a result a new and serious interest was taken in training British airship crews, although the Admiralty Board did not take too well to the enthusiasm of the Air Department. Fortunately Vice Admiral Sir John Jellicoe had taken a trip on a Zeppelin during a visit to Berlin in 1911 and remained a supporter. By 1913 the air-minded officers of the Navy had been able to persuade the government to purchase an Astra-Torres airship from France and a small airship from ET Willows Limited for training purposes.

In August 1912 the Naval Airship Section was reformed as 1 Squadron Royal Flying Corps (Navy), enabling airships to take part in army manoeuvres in 1912 and 1913. The airship *Delta* was under the control of the attacking army and unfortunately broke down on its way to Thetford. The wireless telegraphy signals announcing the fact were clearly picked up. The airship *Gamma* was under the control of the defending army and wireless telegraphy messages from this ship were heard over thirty-five miles away. General Grierson in command of the defence noted that reconnaissance information was available each morning concerning the attacking army whilst in the Cambridge area. At the conclusion of the manoeuvres the airship *Gamma* conducted an experimental bombing operation on Cambridge. Subsequently, *Gamma* ran out of fuel, discharged its ballast, free ballooned in the air until dawn and landed safely at Bristol. During the summer of 1913 in Germany the Army was conducting its own manoeuvres in the area of Gotha. Colonel Erich Ludendorff of the German General Staff witnessed a competition between the Zeppelin LZ 13 Hansa and an aeroplane bombing a target with sandbags, proving beyond any doubt the Zeppelin's capability over the aeroplane.

The First World War

With the start of the First World War in July 1914 Germany's air power in airships consisted of seven rigid vessels and three non-rigid vessels. This flying formation was backed by a large industrial group, which within six months of the declaration of war had rapidly expanded, building laboratories, wind tunnels and engine test chambers. Production facilities existed at Friedrichshafen and at Potsdam. Schütte-Lanz GmbH shortly afterwards formed an industrial combine with the Zeppelin Company, which would enable the Zeppelin airships to be mass produced. It is noteworthy that during the coming year the Zeppelin organization alone manufactured twenty-six airships for offensive purposes. During the Battle of Jutland the scouting activity of the naval Zeppelins was considered by Admiral Scheer to be equivalent to the operational value of two extra cruiser squadrons. The importance of aerial operations was understood by the German armed forces that were backed by a population that was enthusiastic and understood this new form of transport.

In the meantime the small force of British non-rigid airships had successfully escorted the British Expeditionary Force to Northern France without the loss of a single ship; an uninspiring job of great importance. During October 1914 Admiral Lord Fisher, the First Sea Lord, called a conference at which he dramatically pointed out the seriousness of the increasing U-boat activities around the coast of Great Britain. Several weeks later he borrowed twenty midshipmen and proceeded to go into the airship production business. At this time Short Brothers and the Airship Company Limited of Merton in Surrey were called up to assist in this programme. The production envisaged was for the building of the SS class airship for anti-U-boat reconnaissance purposes. These airships had a capacity of 65,000 cubic feet and were powered by a 70 or 100hp engine dependent upon whether a British or French motor was available. They were able to attain a speed in excess of 40mph. At first the car containing the crew of two was a primitive affair consisting of a chassis for the attachment of equipment and two seats for the occupants who were protected from the outside elements by means of plywood sheeting in open cockpits. Developments improved the lot of the crew and they became housed in the fuselage of the Royal Aircraft Factory BE2c aeroplane suspended from the overhead gasbag by Eta patches. These patches were named after the army's last experimental airship, the *Eta,* and consisted of fan-shaped pieces of fabric that were attached to the airship's envelope, through which a 'D' ring was fastened so that gondolas and subsequently aircraft could be suspended securely by wires or straps. These airships were assembled by the Royal Navy at Wormwood Scrubs and later at the Royal Naval Air Station, Kingsnorth, at Hoo near the River Medway. The Sea Scout Coastal, twin-engined airship assembled at the Royal Naval Air Station,

Mullion, in Cornwall, was slightly larger with a capacity of 170,000 cubic feet with a length of 195 feet, a diameter of 39 feet 6 inches and a crew of five. These bigger airships were used for bombing the German U-boats and conducting anti-mine detection patrols.

During the course of 1914 and 1915 the production of non-rigid airships was given top priority in an endeavour to stem the successful U-boat campaigns, but little thought had been given to the use of airships on long-range bombing operations. The Germans had begun to utilize their airship fleet for aerial attacks on the United Kingdom, but it was not until the night of 8/9 September 1915 that German Zeppelin *L13*, under the command of *Kapitänleutnant* Heinrich Mathy, attacked the metropolis. The following day the Admiralty ordered the construction of the *R25* rigid airship, which was to be based on the design of the *R90* built by Vickers Limited at Barrow-in-Furness to the design of Dr Barnes Wallis.

In 1916 Short Brothers was awarded a contract to produce the *R23* class airships in association with Vickers at Barrow, William Beardmore & Company at Inchinnan in Renfrewshire and Armstrong Whitworth at Barlow near Selby. The government provided Short Brothers with a loan to enable the company to acquire a site at Cardington near Bedford in Bedfordshire in order to establish airship construction facilities. This enabled Short Brothers to focus its other construction work of heavier-than-air aeroplanes at its plant on the Isle of Sheppey.

Cardington

On the 3 September 1919 the new *R32* airship was walked out of the giant hangar for the first time. The *R32* was built to the same standards as the *R31*, with a wooden construction made up of glued laminated plywood. It was 615 feet long with a diameter of 64 feet 10 inches and a capacity of 1,535,000 cubic feet of hydrogen. The hull was of a special low drag shape designed from wind tunnel tests to reduce the loss of speed due to a non-aerodynamic cross section. The wooden parts were fireproofed and varnished to resist the weathering. The forward control cabin was attached to the hull and faired into a walkway that extended to the tail providing access to the engine gondolas by means of ladders. The 250hp Rolls-Royce Eagle engines drove two-bladed propellers 17 feet in diameter, which gave the airship a top speed of 65mph. The R32 left Cardington on its maiden voyage piloted by Captain Elmsley to the cheers of everyone from the base that had been given permission to take time off to see the new airship on its way. Subsequently, the *R32* was used for experimental work for the National Physical Laboratory at Teddington, which covered a period of eighty-four hours during which time Mr SJ Durston flew aloft with electrical test equipment in the corridor. Due to the danger from the hydrogen gas it was not possible to use electric light bulbs and the test engineer sat cold and frozen, at times in complete darkness. The airship was based at Howden, near Hull on the

Humber Estuary, where it was used to train the United States naval crew destined to take over the forthcoming *R38* on her completion and some 260 hours of training. The financial costs brought the *R32*'s operational role to a close when the frame was tested to destruction on 27 April 1921, whilst it was based at Howden. Unfortunately, Sir Hubert Wilkins, the Arctic explorer, had hoped to borrow the *R32* for a polar flight that would have gone north to Spitzbergen and then on to the Pole and Northern Canada. This would have been a great flight since the *R32* had a range of 2,000 miles, but at the time the government was not interested in Arctic exploration.

In May 1920 the Admiralty's Rigid Airship Committee recommended a programme of local airship flights during the summer months to be followed in 1921 by experimental flights to Egypt, where it was hoped a shed and mooring mast might have been built. The estimated cost of this project in 1920 was £300,000, to be followed by £509,000 in 1921. Such hopes were dashed when on 22 June 1920 the Treasury stated that it could not sanction £809,000 for flights to Egypt. Over £1 million had been sanctioned for the payment of bad debts owed by the Ministry of Munitions. On 29 July 1920 the Cabinet met to debate the issue and disastrously decided to sell or give away airships as long as they incurred no financial obligations. On 16 November the Admiralty was informed that by early 1921 the two airships, *R37* and *R38*, that were under construction at the Royal Airship Works at Cardington would be completed and that further new ships would have to be laid down for the economic health of that station. The Air Minister expected to commence building a new airship every two years, but with financial difficulties and serviceable ships on hand the Air Council wanted Admiralty views. It was difficult to justify laying down another airship and yet to not do so would mean losing the only airship design team in the country. The cost of keeping Cardington was £210,000 per annum, whilst Howden cost £286,000 per annum, not counting the new ships to be constructed, and in early January 1921 steps were taken to disband the airship service. The Chief of the Air Staff, Air Chief Marshal Lord Hugh Trenchard, was anxious to close down the airship branch as quickly as possible to save money. The *R34* had to be maintained to train the American crew for the *R38* when built. The *R32* was temporarily retained. The *R33* was to become a civilian airship along with the *R36*, which was to be stored unless otherwise required for use. The non-erected mast was to be sent to Cardington at a later date. These plans were slightly altered when *R80* had to be retained subsequent to the *R34* crash. Otherwise this ship, which was accepted from Vickers Limited on 15 February, never saw service.

The Beginning of the End

During the early months of 1921 the airship *R38* was being completed for trial flights. This airship was designed by Commander CR Campbell RN. It was the intention to operate this unit to a height of 20,000 feet, but meanwhile it was being used to train the United States naval crews in the United Kingdom. The first flight took place on 23 June 1921 and lasted for seven hours. Unfortunately, trouble arose with overbalancing of the control surfaces; a backlash was experienced in the long control cables, which was further affected by changes of temperature for which no compensating mechanism had been designed. To maintain a stable flight altitude the controls would have to be over compensated to alter the position of the elevators to bring the airship back on to an even keel position. Problems with the long control cables arose due to their considerable length and the diverse route they took to arrive at the control surfaces. Each turn in the system would require the use of a pulley system and movement could be multiplied with the number of cables or pulleys in the system. The second flight took place eight days later and resulted in further modifications to the control surfaces. The tail fin and elevators were reduced by 10 per cent, the fins of the tail had to be strengthened and modifications to the fuel system had to be made to prevent flooding of the service fuel tanks in the engine gondolas. On the third flight, which took place on 17 July 1921, the airship flew under the national markings of the United States Navy. Command of the ship was under Commander LH Maxfield USN and RAF Flight Lieutenant AH Wann, the airship captain. A maximum speed of 57 mph was obtained but the flight was marred by the tail fin flopping over and several mid-ship girders buckling after longitudinal hunting was experienced in mid-air.

Longitudinal hunting consists of the airship following a flight path in a wave formation in which the airship alternates between travelling upwards and then downwards. In the case of the *R38* the height difference above and below the line of flight was 500 feet. All hell was let loose in the gondolas as the airship violently rose and descended and it was only by the timely handling of the coxswain's controls by Wann that a serious disaster was averted and a safe arrival was made at Howden on the Humber. Extensive repairs were undertaken to make the airship airworthy and for it to be in a saleable condition for the United States government. Fitters and mechanics worked night and day in an effort to correct the very serious faults with the airship. The fourth flight on 23 August 1921, under the command of Flight Lieutenant Pritchard, was to Pulham in Norfolk. The voyage went well until they were close to the Pulham airship station, which by then was blanketed in fog. The captain and crew could not see the mooring mast so it was decided that the airship should stand off over the North Sea until better visibility was experienced in the morning. The coast was crossed at Thorpeness and the airship set a course for Hull. They arrived over the city at 5.20 p.m. at a height of 2,500 feet. The view from the control cabin was excellent; the River Humber was clearly visible together with the city and docks sprawling along the northern river bank. With such good weather the airship's commander decided that since yawing manoeuvres had not as yet been attempted now was as good a time as any. So making her way to the mouth of the Humber the *R38* returned at a speed of 62mph going through the motions of the yawing manoeuvres. At 5.37 p.m. observers on the ground realized that the airship was in serious difficulties. The hull had broken in two between transverse frames nine and ten. Immediately the bow half of the airship burst into flames and exploded, falling into the River Humber. All the United States naval personnel were killed and of the forty-nine crew members on-board only Flight Lieutenant Wann, three crewmen and a National Physical Laboratory observer were rescued. The accident claimed the lives of most of the United Kingdom's airship experts.

A memorial to those that lost their lives was erected in 1924 in Hull's Western Cemetery, including that of Air Commodore Maitland, one of the leading authorities in Great Britain on airship design and flying. As far back as 1912 he had a controlling interest in the Airship Company Limited of Merton in Surrey and in 1913 had made an experimental parachute descent from the airship *Delta* near Farnborough. The airship squadron of the Royal Flying Corps had been put under his command, whose work had made considerable contributions towards the efficient use of wireless telegraphy in British airships. Despite his expertise in parachuting Maitland stayed with the officers and crew of the burning *R38* although he could have saved his own life.

A special accident sub-committee was convened under the authority of Lieutenant Colonel Mervyn O'Gorman from the RAF Accident Investigation Branch. Unfortunately, the chief designer of the airship, Commander Campbell, was one of the victims and this resulted in incomplete technical evidence being placed before the committee. It was established that the airship built by Short Brothers at Cardington was constructed in full accordance with the specifications and that the failure in the hull was possibly due to structural weaknesses exerted by high control forces working on already over-compensated fin and tail elevators. It was stated that the *R38* was comparable with the German Zeppelin *L71* surrendered at the time of the Armistice. On the orders of the government all plans and construction work on commercial airships were halted.

During the course of the accident committee's investigation evidence was given by Wing Commander K Brown-Cave, who was then in charge of research and experiment. He alleged that only informal discussions had taken place between Commander Campbell and one or two other engineers interested in airship construction concerning the stresses that the airship would experience during powered flight. However, *R38* incorporated a number of modifications from standard airship design practice. Apparently, the airship had long diagonal external shear wires but no stirrups supporting the internal corridor as in the German Zeppelin design, which possessed similar 15 metre bays between the transverse frames. Furthermore, the method of transferring lift from the gasbags to the hull was normal and similar to the Zeppelin method. The engine cars were higher up on the hull than in previous designs to allow maximum beam and height to be obtained within the limitations imposed by the size of the sheds. The internal corridor was trapezium sectioned instead of the more traditional shape and the two keeled longitudinals were lower than on previous airships. All fifty of the 190-gallon petrol tanks were suspended from the main frames, which would make the stresses uneven. However, it had to be admitted that the *R38* was, in fact, of a German Zeppelin design. The strength calculations were investigated to learn as much as possible from them. They were scattered over some thirty work books, were extremely confused and incomplete, with tentative calculations only. It was possible to obtain from them a more or less connected story about the stresses, which were the subject of a separate report. Regrettably, the *R38* calculations are not likely to be of much more than historical interest. Unfortunately, only static conditions were considered and little ingenuity was shown in dealing with the familiarities of the structural problems of rigid airships in flight.

During 1921 the airship shed at Pulham in Norfolk was dismantled section by section and was conveyed to Short Brothers at Cardington where it was re-erected by the Cleveland Bridge Company. The mooring mast was also dismantled and taken to Cardington for re-erection. And so 1921 ended in bitterness and disaster. But despite the *R38* crash, the loss of so many airship engineers and the government's decision to cancel all new airship construction, this was not to be the end of the story for the airship in British aviation history.

Chapter 2

Short Brothers and the World's
First Aircraft Manufacturer

Eustace Short was born in 1875 and his younger brother Oswald in 1883. They both flew for the first time in a balloon filled with coal gas in 1897 when Eustace was twenty-two and Oswald just fourteen. This singular experience created a passion within them for flying that led the pair, along with their older brother Horace, to establish the world's first aircraft manufacturing company, Short Brothers, in 1908, which today, over 100 years later, is based in Belfast and owned by the Canadian manufacturer Bombardier.

As early as 1900 the pair had begun manufacturing when they had started to develop high-altitude balloons with pressurized gondolas, which included some of the early design principles established by the French airship pioneer Édouard Surcouf who was based at Billancourt in France. Within a short time the business had grown under the direction of Eustace and Oswald into an established sub-contractor that manufactured components for British naval airships. In 1908 Orville and Wilbur Wright had travelled to France to demonstrate their new Wright Flyer and to promote the exciting possibilities of flight. At this time there were no individual aircraft manufacturers that designers could turn to in order to produce their aircraft in volume, only small independent workshops and balloonists who turned their hands to the novelty of lighter than-air-aviation.

Griffith Brewer was a noted balloonist, aviator and later a close friend of the Wright brothers. He recalled that his first contact with the Short brothers was when Eustace and Oswald reconditioned a balloon that Brewer and his co-pilot Claud Brabazon planned to use in the 1907 Gordon Bennett Cup. Later the Short brothers also built Brewer's 18,000 cubic feet, rubber fabric, hydrogen Bee balloon. It is through these associations that Brewer felt able to recommend them to Wilbur Wright whilst he was visiting Pau in France. The Wrights had been seeking a suitable company in England to manufacture their first six Wright Flyers and agreed to meet the shorts. Brewer then telegraphed the Short brothers to ask them to visit the Wright brothers in Pau in January 1909 in order to note down the necessary design information that they would need to begin manufacturing.

The Short brothers had already built suitable sheds at Shell Beach adjacent to Muswell Manor on the remote and marshy Isle of Sheppey in the Thames Estuary, which also became the first home of the Royal Aero Club. Once the two Short brothers had secured their contract to manufacture the Wright Flyer, Horace Short left his position as an experimental engineer with Charles Parsons to join his two younger brothers and the newly registered Short Brothers Limited began life as the world's first aircraft manufacturer. The first six aircraft built by Short Brothers were purchased by the following customers:

1. Charles Rolls, co-founder of Rolls-Royce, who died on 12 July 1910 when the tail of his Wright Flyer broke off. He was the first Briton to die in a flying accident.
2. Lieutenant Colonel Alexander 'Alec' Ogilvie.
3. Frank McClean, later Sir Francis McClean AFC.
4. Maurice Egerton, later Lord Egerton of Tatton.
5. Cecil Grace, the noted aviator who disappeared in 1910 whilst flying over the sea.
6. Charles Rolls, his second purchase later bought by Alec Ogilvie from Rolls' executors.

In 1910 Short Brothers moved to more suitable accommodation three miles away at Eastchurch and it was here that they began manufacturing aircraft by the noted aircraft designer John Dunne, which included the Short-Dunne 5, the world's first tailless aeroplane. Horace Short was convinced that if sufficient power could be given to an aircraft then there would be no limit to what it could achieve. However, engines of the day lacked sufficient horsepower for Horace's designs and so the solution seemed a simple one, to add a second engine. The Tandem Twin was built for Frank McClean and was powered by two Gnôme rotary engines; one powered a tractor propeller and the other a pusher, with the pilot sitting precariously between the two. Later in 1911 came the Triple Twin, which is regarded as the first twin-engined aeroplane in the world. This was superseded by the Double Dirty, a twin-engined monoplane with two 70hp Gnôme engines positioned in tandem that was built for the Royal Navy in 1912.

Anxious to move away from the box kite design, Short Brothers developed the 70hp Short tractor biplane in 1911, again for Frank McClean. Initially it was designed as a landplane, but was equipped with a central float and outboard wing floats and became a successful seaplane. The Admiralty were so impressed with the concept that they bought one of the aircraft, which marked the beginning of Short Brothers as primarily a marine aircraft manufacturer. In 1912 the S47, the inevitable twin-engined version, emerged. It was powered by two 50hp Gnôme engines, one was a direct drive engine that was mounted in the nose and the second was a chain drive motor positioned behind it, driving two tractor propellers on the wings.

Charles Fairey joined Short Brothers at this time and worked for the company for two years before leaving them in 1915 to establish his own aircraft manufacturing company, Fairey Aviation. Fairey was not the only notable British aviator to work with Short Brothers who subsequently established their own successful aviation business. Over twenty years later in 1938 a young Freddie Laker joined Short Brothers at the age of sixteen as an apprentice and stayed with the company until he joined the Air Transport Auxiliary in 1941.

The S41 was completed in early 1912 and was a land aircraft equipped with a wheel-based undercarriage, but this was soon changed to twin floats. Seven Short Brothers aircraft were involved in the daring raid on the north German port of Cuxhaven on Christmas Day, 1914, three of which were improved S41 aircraft.

Short Brothers' dominant role as a seaplane manufacturer became clearer when on 10 January 1912 Lieutenant Charles Samson flew a Short Improved S27 pusher seaplane from the deck of HMS *Africa* while the ship was at anchor in the River Medway in Sheerness harbour. The ship had been fitted with a 100-foot downward-sloping runway on her foredeck and with this single successful experiment began shipborne aviation in the Royal Navy.

By 1913 Short Brothers had begun to outgrow their factory at Eastchurch and the company recognized the need for new premises nearer the sea that would support their growing number of seaplane developments. That year they bought a little over eight acres of land near Borstal at Rochester in Kent and built three new erecting shops, the last of which was completed in 1917. The float department was the first to be relocated and moved just one week after the outbreak of the First World War, with other departments then relocating over a period of time.

The First World War

One of Short Brothers' most prolific aircraft during the First World War was the two-seater Type 184 reconnaissance, bomber and torpedo 'folder' seaplane, of which 936 were built. The Type 184 first flew in 1915 and was the first seaplane to be specifically designed to carry a torpedo. It was 40 feet 7 inches in length, had a wingspan of 63 feet 6 inches and a height of 13 feet 6 inches. It was powered by a 260hp Sunbeam Gurkha engine, with later models fitted with a 260hp Sunbeam Maori engine. The aircraft could attain a top speed of 88mph, a total flying time of 2 hours 45 minutes and an operational ceiling of 9,000 feet. The Type 184 was armed with a .303 Lewis machine-gun fitted in the rear cockpit and it could carry either a bomb payload of 520lb or a 14-inch torpedo. The first attack using a Type 184 took place during the Battle of Gallipoli, when on 15 August 1915 Flight Commander Charles Edmonds took off from the packet steamer and Royal Navy seaplane carrier HMS *Ben-my-Chree* and attacked a Turkish supply ship in the Dardanelles. Short Brothers had further developed their seaplane reputation when during the war they manufactured the Felixstowe F3 and Felixstowe F5 flying boats designed by Lieutenant Commander John Cyril Porte of the Seaplane Experimental Station in Felixstowe. The Felixstowe F3 was developed from the F2 patrol aircraft that was manufactured by SE Saunders from 1917. The F3 was larger and heavier, but importantly had a much greater range. The prototype was fitted with a 320hp Sunbeam Cossack engine and first flew in February 1917. The production models were fitted with two 345hp Rolls-Royce Eagle VIII V12 inline piston engines. The F3 had a crew of four and was 49 feet 2 inches long, with a wingspan of 102 feet. It could reach a maximum speed of 91mph at 2,000 feet, had an endurance of six hours and could operate at a ceiling of 8,000 feet. It was armed with four Lewis machine-guns and could carry a bomb payload of up to 920lb beneath its wings. The F5 variant first flew in May 1918 and attempted to build upon the best design concepts from the F2 and the F3. The F5 had a slightly reduced maximum speed of 88mph, but did have a greater endurance of some seven hours.

In April 1917 Horace Short, the company's chief designer, died at the age of forty-four and was buried with a modest stone memorial simply marking the outline of his grave in Hampstead Cemetery. Horace's untimely death meant that the heavy burden of responsibility for running the business fell to Oswald and Eustace. Fortunately the brothers had already built a strong team around them, including Arthur Gouge, the general manager and chief engineer who had joined the company in 1915, and Mr AE Bibby, the works manager who had been with the firm since 1910.

Unhappy Experiences at Cardington

In 1915 Admiral Lord Fisher, the First Sea Lord of the Admiralty, called for the rapid construction of small non-rigid submarine scout airships to combat the growing German U-boat menace. At this time Short Brothers' airship activities were mainly as a component manufacturer supplying Airships Limited of Merton, Surrey, whose managing director was George Holt-Thomas. In 1912 Holt-Thomas had established the Aircraft Manufacturing Company (Airco) at The Hyde in Hendon. Short Brothers was asked by the Admiralty to submit designs and prototypes to fulfil the government orders and they began by converting a *Willows IV* airship to create the Short SS1. Shortly afterwards the SS3 was successfully built and carried out trials at the RNAS Air Station Kingsnorth on the Isle of Sheppey. In the same year Short Brothers was responsible for constructing the airship facilities at Cardington, including the 700 foot Shed No. 1, which enabled them to work on the *R31* and *R32*. The company also built a housing estate called Shortstown opposite the airship station to house essential workers. The company received payment for this development from the government by way of a loan. The company had bought the land at Cardington from the wealthy Whitbread family and paid £110,000 for it plus 70 per cent of the cost of the buildings, which included a 30 per cent allowance for wartime price inflation.

On 14 March 1915 the Admiralty informed Short Brothers that they felt that their designs were not sufficiently practical and would therefore be required to build a new airship to an Admiralty design that was to be 594 feet long and with a diameter of 64 feet. Short Brothers were somewhat amazed at the way they had been handled, but on 21 March, due to the possession of the large facilities at Cardington that had put the company in some considerable debt, the company decided that it had no alternative but to agree to the construction of the Admiralty designs.

In January 1916 Short Brothers was invited to build two R23 class rigid airships, which had been designed by the Admiralty and were derived from the Vickers Airship No. 9. These were based exclusively on the designs and methods of construction used by the Zeppelin Airship Construction Company of Potsdam. However, the Admiralty had a sudden change of heart and hurriedly scrapped the *R23* construction programme when they came into the possession of engineering drawings for a Schütte-Lanz airship, secret information provided by a Swiss engineer from the same company and intelligence reports on the Zeppelin *L33* that had been shot down over Little Wigborough in Essex on 23 September 1916.

The Swiss engineer, who went by the name of Müller, had worked in the engineering department of Schütte-Lanz GmbH, which was part of the German Zeppelin Company. He had approached British military intelligence during the early years of the war with the idea of supplying airship designs. At first the British Cabinet had not been keen on the idea, but towards the end of 1915 the Admiralty once more approached the Prime Minister, who gave them permission to proceed with the operation. Müller stole the German engineering designs, aided by British military intelligence officers. Together with all the detailed paper work that he had brought to London Müller was installed in accommodation in the Strand, London, where detailed interrogation work commenced.

The Zeppelin *L33* brought down in Essex had been under the command of *Kapitän* Bocker and had raided the southeast counties of England, where it was attacked by Second Lieutenant Alfred de Bathe Brandon. Flying high over London he had struck the Zeppelin with a hail of incendiary bullets and forced the airship to a lower level. Anti-aircraft artillery had then seriously crippled the airship and brought it down in Essex north of Mersey Island. The survivors were taken prisoner. Mr SJ Durston and other members of the Admiralty's technical team stayed for three weeks at the *Red Lion* in Colchester to examine the wreckage and to make detailed drawings. Equipment that had survived the fire was carefully examined. As a result of the investigation of Zeppelin *L33*, the interrogation of the engineer Müller and the designs that had been stolen from the Zeppelin Company, the Admiralty decided that Short Brothers was no longer to proceed with the construction of the R23 class but was asked to build a new R33 class, which was effectively a reconstruction of the original German design. The Admiralty's decisions and the immense detail that lay behind them were not properly explained to Short Brothers, which only sought to compound an already strained relationship.

Immediately the war was over, Admiralty papers made it clear that the Armistice was not regarded as a truce and the future of the airship programme was reviewed. It was decided that the proposed R32 and R40 would be completed and that one new airship a year would be ordered from Armstrong Whitworth, William Beardmore & Company and Short Brothers. The Admiralty planned to leave Short Brothers to run Cardington so that they could earn back the money they needed to pay off their government loan and also to provide a nucleus for future expansion at the station. Vickers had been left out of the plans, probably due to the fact that their Walney Island facilities were bombarded by a surfaced German U-boat during 1917 and although defence batteries had driven the intruder away the vulnerability of the facilities could not be ignored. Vickers Limited felt considerably slighted and some animosity grew against the senior officers of the Navy.

The financial arrangements with Short Brothers were not the same as those negotiated with William Beardmore & Company and Armstrong Whitworth Limited. On 7 January 1919 Short Brothers complained to the Admiralty that the arrangements were costing the company £136 in taxes and other payments for every £100 of profit. On 17 February managing director Oswald Short found himself ushered into a meeting at the Admiralty and seated next to Sir Vincent Rowen, controller of armament production and Sir Eric Geddes, chairman, to be told that the government proposed to nationalize the Cardington Airship Works. Short vigorously protested and a heated exchange resulted. Oswald Short pointed out how the original agreement would be broken and how his firm would be left with totally inadequate facilities for peacetime airship construction. He was told by the chairman that the Defence of the Realm Act would be used since the peace had not as yet been signed and that if he wished he could claim compensation. Oswald Short left the meeting shattered but did receive £40,000 in compensation and the company did receive payments for their work on the remaining airships.

On 1 April 1919 the Air Ministry took over Cardington and Short Brothers terminated their unhappy association with the Admiralty as an airship constructor. The company quietly moved away to the slipways of Borstal, Rochester in Kent where their seaplanes and flying boats were constructed. Their work in this field had been assisted by the knowledge gained in the use and handling of duralumin. Soon the Short Empire flying boats were spanning the Empire, where airships had proven themselves to be a disastrous failure. This work culminated during the early part of the Second World War with the successful operation of the Short Stirling heavy bomber and the Short Sunderland flying boats, which conducted operations over the North Atlantic, South East Asia and the South Pacific. When peace came the Sunderland continued in operation until the late 1950s, when it was withdrawn from active service and replaced by the Avro Shackleton maritime reconnaissance bomber.

Shortening the Empire

During the inter-war years Short Brothers continued with their experiments with stressed skin metal aircraft coverings and by 1924 they had completed their first all-metal flying boat that became known as the Cockle. They completed their first all-metal landplane the same year. However, they found themselves diversifying into the construction of bus and tram bodywork in order to survive the turbulent years of the Depression and to keep their skilled workforce together. In August 1926 Sir Alan Cobham flew from England to Australia in a de Havilland DH50 fitted with two floats built by Short Brothers. The development of the Short Cromarty twin-engined biplane flying boat powered by Rolls-Royce Condor engines was heavily influenced by the F5 flying boats that Short Brothers had manufactured during the First World War. It was this aircraft that led to the development of the highly successful Short S5 Singapore, the first large all-metal flying boat. The metal construction, in particular the hull, meant that the aircraft was relatively free from leakages and could carry much heavier payloads. Sir Alan Cobham and a crew of five that included Lady Cobham, made detailed aerial surveys around Africa in a Short Singapore, covering 9,950 miles in 100 hours and 34 minutes. The first design of the Singapore was fitted with two Rolls-Royce Condor IIIA engines. However, the S12 Singapore I and the S19 Singapore II variants were four-engined machines. The Singapore III had a crew of six and was 76 feet long with a wingspan of 90 feet. It was powered by four 560hp Rolls-Royce Kestrel VIII/IX piston engines in a pusher/tractor configuration that gave the aircraft a maximum speed of 145 mph at 5,000 feet. The Singapore was operated by Imperial Airways and was joined by the Short S8 Calcutta biplane flying boat that first flew on 14 February 1928 and was used on the Mediterranean stages of the airline's flights from England to India. Yet it would be the Short Empire that would truly open the skies to the various outposts of the British Empire. On 5 July 1937 the aircraft was used for the first westbound transatlantic service from Foynes in County Limerick in the mid-west of Ireland to Newfoundland.

The Air Ministry had set a requirement for suitable passenger and mail aircraft to serve a number of prominent colonies, in particular South Africa and Australia. Short Brothers' response was the development of the C class Empire flying boat to be built at their Rochester facilities. The first Empire, G-ADHL *Canopus*, made its maiden flight on 3 July 1936 and was operated by Imperial Airways, Queensland and Northern Territories Aerial Services (Qantas) and

Tasmanian Empire Airways Limited (TEAL). The Empire 5.23 was 88 feet long, had a wingspan of 114 feet and stood 31 feet 9¾ inches high. It was equipped with four 920hp Bristol Pegasus radial engines that gave it a maximum speed of 200mph. The aircraft could carry a crew of 4, 24 passengers and 4,480lb of cargo over a range of 760 miles, with an operational ceiling of 20,000 feet.

The Caledonia and Cambria were adapted and equipped with long-range fuel tanks to enable them to attempt a true transatlantic service. However, they were not able to carry sufficient fuel and experiments with in-flight refuelling took place. The S30 variants had 815hp Bristol Perseus sleeve valve engines, which combined with reinforcements to the airframe enabled the take-off weight to increase to 46,000lb. A range of 1,500 miles meant that, with in-flight refuelling by Handley Page bombers, the aircraft was able to operate transatlantic mail services. However, experience of handling overweight aircraft during the Second World War demonstrated that the Empire could take off with significantly more fuel than first estimated by Short Brothers and the aircraft could manage the transatlantic crossing without the need for in-flight refuelling.

The Sunderland

The Short Sunderland made its maiden flight on 16 October 1937 and was introduced into service with the RAF the following year, where it served with distinction until its retirement over thirty years later in 1959.

The Sunderland was based in no small way on the successful Empire flying boat but with a much deeper profile hull. The accommodation for the crew of eleven was significant. The fuselage contained two decks and on the lower were six bunks, a galley kitchen, flush toilet and a small workshop for repairs. Variants of the all-metal, flush-riveted aircraft were generally powered by either four nacelle-mounted Bristol Pegasus engines or Pratt & Whitney motors. With additional long-range fuel tanks the Sunderland was able to carry over 2,550 imperial gallons of fuel, giving it a range of 2,980 miles.

The Sunderland served with Australian, Canadian, French, New Zealand, Norwegian, South African and British armed forces. On 21 September 1939 two aircraft rescued the thirty-four crew members of the SS *Kensington Court* after it was torpedoed by a German U-boat in the mid-Atlantic. One of the Sunderlands landed next to the survivors, while the other kept guard above. On 17 July 1940 a Royal Australian Air Force Sunderland from 10 Squadron made the first U-boat kill unaided. In another famous incident a single Sunderland flying off the Norwegian coast on 3 April 1940 successfully fought off an attack by six German Junkers Ju 88 medium bombers. One of the attackers was shot down, another crash-landed and the remaining four were driven off. The attack was recreated in a one-page advertisement in *Flight* magazine. In the Mediterranean Sunderlands played an important reconnaissance role ahead of the noted attack on the Italian fleet at Taranto Harbour by Fairey Swordfish torpedo bombers in November 1940. With the introduction of ASV MkII and

Mk III airborne radar sets the Sunderlands were able to play a more combative anti-submarine role, enabling them to identify and then attack U-boats that may have surfaced, by day or by night.

The Sunderland's .303 machine-guns were not a match for other *Luftwaffe* aircraft or indeed the subsequent armament that was fitted on-board the German U-boats. However, the crews that flew the Sunderland respected its abilities and had built a deservedly fearsome reputation for being able to defend themselves against enemy aggressors. On 2 June 1943 a Royal Australian Air Force Sunderland from 461 Squadron was searching for survivors from BOAC's Flight 777 that had taken off from Lisbon and was attacked by the *Luftwaffe* the day before. The passengers of Flight 777 included the actor Leslie Howard who had starred in the 1942 British film *The First of the Few* (*Spitfire* in the United States of America) that told the story of the Spitfire's designer RJ Mitchell. The aircraft had been attacked by eight Junkers Ju 88 C long-range heavy fighters. The crew of the Sunderland, two British and nine Australians, disposed of their bombs and depth charges in preparation for a truly disproportionate air battle and attempted evasive actions as two aircraft strafed them with machine-gun fire, knocking out one engine. Soon two of the attackers had been shot down; a third was then shot down by the tail gunner whilst attempting an attack. The nose gunner hit a further attacker whose engines were soon engulfed by fire, before another two aircraft were hit. The remaining pair of Junkers ran for home. The Sunderland's pilot, Colin Walker, was able to get the aircraft back to Cornwall and landed at Praa Sands. He received the Distinguished Service Order. Apart from Walker the crew continued to fly together in another Sunderland, but were all lost two months later over the Bay of Biscay after coming under attack by six Ju 88s.

The Short Sunderland Mk III had a crew of between eight and eleven that included two pilots, a radio operator, navigator, engineer, bomb-aimer and three to five gunners. The aircraft was 85 feet 4 inches in length, had a wingspan of 112 feet 9 inches and was 34 feet 6 inches high. The four 1,200hp Pratt &Whitney Twin Wasp fourteen-cylinder engines gave the Sunderland a maximum speed of 219mph and could carry the aircraft to 17,900 feet. The machine was armed with .303-inch machine-guns, as well as a range of bombs, mines, depth charges, smoke-floats and sea markers.

The Sunderland continued in service with the RAF until 1959 and the Royal New Zealand Air Force until 1967. Several surplus aircraft were towed out to sea and scuttled after the war, a practice that was quite common as scrap yards were already full and the resale value was minimal. The growth of land-based civil aviation meant that the flying boats were no longer needed as once they were, except for less developed routes in the Far East. Interestingly ten Sunderlands took part in the Berlin air lift between July 1948 and September 1949. They took off from Finkenwerder on the Elbe at Hamburg and landed at the RAF Gatow airbase on Havelsee Lake. Sunderlands also played an important role during the

Korean War with 88, 205 and 209 Squadrons, as well as during the Korean Armistice period until September 1954.

Fortunately there are still examples of Short Sunderlands that can be seen around the world today, including ML824 at the RAF Museum in Hendon and ML796 at the Imperial War Museum at Duxford in Cambridgeshire. Sunderland T9044 was one of twenty Mk I aircraft to be built and now lies on the seabed off Pembroke Dock in Wales, having sunk during a gale on 21 November 1940. The aircraft was the subject of an episode of the Channel 4 British television documentary series *Wreck Detectives* and the Pembroke Dock Sunderland Preservation Trust hopes to recover the aircraft in the future. One other Mk I, Sunderland T9049, is located in Loch Ryan having been scuttled on 11 December 1946.

The Stirling

The Short Brothers' Stirling was designed by Arthur Gouge and was the RAF's first four-engined heavy bomber. It made its maiden flight on 14 May 1939 and entered service in 1941, remaining with the RAF until 1946. In all some 2,375 were manufactured. The Stirling played an important role during the course of the Second World War but was soon overshadowed by other more well-known aircraft, in particular the feted Avro Lancaster that first flew on 9 January 1941 and the Handley Page Halifax HP57 that made its maiden flight on 25 October 1939.

The RAF first began to seriously look at four-engined bombers in 1936, particularly as the engines being developed in Britain at that time were not able to suitably equip the twin-engined bombers with power units of sufficient size. The Air Ministry issued specification B12/36 for an aircraft capable of carrying a 14,000lb bomb payload 2,000 miles or an 8,000lb payload 3,000 miles, that had a cruising speed of 230mph at 15,000 feet, that would be able to carry 24 personnel and take off in less than 500 feet. Short Brothers adapted the Sunderland design to create the S29 in response to the Ministry's specification. Following redesign recommendations by the Ministry, including swapping the Napier Dagger engines for Bristol Hercules units, increasing the ceiling to 28,000 feet and a reduction in wingspan from the Sunderland's 112 feet to less than 100 feet, an initial order was placed for the aircraft. Production started in Rochester in August 1940. During the first few days of the Battle of Britain the Short Brothers factory was raided by German bombers, including a notable low-level raid by a number of Dornier Do 17s. Several Stirlings were destroyed during the raid and production was put back by almost a year. The persistent bombing raids necessitated moving production to Belfast and a number of satellite factories nearby at Aldergrove and Maghaberry. Short Brothers also established a temporary factory at White Cross Bay by Lake Windermere in the Lake District, which produced a small number of Sunderland Mk IIIs. Austin Motors' Longbridge plant in Birmingham was used to manufacture more than

600 Stirlings and Blackburn Aircraft's plant at Dumbarton in Scotland manufactured 240 Sunderlands. The Stirling was ordered as a second four-engined bomber, with Supermarine's Type 316 as the Air Ministry's first choice. However, following further bombing raids in November 1940, this time on the Supermarine plant at Woolston in Southampton, production of the Type 316 was ceased.

The Handley Page Halifax and the Avro Lancaster, which was a re-engined Manchester, were both smaller than the Stirling, having originally been designed as twin-engined bombers. The Stirling was the only British bomber designed as a four-engined aircraft right from its inception.

Initial Stirling Mk I aircraft were equipped with Bristol Hercules II engines, but subsequent examples of this variant were fitted with the 1,600hp Hercules XI. The Mk IIIs, which came into service in 1943, were powered by the Hercules VI or XVI engines, which generated 1,650hp and increased its top speed from 255 to 270mph.

The first operational Stirlings were deployed in January 1941 to RAF 7 Squadron. On the night of 10/11 February 1941 the first three Stirlings to see active service took part in a bombing raid to destroy fuel storage facilities at Vlaardingen near Rotterdam. The aircraft's thick wing meant that it could out-turn the Junkers Ju 88 and Messerschmitt Bf 110 night fighter, but it did restrict the operational ceiling and a number of operations were flown as low as 12,000 feet, which meant that raids on Italy necessitated flying through rather than over the Alps. On other missions, where accompanying aircraft were able to fly at much higher altitudes, the *Luftwaffe* focussed their attentions on the lower Stirlings. Consequently, sixty-seven of the eighty-four Stirlings delivered within their first five months of service were destroyed.

The Short Stirling Mk III's crew consisted of two pilots, flight engineer, navigator/bomb-aimer, a front gunner/wireless operator and two air gunners. The aircraft was 87 feet 3 inches long, had a wingspan of 99 feet 1 inch and was 22 feet 9 inches high. It was fitted with four 1,650hp Bristol Hercules XVI radial engines. The aircraft had a maximum speed of 270 mph, an operational ceiling of 17,000 feet and a range of over 2,000 miles. The Stirling was equipped with eight .303-inch Browning machine-guns and could carry a 14,000lb bomb payload. In all, some 2,375 aircraft were manufactured.

The Stirling's limited range of 590 miles when carrying its maximum payload restricted its uses as the war progressed, where on longer-range missions it could only carry 3,500lb of bombs, which was comparable to the twin-engined Wellingtons and later the de Havilland Mosquitoes. When in 1943 the Lancaster became available in sufficient quantities, the Stirlings were relegated to second-line duties to make way for the faster, higher and more flexible Lancaster. The Stirlings found themselves used for laying mines, dropping agents behind enemy lines and later for towing heavy transport gliders including the GAL Hamilcar and Airspeed Horsa. The Stirling continued to play a vital role during the later years of the Second World War, including the Battle of Normandy, Operation *Market Garden* and as part of Operation *Glimmer* on D-Day, 6 June 1944, when they dropped patterns of small aluminium strips as an anti-radar countermeasure. The strips, which were code-named Window, resonated and re-radiated the radar signal so as to overwhelm the enemy's screens with spoof radar images of a non-existent invasion force away from the Normandy beaches. A similar system had been developed in Germany at around the same time and was known as *Düppel*.

The Post-war Era
Short Brothers were nationalized for the second time in their history in 1943. The Emergency Powers (Defence) Acts of 1939 and 1949 laid down the regulations that governed the day-to-day lives of British people during a time of war, including the acquisition of a company's assets, such as an aircraft factory that was considered essential for the war effort. Sir Richard Stafford Cripps announced to the House of Commons in March 1943 that he intended to acquire Short Brothers (Rochester and Bedford) Limited using Defence Regulation 78. Under the new arrangement Oswald Short, the former chairman who had stood down three months earlier in January 1943, was asked to stay on in the position of Honorary Life President.

As with most aircraft manufacturers after the Second World War, Short Brothers contracted and cut its production facilities in line with the much lower levels of demand, particularly for military aircraft. By 1948 all of the company's factories had been closed except for those in Belfast, which became the manufacturing and administrative headquarters. During 1936 the Air Ministry had set up a joint venture with Harland and Wolff and Short Brothers to manufacture aircraft and parts in Belfast. The business was aptly named Short & Harland Ltd, which was half owned by the government. In 1947 the nationalized Short Brothers (Rochester and Bedford) Limited was merged with Short & Harland Limited and became Short Brothers and Harland.

During the course of the 1950s Short Brothers was involved in a range of research projects, in particular around the establishing of Britain's own independent nuclear deterrent that led to the development of aircraft such as the Short Sperrin of which only two were built. The first Sperrin prototype flew on 10 August 1951. The aircraft was intended as a fall back in case the planned V bombers were delayed but the aircraft did not go into production and both prototypes were retired by 1958. Short Brothers were also noted for developing Britain's first vertical take-off and landing aircraft, the SC1, which made its first conventional take-off and landing on 2 April 1957 and its first vertical take-off and landing (VTOL) on 26 May 1958. The SC1 was an experimental aircraft designed to develop understanding of VTOL flight. Two prototypes were built and were used by the Royal Aircraft Establishment until 1971.

During the 1960s Short Brothers developed the Skyvan nineteen-seater twin turboprop short haul freighter that was developed into the Short 330 in the 1970s and could carry up to thirty passengers. The Short 360 became the natural successor in 1981 and had capacity for thirty-nine passengers. Over 165 Short 360s were delivered and production ceased in 1991. In 1954 the government had sold 15.25 per cent of Short Brothers to the Bristol Aeroplane Company, which had plans for Short Brothers to build a number of their Britannia turboprop airliners. Short Brothers and Harland changed its name back to Short Brothers in 1977 and was privatized in 1984 when the government sold-off its remaining stake in the company. Short Brothers was later bought by the Canadian company Bombardier in October 1989.

Horace Short had died in 1917 at the early age of forty-four. Eustace Short died in 1932 at the age of fifty-seven and the business remained under the stewardship of Oswald Short as Honorary Life President after nationalization in 1943. Oswald died in 1969 at the age of eighty-six. All three Short brothers are remembered on a memorial to early aviation pioneers in the centre of Eastchurch, on the junction of Church Road and High Street. The memorial commemorates the home of British aviation, the flights and experiments that were made by members of the Aero Club of Great Britain, the establishment of the first aircraft factory in Great Britain by the Short brothers and the formation of the first Royal Naval Air Service station in 1911. The aviators listed on the monument are JTC Moore Brabazon, The Hon. Charles S Rolls, Frank K McClean, Prof. AK Huntingdon, Lieutenant James W Dunne, The Hon. Maurice Egerton, TOM Sopwith, Cecil Grace, Alec Ogilvie, Percy Grace, Ernest Pitman, GPL Jezzi and James L Travers. The designers and constructors remembered are Horace Short, Eustace Short, Oswald Short and the craftsmen of Sheppey. In addition, the Royal Naval Air Service personnel Lieutenant Commander CR Samson, Lieutenant AM Longmore, Lieutenant R Gregory, Captain EL Gerrard and twelve RN technical ratings are listed. The memorial was unveiled by Lord Tedder GCB, Marshal of the Royal Air Force, on Monday 25 July 1955. Next to the memorial is All Saints Church, where a stained glass window was dedicated to Charles Rolls and Cecil Grace, who both lost their lives in flying accidents in 1910.

Chapter 3

Geoffrey de Havilland and the Race to Australia

The most surprising thing about Sir Geoffrey de Havilland's knighthood was that rather than being for his singular contribution to the war effort, the Mosquito fighter bomber, it was for his outstanding contribution to the development of the British light aviation industry prior to the Second World War.

It is quite remarkable that up to 1939, at a time of serious economic recession, when Wall Street had crashed, six million were unemployed in Germany, Adolf Hitler had embarked upon the road to war and unemployment in Britain had reached over two million, Geoffrey de Havilland had built and sold 2,674 aircraft.

By far the most important pre-war design concept was the DH88 Comet twin-engined racing monoplane, not only because this machine won the 1934 MacRobertson England to Australia air race but because of its importance in the development of what was to be a most significant aviation design to come, the Mosquito.

However, the 1934 air race was not de Havilland's only record-breaking connection with pioneering aviation and Australia. Five years earlier, in 1929, he had won the prize for the fastest overall time in the Western Australian Centenary Air Race organized as part of West Australia's centenary celebrations. In total, seventeen competitors took off from Mascot Aerodrome in Sydney, New South Wales, on Saturday 29 September 1929. Fourteen aviators managed to complete the course, landing eight days later on Sunday 7 October 1929 at Maylands Aerodrome in Perth, West Australia.

De Havilland, flying in a modified Gipsy Moth, completed the six-leg, 2,450-mile race from Sydney to Perth in a total of 22 hours, 50 minutes and 23 seconds, winning the prize for the fastest overall time. Remarkably he was the only competitor to fly the course solo. The handicap prize was won by aviator Horace Clive 'Horrie' Miller, who two years earlier had co-founded MacRobertson Miller Aviation with MacPherson Robertson.

De Havilland's association with Australia continued when in 1930 the British aviator Amy Johnson achieved international fame as the first woman to fly solo from England to Australia in a second-hand de Havilland Gipsy Moth named *Jason*. The 11,000-mile flight started when Johnson took off on 5 May from Croydon Aerodrome in Surrey and landed in Darwin, Northern Territory, Australia, nineteen days later on 24 May. Her aeroplane for the flight was G-AAAH, which now forms part of a Johnson collection at London's Science Museum and can be seen in the museum's Flight Gallery.

Many of Johnson's record-breaking flights were, in fact, achieved in de Havilland aircraft. In 1931, flying a de Havilland Puss Moth, Johnson and co-pilot Jack Humphreys became the first to fly to Moscow in a single day, covering the 1,760 miles in around 21 hours. They both then flew on to Tokyo, achieving the record for an England to Japan flight.

In 1932 Amy married the hard-drinking aviator Jim Mollison. Their romance captured the imagination of the public and the press dubbed them *The Flying Sweethearts*. The year after their marriage Amy, flying in a de Havilland Puss Moth, broke her husband's record for a solo flight to Cape Town, South Africa. In 1933 Amy and Jim Mollison flew G-ACCV, a de Havilland Dragon Rapide named *Seafarer*, nonstop from Pendine Sands, South Wales, to Connecticut in the United States of America. The couple reached the American coast in bad weather and following an argument over where to land they crashed the aircraft. Fortunately they managed to escape the wreckage and spent some time recovering in hospital.

The MacRobertson England to Australia Air Race
In 1934 the Lord Mayor of Melbourne proposed organizing an air race from England to Australia as part of the centenary celebrations marking the founding of the State of Victoria. Australian confectionery magnate Sir MacPherson Robertson agreed to offer a prize fund of $75,000 AUD providing that the race was named after his company. The race was organized by the Royal Aero Club and the course covered some 11,300 miles from RAF Mildenhall in Suffolk to the Flemington Racecourse in Melbourne, Victoria.

The competitors chose many of the leading aircraft of the day, including a Douglas DC-2, Boeing 247D, Fairey III F and a Miles M3 Falcon. However, de Havilland was determined to win the race and set about designing a revolutionary new aircraft. The result was the de Havilland DH88 Comet racing plane, which not only incorporated some new design concepts, including a retractable undercarriage and two-pitch propellers, but was the forerunner of the Mosquito. In just nine months on 9 October 1934 the new plane received its certificate of airworthiness, having first flown a month earlier on 8 September. It emerged as a streamlined low-wing twin-engined monoplane of wooden stress-skinned construction, powered by two 230hp de Havilland Gipsy Six R high compression engines, which gave a top speed of 237mph, a cruising speed of

220mph and an operational ceiling of 19,000 feet. It stood 10 feet high, was 29 feet in length and had a wingspan of 44 feet.

A total of three machines of this type were manufactured and all three competed in the race. The first was Comet G-ACSR, which was built for Bernard Rubin and painted green. It was piloted by Owen Cathcart-Jones and Ken Waller. The second Comet was G-ACSP, which was named *Black Magic* and was painted black and gold. It was piloted by its owners Amy and Jim Mollison. The third was Comet G-ACSS, which was ordered by Mr AO Edwards, the managing director of the *Grosvenor House Hotel* in Park Lane, London. It was painted a distinctive scarlet and was aptly named *Grosvenor House*. The pilots were Charles Scott, the former record holder for the route, and Tom Campbell-Black.

The race included five compulsory stops at Baghdad, Allahabad, Singapore, Darwin and Charleville. In addition to these the organizers had prepared a further twenty-two refuelling stops. By the time the race was due to start on 20 October 1934 an ambitious array of some sixty entrants had been cut to a mere twenty.

At 6.30 a.m. on a crisp autumn morning Amy and Jim Mollison were the first into the air in G-ACSP *Black Magic*. They flew without incident to Baghdad and went on to reach Karachi by 10.00 a.m. on day two, setting a new flying record from England to India. However, they soon ran into a catalogue of difficulties. After leaving Karachi they had problems retracting their landing gear and were forced to return for repairs. A refuelling stop at Jabalpur became chaotic when they found that there was no aviation fuel available. Jim Mollison, against Amy's wishes, chose to fill up using fuel from the local bus company. Shortly after they took off the aircraft developed irreparable engine trouble and they were forced to pull out of the race at Allahabad.

The race lead now fell into the hands of Charles Scott and Tom Campbell-Black in G-ACSS *Grosvenor House*. They flew through particularly heavy storms over the Bay of Bengal and across the Andaman Sea to land at Singapore eight hours ahead of their closest rivals in the DC-2.

On the next leg of the race from Singapore to Darwin G-ACSS developed an oil pressure problem in the port engine, which caused it to lose power. Following urgent repairs at Darwin they were able to continue in the race but were forced to fly the final legs to Charleville and Melbourne with one engine throttled back. Despite their engine problems Scott and Campbell-Black developed a commanding lead and crossed the finish line at Flemington Racecourse, Melbourne, at 3.33 p.m. on 23 October 1934, with a total elapsed time of 71 hours, some 18 hours 47 minutes ahead of the DC-2. G-ACSS *Grosvenor House* qualified for both the fastest time and handicap prizes. Unfortunately, the race rules only allowed one prize per aircraft and so G-ACSS was only awarded the fastest time.

Owen Cathcart-Jones and Ken Waller in G-ACSR arrived safely, crossing the finish line in fourth place. Shortly after touching down they were loaded with newsreel footage of the race and took off again for RAF Mildenhall. Their return journey set a new record for a round-trip, completing the whole journey in a little over thirteen days.

G-ACSS was later evaluated by the RAF but following an accident on 30 August 1935 when the undercarriage failed to lock and another on 2 September 1936 at RAF Martlesham Heath the aircraft was sold for scrap. Fortunately, it was bought by architect Mr FE Tasker and it was restored at Essex Aero Limited at Gravesend, where it was given the name *The Orphan*. In 1937 it came fourth in the Marseilles Damascus Paris air race. Later, under the name of *The Burberry* the aircraft achieved a number of new records, including cutting the out-and-home record to the Cape in South Africa to just 15 days and 17 hours. The following year Arthur Edmond Clouston and Victor Anthony Ricketts flew a 26,450-mile round trip to New Zealand in just 10 days, 21 hours, 22 minutes.

G-ACSS was restored for the Festival of Great Britain in 1951 by de Havilland apprentices, where it was put on display hanging from the roof. The aircraft was given to the Shuttleworth Collection in 1965 and following an appeal for funds it was restored to full flying condition. It flew for the first time in forty-nine years on Sunday 17 May 1987.

The other two Comet DH88 aircraft that were built for the race also went on to have momentous flying careers. In 1934 G-ACSR was renamed *Reine Astrid* and was used to fly mail from Brussels to Leopoldville in the Belgian Congo. Following its subsequent sale to the French government it set a record on 5 July 1935 flying between Croydon Aerodrome and Le Bourget in just fifty-two minutes.

Black Magic G-ACSP was sold to the Portuguese government which had ambitious plans to operate it flying between Lisbon and Rio de Janeiro. Unfortunately, these plans failed to come to anything and the aircraft disappeared from the skies until it was found, derelict and decaying on a farm in the 1970s. G-ACSP was brought back to the UK and is being restored by the Comet Racer Project Group at Derby Airfield at Egginton in Derbyshire. Copies of letters that have come to light written by Amy Johnson to Lord Swinton and Colonel Jellicoe suggest that in 1936 she unsuccessfully attempted to buy *Black Magic* back from the Portuguese government for a 'Johannesburg race'.

A fourth Comet DH88, F-ANPZ, was built for the French government and had its nose specially adapted to carry mail.

A fifth Comet, G-ADEF, named *Boomerang*, was ordered by Cyril Nicholson who had intended to make a number of attempts on a whole series of long distance records. The aircraft was piloted by Mr JC McArthur and Tom Campbell-Black, co-pilot on G-ACSS during the 1934 MacRobertson England Australia race. On 8 August 1935 they set out on an attempt on the record for the nonstop London to Cape Town flight. They covered the 2,240-mile first stage to

Cairo in a record breaking 11 hours 18 minutes, but they developed engine trouble and were forced to abandon the remainder of the flight. They returned to England in 12 hours 15 minutes and set a new record for the out-and-home London to Cairo flight. *Boomerang* was entered in the 1935 Round Britain King's Cup Race but failed to start. A second attempt on the Cape record was made in 1935, however on 22 September while flying over the Sudan the aircraft developed severe airscrew trouble and crashed. Fortunately, McArthur and Campbell-Black were able to escape and parachuted to safety.

Both G-ACSR and F-ANPZ ended up owned by the French government and in June 1940, during the Battle of France, the aircraft were kept at Istres Airbase near Marseilles in the south of France. A major fire broke out at the airbase and both aircraft were destroyed.

Early Life
Captain Sir Geoffrey de Havilland, OM, CBE, AFC, RDI, FRAeS was born on 27 July 1882, near High Wycombe, Buckinghamshire, the second son of Alice and Reverend Charles de Havilland. His elder brother, Ivon, was born three years earlier. The family moved to a parish in Nuneaton, Warwickshire, where de Havilland's sisters Ione and Gladys and younger brother, Hereward, were born.

It was generally expected that de Havilland would follow in his father's footsteps and train for the clergy when he left St Edward's School, Oxford. However, an overriding passion for mechanics and engineering meant that in 1900 he began studying at the Crystal Palace Engineering School instead. It was while he was a student there that he designed and built his first motorcycle.

After leaving the engineering school he took up an apprenticeship at Willans & Robinson at Rugby in Warwickshire. While working there he designed and built his second motorcycle, which he gave to his brother Hereward who drove it for many years. As an apprentice he often found himself in need of funds and on one such occasion he sold the drawings of his second motorcycle to two student friends for just £5. These friends used his design and went on to form the Blackburne Motorcycle Company.

De Havilland moved to the Wolseley Tool & Motor Car Company at Adderley Park in Birmingham as a draughtsman in 1905 and then a year later to the Motor Omnibus Construction Company in Walthamstow. It was here that he met and became friends with the Cornish engineer Frank Hearle, a friendship that was instrumental in his move into aviation.

In 1907 de Havilland moved into a flat in Kensington with Hearle. His sister Ione became their housekeeper and later married Hearle. The following year the Wright brothers demonstrated their aircraft at Le Mans and de Havilland, captivated by the aircraft, decided then and there that his future lay in aviation. He borrowed £1,000 from his maternal grandfather and began setting about building his first aeroplane and power unit. The engine was a 45hp flat four-cylinder motor, which was built by the Iris Motor Company of Willesden in London, where de Havilland's brother Ivor had been appointed chief engineer.

Work on this initial design proceeded at Fulham in London. The machine was to be a wire-braced, front elevator, twin-pusher propeller biplane and assistance in the construction was given by Frank Hearle, who was by then de Havilland's brother-in-law. In December 1909 de Havilland made his first flight at Seven Barrows, near Litchfield in Hampshire. Due to his piloting inexperience he crash-landed the aircraft from a height of just 15 feet and over stressed the structure. A memorial stone adjacent to the A34 now marks the spot where this short but momentous flight took place.

By 10 September 1910 a second prototype had been built. This time it was equipped with a single propeller shaft and constructed in spruce and ash. Though used for carrying passengers it was sent to the Balloon Factory at Farnborough for army evaluation tests, which proved successful and acceptance soon followed. Both de Havilland and Hearle were appointed to the staff of the Balloon Factory, which was later to become the Royal Aircraft Factory. De Havilland sold his second aeroplane, the FE1, to the factory and it became the first aircraft to have an official Royal Aircraft Factory designation.

In 1912 de Havilland designed the BE2 and established a new British altitude record, reaching 10,500 feet. His brother Hereward was the test pilot. During that year the *Graphic* newspaper proprietor, George Thomas, had founded the Aircraft Manufacturing Company at Hendon Aerodrome and two years later in June 1914 had appointed de Havilland as chief engineer. At the time this company was assembling imported French Maurice Farmen aircraft built under licence, which were powered by imported Renault engines.

In 1914 the DH1 Pusher reconnaissance biplane had been designed and successfully flown, soon followed by the DH2 single-seater fighter, which won fame with Royal Flying Corps squadrons in France during the First World War. Eventually, the DH4 and its successor, the DH9 day-bomber, were delivered to British squadrons, the latter a highly successful design that was mass produced in America for the new United States Army Air Force, which continued in service with the RFC and subsequently the RAF long after the Armistice of November 1918.

Far-sightedly an attempt was made to organize an airline service on 5 October 1916 when the Aircraft Transport and Travel Company was established as a subsidiary of the Aircraft Manufacturing Company. By 31 March 1920 the de Havilland DH18 single-engined cabin biplane was in service with AT&T, which carried eight passengers in a cabin and a pilot in an open cockpit on the Croydon to Paris route. Unhappily during the same month both AT&T and Airco were sold to the Birmingham Small Arms Company and AT&T was closed down by the following December.

Family Triumphs and Tragedy

In 1909 de Havilland had married Louise Thomas, who some years earlier had been governess to his sisters. They had three sons together, but two died tragically as test pilots for the de Havilland Aircraft Company. Their youngest son, John, was killed in a collision involving two Mosquitoes in 1943. Geoffrey junior was the company's chief test pilot and was the first person to fly both the Mosquito and the Vampire. He was killed in 1946 while testing the experimental de Havilland DH108 Swallow. The aeroplane failed to pull out of a steep dive and crashed into the mud of the Thames Estuary. Wreckage was subsequently recovered from Egypt Bay near Gravesend in Kent. David Lean's 1952 film *The Sound Barrier*, with a screenplay by Terrence Rattigan, was broadly based upon these events. Sadly Louise de Havilland was not able to recover from the shock and heartache of losing two of her sons and suffered a nervous breakdown. She died in 1949. Two years later de Havilland married divorcee Joan Mary Frith and they remained together until his death in May 1965.

De Havilland's cousins were Hollywood actresses Olivia de Havilland and Joan Fontaine, the daughters of Lillian Augusta Ruse, whose stage name was Lillian Fontaine, and Walter Augustus de Havilland, a patent lawyer practising in Tokyo, Japan.

Olivia displayed much of her cousin's tenacity and determination during her career. She achieved great acclaim as an actress, with numerous successful film appearances to her name including roles opposite Errol Flynn in *Captain Blood* and *The Adventures of Robin Hood*. Despite her success Warner Brothers arbitrarily decided to add six months to her contract to cover time that she had spent on suspension. Bette Davis had failed to have a similar extension overturned in the courts in the 1930s. Undaunted, Olivia de Havilland, with the support the Screen Actors Guild, successfully sued Warner Brothers in 1943. The case put a limit of seven years on a performer's contract and became known as the 'de Havilland decision'. Her success won her great praise from her fellow actors. Warner Brothers, however, decided never to put her in one of their films again.

The de Havilland Aircraft Company

The de Havilland Aircraft Company, financed by the *Graphic* newspaper proprietor George Thomas, was established on 25 September 1920. Frank Hearle was appointed general manager, with Charles Walker as chief engineer and Arthur Hagg as the assistant designer. The new venture was based at Stag Lane, Edgware, north London. The company's premises consisted of just two wooden sheds, formerly the offices of the London and Provincial Aviation Company which had operated a flying school there.

One of the first customers was Alan S Butler, a wealthy private owner who had purchased a DH37 Tourer, a fast open cockpit biplane accommodating a pilot and two passengers. The aircraft was so successful that Butler decided to invest in the company, eventually becoming Chairman.

Much of the work in the early days consisted of reconditioning DH9 and DH9A aircraft for use by the RAF. Between 1924 and 1926 Sir Alan J Cobham used a DH50 machine on three long distance survey flights pioneering forthcoming Commonwealth air routes. At the same time production licences were negotiated with companies in Australia, Belgium and Czechoslovakia. Unfortunately, a glider venture was unsuccessful as indeed was the design of an ultra-light aircraft, but de Havilland remained undaunted.

The de Havilland DH51 of 1924 was a single-engined open cockpit biplane initially manufactured for the private owner as a cheap means of air transport and was powered by a war surplus 90hp Royal Aircraft Factory 1a engine (later replaced by a 120hp Airdisco engine), but only three were ever made. One of these, namely VP-KAA, was the first aircraft on the Kenya Air Register where it remained for some forty years before forming part of the Shuttleworth Collection as G-EBIR at Old Warden Aerodrome.

The following year the de Havilland DH60 Cirrus Moth first flew on 22 February 1925. This machine was a single-engined, open cockpit, two-seater biplane powered by a 60hp ADC Cirrus I, a reworked surplus wartime Renault aero engine. The aircraft was a scaled down version of the DH51 and in size would relate between the DH51 and DH53. However, the production aircraft of this type were re-engined with 85hp ADC Cirrus II engines of which 461 were delivered. Eventually, a number of engineering changes were made that necessitated the machine being redesignated as the DH60X Hermes Moth, signifying the split or X axle type in which a 90hp ADC Cirrus III was installed. The later production run of this aircraft utilized the 105hp ADC Cirrus Hermes I engine.

The ADC engines supplied for amongst others the DH51 and DH60, were wartime Renault aircraft engines now surplus to requirements, which were specially adapted for light aviation applications. Since this source of supply was now no longer available Major Frank Halford of the Air Disposal Company had designed a 100hp aero engine for de Havilland's use known as the Gipsy I. It was used on the DH60 and Gipsy Moth of June 1928, a single-engined open cockpit biplane destined to win the King's Cup Air Race at an average speed of 108mph; later production models were equipped with a 120hp Gipsy II engine.

At the same time the design of the DH60 Cirrus Moth had been a great success as it was cheap, reliable and rugged. Sales exceeded all others within the British aviation industry. Licensed manufacturing started in the United States of America, Sweden, Norway, Portugal, Finland, France and Australia, with the output of the DH60G reaching 696 machines.

The prototype de Havilland DH80A Puss Moth, an all-wooden high-wing cabin monoplane powered by an inverted 120hp Gipsy III engine, first flew on 9 September 1929. Production commenced with an all-steel tubular fuselage frame replacing the hitherto wooden structure. Carrying a pilot and two passengers, manufacture continued at the de Havilland Canadian plant in

Downsview, Toronto, and eventually a total production run of 286 was achieved, including twenty-five for the RCAF.

By 1930 the aviation design, development and production facilities had outstripped the Stag Lane plant and larger premises were built in Hatfield, Hertfordshire, though the Edgware plant was retained for aircraft engine production.

The first flight of the de Havilland DH83 Fox Moth, which had been designed as an open pilot cockpit single-engined biplane incorporating a small enclosed cabin for four passengers, took place on 29 January 1932. A low cost of production was achieved by using a wooden construction for the fuselage and incorporating many common components into the design from other de Havilland machines, with 154 being produced.

During February 1936 the first flight took place of the de Havilland DH87A Hornet Moth. This aircraft was a single-engined cabin biplane with pointed wing tips, and an all-welded steel tubular front fuselage frame with spruce and plywood framing at the rear as had been built into the design of the Leopard Moth. The sixtieth production machine introduced square ended wing tips that cured the original stalling problems and was known hence as the DH87B. Powered by a 139hp Gipsy Major engine, four float plane versions of the 165 that were built were supplied to the Royal Navy's Fleet Air Arm for evaluation purposes.

The DH89 Dragon Rapide, a twin-engined cabin biplane with a fixed undercarriage and trailing edge landing flaps below the lower wings, first flew in April 1934. Intended as a replacement for the DH84 it incorporated improvements from the DH86 powered by two 200hp Gipsy Six engines. With a capacity for one pilot and seven passengers, the improved DH89A was the ninety-third aircraft off the production line followed by the DH89B Dominie.

The Dominie was a militarized version of the Dragon Rapide developed in response to Air Ministry specification G18/35, but the aircraft lost out to the Avro Anson. Nevertheless, RAF contracts were awarded to the DH89B Mk I, which was used for navigation training and the Mk II for radio training. The Gipsy Six engines were installed in the 253rd and all subsequent planes. Production was transferred to the Brush Coachworks after the 392nd and total production of the DH89 series amounted to more than 700 aircraft.

The DH90 Dragonfly made its maiden flight on 12 August 1935. Designed as a luxury five-seater with two pilots and dual controls, it was powered by two 142hp Gipsy Major I engines. It was a cabin biplane manufactured in a wooden monocoque construction, which became the hallmark of the de Havillands. Only sixty-seven were built, some of which were supplied to the Royal Canadian Mounted Police as well as to army co-operation contractors.

On 15 May 1939 a certificate of airworthiness was issued for the DH94 Moth Minor, a low-wing, two-seater monoplane with high aspect ratio plywood covered wings, powered by a single 90hp Gipsy Minor motor. The aircraft first flew two years earlier on 22 June 1937 and was intended for use as a tourer and a trainer, to be used alongside the Tiger Moth. At Hatfield important designs were conceived, resulting in the production of the DH84, a twin-engined biplane airliner seating six passengers, which first flew on 12 November 1932, as well as the DH86, another airliner powered by four 200hp Gipsy Six inline engines, accommodating ten passengers and a crew of two, designed primarily for Australian airlines.

In 1938 Ronald Bishop, working with de Havilland, designed the Mosquito. Known as the Wooden Wonder its initial concept was as an unarmed bomber capable of speeds in excess of 415mph, powered by twin Rolls-Royce Merlin engines. Its applications spread to include day and night bombing, torpedo bombing and photographic reconnaissance operations.

The favoured use for the aeroplane was for night-time nuisance bombing over Germany and due to their speed only eleven planes were lost during the first 1,000 sorties. By early 1944 they were carrying 4,000lb blockbuster bombs, primarily over Berlin, having made sixty-seven visits to the city in that year alone.

It is significant that these most singular aircraft, rejected by the Air Ministry over twelve months prior to the declaration of war, entered service on 20 September 1941 on a reconnaissance mission, but by the end of 1944 had dropped 12,000 tons on Germany with 2,000 on Berlin.

Rebuffed as early as 1938 the Mosquito only came into being due to the support of Air Chief Marshal Sir Wilfred Freeman. Rather typically, de Havilland decided to go ahead on the project anyway, despite the Air Ministry's views, christening their creation Freeman's Folly. Around 8,000 were constructed in a very wide variety of versions, more latterly converted to take Barnes Wallis' bouncing bomb and used to attack the Japanese fleet in the Pacific.

In 1944 de Havilland was knighted, not for his outstanding work on the DH98 Mosquito fighter bomber but because he had successfully promoted the interest of the British light aviation industry over many years before the Second World War.

The pioneering spirit of Geoffrey de Havilland is illustrated by the fact that in 1941 he was the first recognized aero engine builder to enter the development of jet engines for quantity production. The new Goblin engine was ready to fly almost two years later and a pair was fitted to a converted Gloster Meteor.

This early exploratory work and its many successes led to de Havilland achieving numerous other aeronautical landmarks, notably the development of the world's first passenger jet airliner the DH106 Comet, which first flew on 27 July 1949. Meanwhile, other designs were being developed, including the DH100 Vampire jet fighter that entered service with the RAF in 1945 and followed the Gloster Meteor to become the second British jet fighter. The de Havilland DH104 Dove was a short-haul twin-engined airliner that succeeded the Dragon Rapide and first flew on 25 September 1945, whilst the DH121 Trident three-engined airliner was designed by de Havilland but built by Hawker Siddeley after the company was acquired by them in 1960.

During its history the de Havilland Aircraft Company had a number of subsidiaries in the UK and overseas, including de Havilland Australia, de Havilland Canada, Airspeed, de Havilland Propellers and the de Havilland Engine Company.

As early as March 1927 the company opened its first subsidiary, de Havilland Australia in Melbourne, to sell and assemble aircraft as well as to provide parts and servicing. Three years later the company relocated to Mascot Aerodrome at Sydney, New South Wales. In 1965, following the de Havilland Aircraft Company's sale to Hawker Siddeley, de Havilland Australia became Hawker de Havilland. The company changed hands several times in the following decades until 1998, when it was sold to Tenix. Hawker Pacific was sold to the Swedish company Celsius. Two years later Tenix sold Hawker de Havilland to Boeing, which then merged the business with Aerospace Technologies of Australia to create Hawker de Havilland Aerospace as a division of Boeing Australia.

De Havilland Aircraft of Canada Limited was established in 1928 in Toronto to manufacture aircraft, in particular Moths that were used to train Canadian airmen. The company was initially based at De Lesseps Field, Toronto, before being moved to Downsview the following year. The original factory is now the location of the Canadian Air and Space Museum. During the Second World War the company became a Crown corporation of the Canadian government. The Avro Canada manufacturing facilities were moved to de Havilland Canada by Hawker Siddeley in 1960. The Canadian government eventually sold de Havilland Canada to Boeing in 1986 on the basis that they would continue to manufacture the then current range of aircraft. Soon after the sale Boeing controversially discontinued the Twin Otter and Dash 7 aircraft. At that time Boeing was competing against the European manufacturer Airbus for a contract to supply new airliners to Air Canada, also a Canadian Crown corporation. Air Canada awarded the contract to Airbus in 1988 and Boeing immediately put de Havilland Canada up for sale. Bombardier Aerospace, based in Montreal, acquired the company in 1992. In February 2006 Viking Air, based in Victoria, British Columbia, bought the original de Havilland type certificates from Bombardier for the DHC1 Chipmunk, DHC2 Beaver, DHC3 Otter, DHC4 Caribou, DHC5 Buffalo, DHC6 Twin Otter and the DHC7 Dash 7.

Airspeed Limited was established in 1931 by AH Tiltman and Nevil Shute Norway, the aeronautical engineer and noted author, with aviator Amy Johnson as one of the first investors. In August 1934 the company was bought by ship builder Swan Hunter & Wigham Richardson Limited and became Airspeed (1934) Limited. The de Havilland Aircraft Company bought Airspeed in 1940 and allowed the company to maintain its own identity after the sale, but as a wholly owned subsidiary. After the Second World War Airspeed produced the

AS57 Ambassador, a twin-engined, pressurised, piston airliner that was operated for many years by British European Airways. Airspeed Limited was finally merged into the de Havilland Aircraft Company in 1951.

De Havilland Propellers was established in 1935 when de Havilland acquired a licence to manufacture variable pitch propellers from the American company Hamilton Standard. Following the Second World War and the evolution of the jet engine, de Havilland Propellers diversified, becoming involved in the development of guided missiles and the development of Britain's own nuclear missile Blue Streak.

The de Havilland Engine Company was established in 1944 and was based at Leavesden, near Watford in Hertfordshire. Originally the company was the engine division of the de Havilland Aircraft Company and was responsible for the de Havilland Gipsy engines. The company was merged into Bristol Siddeley Engines in 1961, which was sold to Rolls-Royce in 1966. The factory is now the location of Leavesden Film Studios, home to many major film productions, including the Harry Potter series.

The End of the Runway

By 1956 Geoffrey de Havilland had been appointed President of the de Havilland Aircraft Company and two years later the company joined with others to form an aviation manufacturing consortium under the revived name of Airco, comprising the de Havilland Aircraft Company, the Fairey Aviation Company and Hunting Aircraft.

During 1959 the British government under the Conservative Prime Minister Harold MacMillan were actively encouraging the UK's aircraft manufacturing industry to amalgamate into two major groups, a proposal that received a great deal of opposition from aviation boardrooms. The government made it clear that failure to comply could result in the cancellation of lucrative contracts, particularly as they considered that the era of manned military aircraft was rapidly drawing to a close and saw Britain becoming more reliant upon rocketry. The Handley Page Aircraft Company had resisted pressure to join these mergers and was effectively driven out of business by the government in retaliation for their noncompliance with the policy. By 1960 the de Havilland Aircraft Company had been acquired by the Hawker Siddeley Group and like the other proud aviation companies in the group, was soon required to abandon its name and independence. The Airco Consortium was disbanded and the Hawker Siddeley Group was reorganized. It took over all design work and production facilities from the de Havilland Aircraft Company and other aviation companies brought into the group during the course of 1960. From this point all further aircraft designs ceased to contain the initials DH for de Havilland and were replaced with HS for Hawker Siddeley.

Five years later on 26 May 1965 Sir Geoffrey de Havilland, the chief designer of so many pioneering aeroplanes, died. Following his cremation his ashes were scattered over Seven Barrows in Hampshire, where he had made his first flight. During his lifetime he had received many awards and honours, including the Order of the British Empire (OBE) in 1918 and the Air Force Cross in 1919; he was made a Commander of the British Empire (CBE) in 1934 and in 1944 he was knighted. In 1979 his autobiography *Sky Fever* was published posthumously by Peter and Anne de Havilland. A statue of Sir Geoffrey de Havilland by Keith Maddison was erected at the University of Hertfordshire's College Lane Campus in 1997 and was unveiled by the Duke of Edinburgh. Six years later in 2003 the University of Hertfordshire opened its de Havilland campus.

Today many examples of de Havilland aircraft can still be seen at museums around the UK, including the Shuttleworth Collection at Old Warden Aerodrome in Bedfordshire, the Imperial War Museum at Duxford in Cambridgeshire, the Tangmere Military Aviation Museum near Chichester in West Sussex, the Science Museum in London, the RAF Museum in Hendon and the de Havilland Aircraft Heritage Centre at London Colney in Hertfordshire. The Centre was formerly the Mosquito Aircraft Museum and is based at Salisbury Hall where in 1939 the de Havilland Aircraft Company set up the Mosquito design team and built the Mosquito prototype. DH98 Mosquito fighter bombers were found still in operational service in the 1980s in South America. Sir Geoffrey de Havilland's name will always be associated with a brilliant period of British light and military aviation prominence.

Chapter 4

Vincent Richmond, the *R101* and the End of British Airship Ambitions

The *R101*'s maiden flight was intended to be a momentous voyage from Cardington in Bedfordshire, to Karachi in India, with a refuelling stop at Ismailia in Egypt. The flight was intended to not only demonstrate Britain's prowess in the sky but also to connect the four corners of the Empire. However, within a few hours of the airship's departure the much trumpeted flight had ended in disaster and with it came the end of Britain's airship ambitions.

On the evening of 4 October 1930 the *R101*'s commander, Flight Lieutenant Carmichael Irwin, had intended to have the airship gently slip away from its mooring at Cardington and gracefully head into the night. A crowd of 3,000 eager spectators had gathered to watch the airship depart but instead of an elegant departure they witnessed the *R101* struggle to pull away from the mast and limp into the night. Overloading had made the airship dip violently as it left the mast and four tons of ballast had to be immediately dumped from the nose section to bring the airship back to true and compensate for the uneven handling. As the winds picked up the *R101* was tugged and buffeted as it moved away from the mast and then, as if to add insult to injury, one the aft engines failed to start. Eventually at 6.24 p.m. the largest airship ever built departed. On-board were forty-two crew members, six passengers and six officials, including Lord Thomson the Secretary of State for Air, Sir Sefton Brancker the Director of Civil Aviation, Squadron Leader William Palstra, Royal Australian Air Force air liaison officer to the British Air Ministry, Lieutenant Colonel Vincent Richmond who had led the *R101* design committee and Squadron Leader EM Rope, assistant designer. In the early hours of the morning of 5 October 1930 the *R101* was flying at just 300 feet over Beauvais in northern France, around fifty miles north of Paris, when suddenly the airship went into a steep dive. After releasing ballast the crew brought the airship back to a level position before it went into a second steep dive and gently clipped the hill below. Frantically the crew tried to pull up again, to level off and regain control, but it was to no avail. The *R101* burst into flames and crashed, killing forty-seven of the people on-board.

Imperial Airship Scheme

In 1924 the British government established the Imperial Airship Scheme to develop Britain's long-distance passenger and mail services to the further reaches of the Empire. Under the scheme the government sought designs for airships that could carry 150 passengers, 40 crew members and cargo to such destinations as Canada, Australia and India. The requirements specified by the Air Ministry meant the possibility of building an airship with a capacity of up to 8 million cubic feet, significantly larger than anything that had been built before. The government wanted to establish whether rigid airships could provide the answer to the need for long-distance high-speed flights and planned to invest a total of £1,350,000 in the construction of two new large airships. On 14 March 1924 the Cardington and Pulham air stations were recommissioned and shortly afterwards the Air Ministry awarded contracts for the construction of two new rival airships, the *R100* and the *R101*. The *R100* was built by the Airship Guarantee Company at Howden just outside Hull on the Humber Estuary with the development led by Sir Dennistoun Burney RN MP. The *R101* was designed by Lieutenant Colonel Vincent Crane Richmond of the Royal Airship Works and was built at Cardington. To enable development of the airships to begin the Airship Guarantee Company was paid an initial sum of £150,000 on account out of a total provision of £500,000 for the *R100*, whilst the sheds at Cardington were lengthened to make room for the construction of Richmond's *R101*.

Richmond was born in London on 21 January 1893, the son of a mechanical engineer and model maker. He attended the Royal College of Science before joining S Pearson & Sons as an engineer. During the First World War he served with the Royal Naval Air Service from 1915, where he developed envelopes for non-rigid airships and devised a method for doping linen before it was applied to an airframe, which managed to earn him the nickname Dope.

In 1920 Richmond joined the Military Inter Allied Commission of Control and was posted to Germany, where as part of the Naval Sub-Commission he oversaw the surrender of airships and seaplanes. The following year he was posted to the Air Ministry's Airship Research Department where he held a number of research posts and in 1923 became lecturer in airship design and construction at the Imperial College of Science. Richmond moved to the Royal Airship Works in 1924 and lived just north of Bedford. He was appointed Officer in Charge of Design and Research. Richmond led the *R101*'s design committee and was assisted by Squadron Leader EM Rope, who in 1915 had been lead designer for the highly successful Sea Scout (SS) Zero reconnaissance and anti-submarine airships of the First World War. Rope transferred to the RAF on its formation and after a spell in the Far East was posted to the Royal Airship Works at Cardington. He was responsible for a number of pioneering airship design features, including a new method of preventing the gas bags from chafing against the hull of the great airship by surrounding each of the seventeen bags with a parachute-type harness, an automatic gas valve and a variable-pitch wind-driven propeller that was used to generate electricity while the airship was in flight. Rope perished along with Richmond in the *R101* disaster.

In April 1924 a programme of research and development into high-speed flights was started using the *R33* airship, which was flown from Pulham in Norfolk to Cardington. The *R33* arrived on 15 April 1924 and after it was successfully moored the majority of the crew departed leaving only a skeleton crew on-board. The following night the weather turned and a severe gale began to tear the airship away from its mast. At first the mooring mechanism appeared to be able to take the strain and the crew began to relax. However, at the height of the gale the nose section was torn away from the hull and the airship was blown out over the North Sea. Flight Lieutenant Booth had remained on-board and with the aid of the skeleton crew took command and made numerous attempts to bring the airship back under control as it continued to drift out to sea. With the wind blowing hard and the caps of the breakers frothing white below the engines were feverishly started as the airship proceeded to cross the Dutch coast. At last, while over Holland, Booth managed to gain control of the airship and re-crossed the Dutch coast heading back for East Anglia. In the meantime the destroyer HMS *Godetia* had been ordered out of Harwich and raced across the North Sea to act as an escort to the airship in case its precarious situation worsened. At the height of the gale the airship was being blown astern across the North Sea but was able to eventually make landfall at 3.20 p.m. on 17 April at Pulham in Norfolk.

By October 1925 the nose cone on the *R33* had been replaced and reinforced, which enabled a further series of flying experiments to take place that were used to gather data that would be useful in the design of the *R101*. In December 1925 a lightweight DH53 Hummingbird aircraft was attached to the *R33* below one of the gondolas and after a number of attempts a successful launch and recapture in mid-air was achieved. During this time a hangar was erected at Karachi and mooring masts were built in Egypt and in Montreal, Canada. However, the funding for the *R33* experiments ran out and further work was cancelled. The *R36* airship had been repaired and made ready to undertake a number of test flights to Egypt, but again due to funding difficulties this part of the programme was also discontinued. The *R33* was under the command of Flight Lieutenant Irwin and Major GH Scott whose disappointment can only be imagined after the *R33* had broken away from its mooring mast and the subsequent government decision not to finance any further test work. However, despite limited funds and the cancellation of the *R33* research programme the Cardington air station was prepared for its new task. The carcase of the *R37* that had been dismantled in 1921 after its construction had been halted by the government, was cleared from the Cardington shed and sold as scrap. Mooring mast investigations took place and a limited research programme was carried out to improve gas bag material.

Construction work on the *R101* commenced in earnest in 1926 and a test section that was bolted to the floor of the Cardington shed was demonstrated to the Imperial Conference that year. The 1926 Imperial Conference was the sixth such conference and was held between 19 October and 22 November. It was hosted by the British Prime Minister Stanley Baldwin. The delegates, who included the Prime Ministers of Australia, Canada, the Irish Free State, Newfoundland, New Zealand and South Africa were suitably impressed with the demonstration, particularly after it was pointed out the shed had been enlarged at the cost of £95,000 and that the ship was expected to be ready to fly to India by 1927. However, work on the *R101* was considerably slower than that of the *R100* due entirely to the highly experimental nature of the *R101* and the comparative inexperience of the designers at Cardington. The shed was lengthened to 812 feet and the roof was raised from 110 feet to 156 feet. Improvements in the water and electrical supplies were also made at a cost of £105,800. The mooring mast was a highly elaborate affair 200 feet high that was made of latticed steel and included connections for fuel, gas, water and electric mains. On the top of the enclosed tower was a swinging attachment that enabled the anchored airship to float in any direction the wind was blowing. The mooring equipment consisted of a receiving arm on top of the tower that could swing through 30 degrees to follow an airship's movement or when the vessel was blown by the wind. The mooring wire was attached to a steel cone on the airship's bow and ran through the centre of the receiving arm. The bow locked automatically into the receiving cup on top of the arm, whilst yawing was prevented by guide ropes stretched from side to side of the airship's nose to anchor blocks 750 feet away and buried within the grass of the fields. A 12-inch gas main ran up the mast and the top of the tower was capable of taking a 30-ton pull. Underground fuel tanks holding 10,000 gallons of fuel were alongside with a pumping mechanism capable of sending 2,000 gallons of fuel an hour to a height of over 400 feet. Two other pumping houses were built from which water ballast could be pumped at the rate of 5,000 gallons an hour.

Richmond's design for the *R101* was characterized by the use of many new and untried design concepts. The gas bags were retained in position by the use of a slack wire system that surrounded the gas bags like parachute rigging to retain them in position. The girders for this giant ship were made by Boulton & Paul Limited of Norwich and the outer covers for the hull were constructed at Cardington in the new Top Shop, which had been erected by Stephen Eaton Limited of Wallsend-on-Tyne. In all, 354 people worked on the construction and with a serious shortage of housing in Bedford it was recognized that the workers would have to be provided with special accommodation at Cardington and so a limited number of houses were built opposite the air station in an area that was named Shortstown, after Short Brothers.

The *R101* cost a total of £438,000 to build and had a capacity of 5 million cubic feet that was filled with hydrogen. It was 732 feet long, 132 feet in diameter and was expected to be able to lift 150 tons. A considerable amount of experimental work was undertaken to develop a suitable lightweight aero–diesel engine for the airship, but the lack of government funds meant that this work was soon stopped. Richmond decided to equip the *R101* with five 585hp Beardmore diesel engines that had been originally designed for use on Canadian railway locomotives. This was a disastrous decision as the engines were far too heavy for the *R101* and were not able to provide it with the amount of lift that it needed to reach its optimum altitude. On 14 October 1929 the *R101* was walked out of its Cardington shed and preparations for its maiden flight began. The following month on 23 November 1929 seventy-five Members of Parliament were taken up in the *R101* for a short test flight.

The *R100* had been undertaken by the Airship Guarantee Company, an offshoot of Vickers Limited under the controlling interest of Sir Dennistoun Burney RN. The chief designer was Dr Barnes N Wallis and the chief mathematical calculator was Nevil Shute Norway. Unhappily for the Royal Airship Works at Cardington it had been necessary to hurriedly enlist the services of technicians, engineers and scientists who were not as familiar with airship construction as those retained by the Airship Guarantee Company who had been involved in previous airship development work.

The *R100* was completed in November 1929 but was deliberately held back due to the bad flying weather during the course of the trials of the *R101*. A delay of three weeks ensued until a break in the weather allowed the *R101* to be housed again. A further delay of a week occurred before the *R100* could be flown from Howden to Cardington, which might have been avoided if a mast had been erected at Howden as hoped in 1921. However, in the cold blue light of dawn on 16 December 1929 the *R100* rose into the morning sky for the first time and headed for its new home at Cardington.

At the time Ramsay MacDonald was the Prime Minister of a Labour government and the somewhat eccentric Lord Thomson of Cardington was the Secretary of State for Air. The development of British rigid airships came under the direction of the Air Member for Supply and Research at the Air Ministry who was directly responsible to the Chief of the Air Staff and the Air Council. By arranging for the construction of the airships by two parallel organizations it is understandable that an unpleasant air of competition existed rather than the dignified co-ordination of ideas and resources. On the one hand Vickers Limited and Airship Guarantee Company key personnel included Sir Dennistoun Burney, Dr Barnes Wallis, JE Temple, Nevil Shute Norway and Squadron Leader RS Booth, commander of the *R100*. On the other hand the personnel at the Royal Airship Works at Cardington included Wing Commander RBB Colmore, Director of Airship Development and Major GH Scott, Assistant Director, who were responsible for overall direction to Air Vice Marshal Sir Sefton Brancker, Director of Civil Aviation. During its construction the *R101* consumed two miles of longitudinal steel girders, six miles of booms or smaller girders and eight miles of side and base struts, making 18,000 struts in all. There were eleven miles of bracing cables, twelve miles of webs, twenty-seven miles of tubing and and the whole thing was held together with over 450,000 rivets.

Into the Air

The *R100* was the first to make its formal maiden voyage when it slipped from its mooring mast at Cardington at 3.48 a.m. on 29 July 1930 as it set course for Montreal, Canada, across southern Scotland and Northern Ireland. The crew were able to make out the street lights and towns below before they turned westward and made their way out over the Atlantic. A stream of intelligence on the changing meteorological situation was transmitted to the navigating officer and by following the German method of constantly changing course storms were by-passed and accidents caused by lightning were avoided. On 1 August 1930 the *R100* arrived at St Hubert's Aerodrome, Montreal, to the acclamation of the crowd that cheered madly as they approached. The journey had covered 3,300 miles in little over 78 hours with accommodation for passengers that would favourably compare with any North Atlantic Ocean liner. Damage caused to the tail fin by a severe gust of wind 200 miles from Montreal was quickly repaired. On 16 August the *R100* returned to England in just over 47 hours. The success of the Airship Guarantee Company was not in any doubt and the intentions set for the North Atlantic run by Sir Dennistoun Burney and Dr Barnes Wallis had been met in every instance. It only remained for an air service to be opened to make the *R100* adventure an undoubted success.

The *R100* had a crew of thirty-seven, was 709 feet long and had a diameter of 133 feet, with a total volume of 5,156,000 cubic feet. The six 650hp Rolls-Royce Condor IIIB 12-cylinder engines gave the airship a maximum speed of 81.5mph, a range of over 4,095 miles and an endurance of 64 hours.

Towards the end of 1929 the *R101* had been undergoing further flight tests. On 17 November 1929 an endurance flight was undertaken from Cardington to Scotland and eastern Ireland that crossed the Irish Sea four times during a flight that lasted 30 hours 35 minutes. It became clear that the airship was too heavy and she was confined to her shed for gas bag netting adjustments in an effort to increase the amount of lift, but in reality the airship was underpowered. In 1930 the *R101* flew at the Hendon Air Display and almost plunged into the ground. Its unpredictable handling and poor lift led to it being taken back into the shed at Cardington and lengthened by 35 feet, with additional gas bags fitted to the new longer airframe. The modifications were completed by 26 September 1930 and the *R101* was supposed to have been given an Airworthiness Certificate. Following the extension the *R101* was 777 feet long, had a diameter of 131 feet 4 inches and was 140 feet high. The five 585hp Beardmore Tornado 8-cylinder diesel engines were fitted with two bladed propellers 16 feet in diameter that gave it a maximum speed of 71mph, a cruising speed of 63mph and a range of some 4,000 miles, with a crew of forty-five and capacity for 100 passengers. The airship then underwent an almost idyllic endurance flight for more than 16 hours, where to many the airship appeared to perform well, even though no full speed trials were undertaken during the flight due to engine difficulties and the gas bags were later found to have been chafed by the netting that held them in place and numerous leaks had developed.

On 4 October 1930 the great airship was moored in the semi-gloom of the cool evening as the lights of Bedford illuminated the sky in the distance. People had been assembling at the Royal Airship Works since midday, standing around in a sea of mud, wrapped up warmly in raincoats and armed with umbrellas against the persistent drizzle. Crewmen had been arriving from their lodgings; those that were married and lived across the road in Shortstown bade farewell to their wives and children. They made their way to the lift shaft at the mast that gave access to the interior of the great ship. Fuel and water were still being pumped up the mast to fill the tanks located in the lower portion of the hull. The vessel's officers had arrived and already the navigating officer was working out the route the ship would take to Karachi. It had been proposed that the great airship should fly across France and the Mediterranean to Egypt and land at Ismailia.

By now it was dark and the cloud had increased in density but despite the bad weather everyone had a glorious view of the airship riding at the mast illuminated by searchlights from around the airfield. The Air Minister, Lord Thomson of Cardington, arrived by car and the crowd eagerly pressed around the official party for some indication of feeling on the inauguration of this service. Lord Thomson was not the type of man to disappoint an audience having been a Brigadier General in the Army, a Member of Parliament and now a Minister in a Labour government. The official party commenced the ascent in the lift to the bow of the airship and entered the vast interior of the new vessel.

At 6.24 p.m. the airship was seen to be released from the mast and the crowd stood gazing up in expectant silence as the roar of the diesel engines opened up. All but one of the five engines sprang into life, the fifth started shortly after. It appeared to some that the airship stood motionless before slowly circling the town and bade farewell to the well-wishers below. After leaving Bedford the *R101* headed out towards Hitchin and flew south to London. A local eyewitness recalled that the airship seemed to be flying very low. The airship had, in fact, been rolling and pitching due to the adverse weather and the aft engine had stopped due to faulty oil pressure. It was not widely known at the time but for its inaugural flight the *R101* had only been issued with a partial Airworthiness Certificate by the Air Ministry specifically to cover Lord Thomson's voyage. At 9.30 p.m. the airship had reached Hastings and started to cross the English Channel in very bad weather. At the mid-point the engine that had been dead was restarted, which increased power to the airship whose height had dropped to 70 feet. At the Pointe de St Quentin the time was registered as 11.26 p.m. and the speed of this great ship had become a mere crawl. An observer at Poix

Airport reported the height of the *R101* to be as low as 300 feet and at 1.52 p.m. Le Bourget Airport put the airship just north of Beauvais.

The inhabitants of Beauvais had been in bed for some time, but despite the bad weather the local gendarme had been on his beat. At 2.05 a.m. the airship was observed in a steep dive and with the release of water ballast the airship was brought back to an even keel. Three minutes later the airship again went into a dive and gently hit the hill just outside the town. In seconds 5 million cubic feet of hydrogen had burst into flames. Immediately the inhabitants of Beauvais were rudely awakened by the roar of the explosion and the flames that illuminated the night sky. Those who had heard the droning of the engines as the airship had passed the north of the town realized instantly what had happened. People immediately rushed out of their homes and saw the fire that was burning fiercely. Having rushed to the scene of the disaster they found that it was near impossible to approach the flaming wreck due to the intense heat. The government airship was a burning wreck and only eight survivors managed to reach the safety of the people from Beauvais who stood watching, powerless to help.

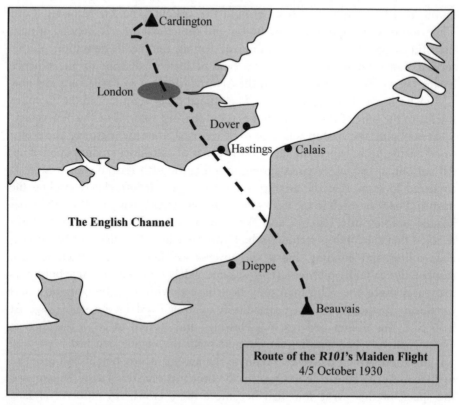

Final route of the *R101* airship, 5 October 1930.

The Aftermath

As soon as the news was cabled from France the disaster was announced and it was a complete shock to all that led to an outpouring of national grief. His Majesty King George V sent the following message to the Prime Minister.

'I am horrified to hear of the national disaster which has befallen the *R101* and the consequent serious loss of life including Lord Thomson, my Air Minister. The Queen and I sympathise deeply with the relatives of those who have perished in the service of their country and also with the injured survivors.'

George RI

Many stories circulated at the time concerning individual incidents or facts. One of the survivors told of how the commander, Flight Lieutenant Irwin, died at his post.

As I fought my way through the flames I saw him standing there quietly giving orders and he died there. Owing to the terrific heat of the flames the rescuers were unable to reach the passengers who were imprisoned in the cabins. The airship, just a mass of twisted metalwork, lay at the side of a hillock. Forty bodies were recovered by 10 o'clock. The majority of the victims were quite unrecognisable as they were terribly burned and charred and their identification was only established by what was in their possession.

In all, eight people managed to escape from the burning wreck of the *R101*, engineers AV Bell, JH Binks, AJ Cook and V Savory, foreman engineer JH Leech, rigger WG Radcliffe and wireless operator A Disley. The eighth was Rigger Church, but despite his miraculous escape he succumbed to his injuries and died three days later.

A total of forty-six of the fifty-four people on-board died at the scene. Their bodies were returned to the UK and were allowed to lie in state at Westminster Hall, within the Palace of Westminster. Following a memorial service on 11 October 1930 at St Paul's Cathedral, London, they were taken by a special train to Cardington and interred in a single grave in the cemetery of St Mary's church. A monument with the names of all those who had been killed was later erected as a lasting memorial.

The skeleton of the *R101* was almost intact following the disaster, but was left where it had fallen into 1931. It was subsequently broken up by Thomas W Ward Limited of Sheffield and the steel girders were scrapped. The German Zeppelin company bought five tonnes of duralumin from the wreck and some have speculated that it may have been used in the construction of the *Hindenburg*.

On 24 October 1930 *The Bedfordshire Standard* recorded that the plot of ground near Beauvais where the airship had crashed was offered to Britain as a memorial by the municipality of Allonne.

> The Municipality of Allonne, near Beauvais, has decided to offer to the British the piece of ground on which the airship *R101* crashed. This spot lies within the confines of the commune and not far from the village of Allonne. The promptitude with which the inhabitants, one and all, came to the help of the survivors of the *R101*, the care they took of the dead and the heartfelt sympathy they showed throughout the trying times preceding the removal of the bodies of the victims will be well remembered. The action the village authorities have now taken is another proof of their sympathy with the British nation in the disaster. At a special meeting held on Monday evening they offered to make over the ground to the British government as the site of a monument to be erected to those who lost their lives when the airship met her fate.

A thirteen-day inquiry into the loss of the *R101* was concluded in December 1930 and the official report was published in March 1931. The inquiry was held at the Institution of Civil Engineers in Westminster, and was chaired by Sir John Simon, who had with him as assessors Lieutenant Colonel JTC Brabazon, Professor CE Inglis, the Attorney General Sir William Jowitt, and the Solicitor General Sir Richard Stafford Cripps. Wilfred Lewis represented the Crown and Mr PL Teed attended to watch the proceedings on behalf of the widow of Flight Lieutenant Irwin who had commanded the flight.

The inquiry took evidence in a number of areas, including fuel control and meteorological forecasting, before dealing with the critical area of lift. It was stated that during trials the airship was found to have had a disposable lift of 40 tons, instead of the expected 60 tons. In a report on the lift of the airship dated 18 November 1929, it was stated 'it would be impossible to attempt to operate the ship on the Indian route even for a demonstration flight with only this disposable lift available'. To overcome this problem the cubic capacity was increased by unscrewing the longitudinal pieces and inserting a new middle section at the request of Wing Commander RB Colmore, Director of Airship Development. The work was authorized by the Secretary of State for Air but did not start until July 1930.

The inquiry had no doubt that the Secretary of State was anxious to start the *R101*'s maiden flight to India as soon as possible and that he believed it would be a notable and dramatic achievement to accomplish the return flight while the Imperial Conference was sitting. Sir John Simon said that one of the things that struck him was the very striking and memorable fact that Lord Thomson was determined to go himself.

'I can well believe that his great desire to go himself may have had something to do with the moment of the start', said Sir John. 'At the same time we have to see very carefully with what degree of care and deliberation the decision was reached that the vessel was fit to fly.'

The Attorney General said that on 14 June 1930 Sir John Higgins wrote to the Secretary of State for Air stating that everything was ready to begin work on the *R101*, but that until *R100* had completed her trial flights the possibility remained that *R101* might be required for the Canadian flight. He did not think that the *R101* should be put out of action until they knew that the airship was not required.

Lord Thomson replied, 'So long as *R101* is ready to go to India in the last week of September this further delay in getting her altered may pass. I must insist on the programme for the Indian flight being adhered to as I have made my plans accordingly.'

During the inquiry a well-known spiritualist medium practising in London claimed to have made contact with Flight Lieutenant Irwin in the world beyond. The attention of Major Scott, the Assistant Director of Airship Construction, was drawn to the affair and he investigated the matter in case the information may have been of use. The medium's contact with Irwin seemed to confirm all that had been said was wrong with the airship. It was claimed that the conflagration had occurred too quickly for any effective action to take place to prevent the disaster. The medium was found to have no knowledge of engineering, least of all airship construction, and therefore the possibility of a series of narrative inventions was ruled out. Nevertheless, the information concerning the technical faults was not accepted by the inquiry, but neither did it deny the possibility of its truthfulness.

Despite the inquiry's endeavour not to place the blame on any one person, the deficiencies in the design were all too clear. In view of the fact that a partial Airworthiness Certificate was issued it was concluded that the Civil Aviation Inspectorate did not consider this airship airworthy. The inquiry considered that the disaster had occurred despite the fact that the airship had been identified as sluggish during the previous Hendon Air Display and when it had left for its maiden voyage. Foolishly, heavy diesel engines had been installed that were not designed for aviation. There was a loss of lift due to the gas bags having been chafed over some considerable period of time that allowed minute holes to form and precious hydrogen to escape, which indirectly brought into question Richmond's design. Lord Thomson, Secretary of State for Air, had pushed for the maiden flight to take place against better judgement. One of the engines malfunctioned as the *R101* had left its mooring mast, causing it to lose speed.

The government had the *R100* confined to its shed for one year, despite fulfilling every objective set by her designers, possessing a full Airworthiness Certificate and having spent £450,000 to build it. She was subsequently broken up, the pieces crushed by a steam roller beyond all recognition before being sold as scrap for just £450. A paragraph that had been written in *The Bedfordshire Standard* on the day the *R101* left for her maiden voyage read, 'It is no extravagant stretch of imagination to assume that with Cardington as the world's largest airport this may mean the development of Bedford into one of the leading cities of England.' Such high hopes had been dashed.

Air Chief Marshal Lord Trenchard had endeavoured to build a defensive air force on a shoestring budget and the government was determined that the limited funds that were then available had to be spent on the development of a sustainable air defence equipped with fighters and bombers, not airships. At the time the airship *R100* was broken up plans had been drawn up at Cardington to build the *R102*. Designs had been laid out on drawing boards that incorporated improvements on the previous airship. However, with the withdrawal of further financial support by the Treasury, the Royal Airship Works at Cardington was unable to commence construction and shut down.

It was not until six years later in 1936 that the Royal Air Force came to Cardington again when they re-opened the station as part of the new RAF expansion programme. With the gathering of the war clouds over Europe RAF Cardington was equipped to become the Headquarters of RAF Balloon Command. The facilities that had been left after the airship days were admirably suited to the construction and servicing of balloons used in the barrages around London and other cities up and down the country. By 1939 RAF Cardington not only housed the headquarters of Balloon Command but had become a major reception centre for recruits called-up for national service.

On 16 July 1959 RAF Cardington was awarded the freedom of the Borough of Bedford. Present at the ceremony were two survivors of the *R101* disaster and one survivor from the *R33*, all still employed at the station.

Chapter 5

Sir George White and the British and Colonial Aeroplane Company

On 22 November 1916 the aviation industry received the news that Sir George White, Bart, who had established the British and Colonial Aeroplane Company six years earlier, had died at the age of sixty-two. White had started his working life in a lawyer's office in Bristol and later formed the stock broking firm Messrs George White and Co. On the day of his funeral the Bristol Stock Exchange, where he had served as president, was closed as a mark of respect. He had begun a long association with trams when he became the secretary of the Bristol Tramways Company in 1875 and later with the Imperial Tramways Company and London United Tramways. White was appointed managing director of the Bristol Tramways Company in 1897 and subsequently chairman by the turn of the century. His achievements in business and his philanthropic support of the sick were recognized in 1904 when he was created a baronet. Sir George White was born in Kingsdown, Bristol on 28 March 1854 and was succeeded in the baronetcy by his son George White who was born in 1882.

White founded the British and Colonial Aeroplane Company with Edwin Henry Dyer in May 1910, with a manufacturing base located in an ex-tramway shed at Filton, near Bristol. The company, which quickly became known simply as Bristol, was managed by experienced, capable businessmen who were able to inject sufficient funds to allow the business to have ambitions of large-scale commercial production. The company also formed a highly successful flying school with bases at Brooklands in Surrey and at Larkhill on Salisbury Plain. Pilots learning to fly at the school between 1910 and 1914 earned 308 of the Royal Aero Club's 664 pilots' certificates that were issued during this period.

Bristol's first aircraft to go into production was the Bristol Boxkite, a two-seater trainer developed from a Henri Farman biplane that first flew on 29 July 1910 from Larkhill. The aircraft was 38 feet 6 inches long, had a wingspan of 34 feet 6 inches and was equipped with a 50hp Gnôme rotary piston engine, which gave the aircraft a maximum speed of 50mph at 1,000 feet. In all, some

76 aircraft were built. In December 1910 four machines were shipped out to the Empire on air missions, with two going to India and a further two to Australia. A total of 61 Boxkites were manufactured for military use in the years before the First World War and were issued to the Royal Naval Air Service in March 1911 and to the Army Air Battalion at Larkhill in April 1912. The military variant had larger upper wings, three rudders, enlarged fuel tanks and an uprated 70hp Gnôme rotary engine. The first export order for the Boxkite was received from the Russian government, which bought four aircraft that were delivered to St Petersburg in April 1911. The Boxkite achieved many firsts in its time, including being the first aeroplane to land at RAF Bicester, the first to land at RAAF Williams at Point Cook in Victoria, Australia, and the first to fly into Perth and Singapore. In fact, the first passenger flight in Australia was made in a Boxkite by Joseph Hammond who took off from Altona in Victoria during February 1911. Hammond's wife was the first woman to fly in Australia. Despite its popularity the Boxkite was not easy to fly and by 1915 most had been withdrawn from military service. The memory of the Boxkite lives on in no small measure due to the 1965 British comedy film *Those Magnificent Men in their Flying Machines, Or How I Flew from London to Paris in 25 Hours 11 Minutes*. The film was set in 1910 and told the story of Lord Rawnsley, the owner of fictional newspaper the *Daily Post*, who offered a prize of £10,000 to the winner of an air race to be run between London to Paris. The film used three replica Boxkites and after filming had been completed one of them was presented to the Shuttleworth Collection at Old Warden Aerodrome in Bedfordshire, where it still takes part in regular flying displays today.

The Western Front
The Romanian Henri Coandă was Bristol's chief designer between January 1912 and October 1914 and was responsible for a number of Bristol aircraft, most notably the Bristol-Coandă monoplane, which won the main prize at the International Military Aviation Contest in 1912. Coandă returned to France in 1915 and worked for the luxury automobile manufacturer Delaunay-Belleville based in Saint-Denis, just north of Paris. They manufactured the most sought after luxury cars in the world at that time and produced the favourite automobile of both Tsar Nicholas II and King George I of Greece. Following Coandă's departure the role of chief designer went to Frank Barnwell, who had made the first powered flight in Scotland in 1909 near the Wallace Monument at Causewayhead. Barnwell was responsible for many of Bristol's most successful aircraft, including the Bristol Bulldog and the Bristol Blenheim. He was awarded the Order of the British Empire in June 1918 and the Air Force Cross in September 1918 in recognition of his outstanding contribution to aviation. Sadly, he was killed in an air crash in 1938 while attempting to take off in an aircraft that he had built himself. His widow, Marjorie, suffered yet further tragedy when all three of their sons, David, Richard and John, were killed in

separate incidents during the early years of the Second World War.

One of Barnwell's first designs was the single-seater scout and fighter biplane the Bristol Scout, which Barnwell had developed with the assistance of the pilot Harry Busteed who at that time was regarded as Harry Hawker's great rival. The Scout first flew on 23 February 1914. In total, 373 aircraft were delivered, with the majority being flown by the Royal Flying Corps, the Royal Naval Air Service and the Australian Flying Corps. Initially the Scout was armed with a standard Lewis machine-gun, but by the time the more flexible synchronized-gear machine-gun was available the aircraft was beginning to be overshadowed by other more capable aircraft. The early variants had been fitted with two rifles that were specifically aimed downwards to ensure that they cleared the propeller. Two of the RFC's Scouts were later equipped with a Lewis machine-gun on the port side and one of these aircraft, Scout B No. 1611, was flown by Captain Lanoe George Hawker. On 25 July 1915, while flying over Passchendaele and Zillebeke, Hawker was attacked by three German aircraft. He shot down two of the enemy aircraft and forced the third to retreat with his Lewis machine-gun; his actions earned him the Victoria Cross, the first to be awarded to a British pilot. Several of the Scout C variants had their machine-gun fitted on the upper wing in a similar manner to the mounting on the Nieuport 11.

Improvements to the design of the Scout C led to the Scout D variant, which represented the majority of the aircraft that were manufactured. The Scout D was 20 feet 8 inches in length, had a wingspan of 24 feet 7 inches and stood 8 feet 6 inches tall. It was equipped with an 80hp Gnôme rotary piston engine that allowed it to reach a top speed of 93mph and to have an operational ceiling of 15,500 feet. By May 1916 the Scout had been successfully tested with the Vickers synchronized-gear machine-gun, but the aircraft was being outpaced by the Sopwith Camel and so was withdrawn from front-line duties and reassigned as a trainer.

On 9 September 1916 Barnwell's Bristol F2A two-seater fighter and reconnaissance biplane took to the air for the first time. A total of fifty-two machines were produced before the F2B made its maiden flight on 25 October 1916. The F2B was the variant that went into mass production with over 5,300 aircraft delivered. It was 25 feet 10 inches long, had a wingspan of 39 feet 3 inches and stood 9 feet 9 inches high. It was originally equipped with a Rolls-Royce Falcon I in-line engine that was later uprated to the Falcon II engine before the introduction of the 275hp Falcon III liquid-cooled V-12 engine, which gave the F2B a maximum speed of 123mph whilst at 5,000 feet and an operational ceiling of 18,000 feet. It was armed with a synchronized forward firing .303-inch Vickers machine-gun, with either one or two .303 Lewis machine-guns in the observer's rear cockpit and a 20lb bomb payload. Production was shared between Bristol, Standard Motor Company, Armstrong Whitworth and the Cunard Steamship Company and it remained in service well into the 1930s in both military and civil applications. Today one example can be found amongst the Shuttleworth Collection at Old Warden Aerodrome in Bedfordshire.

The Bristol F2B fighter entered service in March 1917 and was first deployed on the Western Front the following month in time to provide aerial support during the Battle of Arras. The first sortie was led by Lieutenant William Leefe Robinson VC of the RFC's 48 Squadron, who had previously been awarded the Victoria Cross for his actions on the night of 2/3 September 1916 when he became the first British pilot to shoot down a Zeppelin over Britain. Several years later, it was claimed that the airship was in fact a Schütte-Lanz SL11. However, on this occasion he led a patrol of six Bristol F2 fighters when they ran into Manfred von Richthofen who was leading a flight of five Albatros DIIIs from *Jasta* 11. During the conflagration Robinson and three other F2s were shot down and Robinson was taken prisoner. The F2B saw service with numerous air forces around the world, including in Australia, Belgium, Canada, Ireland, Greece, Mexico, New Zealand, Norway, Peru, Poland, Spain and Sweden, as well as the RAF, which finally retired the aircraft in 1932.

The British and Colonial Aeroplane Company had for many years been affectionately known simply as Bristol, not least because of its manufacturing works located at Filton and Brislington in the city. Bristol had grown significantly by the end of the First World War and had over 3,000 staff. In 1920 the company was dissolved and its assets re-established as the Bristol Aeroplane Company Limited. It was at this point that the company made its first steps in establishing the noted aero engine division with the acquisition of the Bristol-based Cosmos Engineering Company, which became the Bristol Engine Company. At this time Bristol made two important design decisions, first that from then on they would only use all-steel airframes in their aircraft and second that they would only be equipped with Bristol engines.

One of the main Bristol designs of the inter war years was the Bristol Bulldog fighter of which a total of 456 machines were built. The Bulldog was a single-seater biplane fighter designed by Frank Barnwell that served with the RAF until 1935. The Mk I prototype first flew on 17 May 1927 but the main production variant was the Bulldog Mk IIA, which was 25 feet 2 inches long, had a wingspan of 33 feet 10 inches and stood 8 feet 9 inches tall. It was equipped with a 490hp Bristol Jupiter VIIF radial piston engine, which gave the machine a maximum speed of 174mph and an operational ceiling of 29,300 feet. The armament consisted of two synchronized .303-inch Vickers machine-guns and four 20lb bombs. The Bulldog was easy and cheap to maintain, which at a time of deepening economic recession in the late 1920s and early 1930s meant that the aircraft escaped numerous cuts in defence spending. In fact, Britain's balance of payments were boosted by the enormous popularity of the Bulldog abroad, which led to export orders from air forces in Australia, Denmark, Estonia, Finland, Japan, Latvia, Siam, Spain and Sweden. The Bulldog was retired from the RAF in 1937 when it was replaced by the Hawker Hurricane and the Supermarine Spitfire.

In 1931 Douglas Bader, who later became Group Captain Sir Douglas Bader and a Second World War fighter ace with twenty credited victories, was training to compete in the 1932 Hendon Air Display. He had been warned previously not to perform aerobatics below 2,000 feet but despite the warning crashed his Bristol Bulldog Mk IIA, number K1676, at Woodley Airfield on 14 December 1931. The accident was caused when a tip of a wing clipped the ground while he was attempting to perform an aerobatic manoeuvre for a dare. He was taken to the Royal Berkshire Hospital where the famous surgeon J Leonard Joyce was left with no option but to amputate both of Bader's legs, one below the knee and the other just above. For many, such debilitating injuries would have marked the end of their career, but Bader's remarkable story seems to have flourished in the face of such adversity. He fought long and hard to regain his mobility and on 27 November 1939 he was able to fly solo again in an Avro Tutor. By January 1940 he was back in the RAF and at the age of twenty-nine he was posted to 19 Squadron at RAF Duxford in Cambridgeshire. On 9 August 1941 Bader was flying over German-occupied northern France in Spitfire number W3185, when he was attacked and shot down. There is some controversy over the incident, with some sources suggesting that he may have been the victim of friendly fire. Having baled out he was eventually captured by the Germans and following a number of escape attempts was incarcerated at the notorious prisoner of war camp at Colditz Castle near Leipzig in the German state of Saxony. He and his fellow prisoners were liberated in 1945 by the First United States Army.

The Bristol Blenheim

Bristol was floated as a public limited company on 15 June 1935, by which time it was employing over 4,200 people, the majority of whom worked in the aero engine division. The company's growth and solid commercial footing meant that it was in a strong position to support the British government's re-armament plans that began in May 1935. One of the most important new aircraft to be brought into service with the RAF in the years leading to up to the Second World War was the twin-engined Bristol Blenheim light bomber, which first flew on 12 April 1935 and was named after the famous Battle of Blenheim that took place on 13 August 1704 during the War of the Spanish Succession. The aircraft's design was well ahead of its time in many ways. It was the first aircraft to be built with an all-metal stressed skin, the first to have retractable landing gear, the first to be fitted with powered gun turrets and the first to be equipped with variable pitch propellers. The Blenheim Mk IV was 42 feet 7 inches in length, had a wingspan of 56 feet 4 inches and stood 9 feet 10 inches high. It was fitted with two 920hp Bristol Mercury XV radial engines, with three bladed Hamilton Standard propellers that gave the aircraft a maximum speed of 266mph at 11,800 feet, a range of 1,460 miles and an operational ceiling of 22,000 feet. However, the Blenheim was comparatively slow and lightly armed and as such was not a match for the *Luftwaffe*'s Messerschmitt Bf 109 fighter aircraft. As a result the Blenheim was used more and more as a long-range reconnaissance aircraft or as a night fighter. The armament consisted of one .303-inch Browning machine-gun located on the port wing, one or two .303-inch Browning machine-guns fitted in either a rear firing under-nose blister or a Nash & Thomson FN54 hydraulically operated turret and two .303-inch Browning machine-guns located in a dorsal turret. The machine had a total bomb payload of 1,000lb, which could consist of either four 250lb bombs or two 500lb bombs, with a further eight 40lb incendiaries available stowed outside the aircraft. The Air Ministry was so convinced by Barnwell's design that they ordered the Bristol Blenheim straight off the drawing board, with the first machines delivered on 10 March 1937 to 114 Squadron. Flying Officer Andrew McPherson was the first British pilot to fly over the German coast during the war, taking off on the day war was declared. The following day fifteen Blenheims took part in the first bombing raids over Germany.

In all, over 4,000 aircraft were delivered and they served with the RAF until 1944. They saw active service during the Battle of Britain when they raided German airfields between July and October 1940 as well as mounting numerous long-range reconnaissance missions. On 12 August 1941 Wing Commander Nichol, the commanding officer of 114 Squadron, led fifty-four Blenheims on a low-level bombing raid against the Fortuna Power Station at Knapsack and the Goldenburg Power Station at Quadrath in Germany. It was Nichol's first raid in a Blenheim and twelve of the aircraft did not return. The power stations were attacked again twice that year by de Havilland Mosquito bombers on the nights of 2/3 October and 21/22 December. The Blenheim had more success as a night fighter, scoring five victories against German bombers raiding London on 18 June 1940, but by early 1941 the Blenheim was being out-performed by the Bristol Beaufighter. The Blenheims remained in service until 1943, fulfilling front-line duties in the UK as well as in the Middle and Far East, where they helped with the defence of India and with the Burma campaign. The Bristol Buckingham was expected to be the logical replacement for the Blenheim, but with changes to the Air Ministry's requirements and the appearance of the de Havilland Mosquito the aircraft became obsolete before it had a chance to see active service.

The Bristol Fairchild Bolingbroke was developed from the Blenheim Mk IV and first flew on 14 September 1939, with a total of 676 aircraft built by Fairchild Aircraft Limited in Canada. The Bolingbroke was 42 feet 9 inches in length, had a wingspan of 56 feet 4 inches and stood 9 feet 10 inches tall. It was equipped with two 920hp Bristol Mercury XV nine-cylinder radial air-cooled engines, which gave the aircraft a maximum speed of 288mph at 15,000 feet and an operational ceiling of 27,000 feet. The Bolingbroke's armament consisted of one forward-firing .303-inch Browning machine-gun, a second .303-inch Browning in the dorsal turret, a further two Brownings in a Boulton & Paul Type C gun turret and a 1,000lb bomb payload. This variant of the Blenheim was deployed primarily as a long-range maritime patrol bomber by the Canadian Air Force between 1940 and 1944 that was operated along the Canadian Atlantic and Pacific coasts.

Leslie Frise Picks Up the Mantle

Following Frank Barnwell's tragic death in 1938, Bristol appointed Leslie Frise as its new chief designer. Frise had joined the company in 1916 and worked on numerous designs, including the Bristol Fighter in 1916 and the Bristol Bulldog in 1927. Frise left the Bristol Aeroplane Company after the Second World War to become the chief engineer at Hunting Percival Aircraft, where he later designed the Hunting Percival Jet Provost. However, one of his most significant contributions to the war effort while at Bristol was undoubtedly the Bristol Beaufighter. This was a two seat long-range fighter, a night fighter, a torpedo bomber and a ground attack aircraft that was derived from the earlier Bristol Beaufort torpedo bomber.

The Bristol Beaufort Mk I had a crew of four and was 44 feet 7 inches long, with a wingspan of 57 feet 10 inches and a height of 12 feet 5 inches. The aircraft was fitted with two 1,130hp Bristol Taurus 14-cylinder sleeve valve radial engines, which gave it a maximum speed of 265mph at 6,500 feet and an operational ceiling of 16,500 feet. The Beaufort was armed with a total of four .303-inch Vickers K machine-guns and could carry either a 1,500lb bomb payload or a 1,605lb 18-inch Mk XII torpedo. Production was due to commence at the end of 1938, but overheating problems were experienced with the Bristol Taurus engines and manufacturing had to be delayed. The Air Ministry then decided to prioritize the manufacture of the Blenheims, which meant that the Beaufort did not begin to enter service until January 1940. In all, more than 2,000 Bristol Beauforts were delivered, which included 700 aircraft built in Australia that were equipped with two 1,200hp Pratt & Whitney Twin Wasp engines.

The Beaufort was evolved from the Blenheim light bomber and was operated by RAF Coastal Command and the Royal Navy's Fleet Air Arm between January 1940 and the middle of 1943, principally as a torpedo bomber in the North Sea, the Atlantic Ocean and the English Channel. On 16 May 1942 the German heavy cruiser *Prinz Eugen*, escorted by two destroyers, was sighted off Trondheim in Norway attempting to break out into the North Atlantic. The first RAF attack force, which was made up of twelve Beauforts from 42 Squadron, six Blenheims from the Royal Canadian Air Force's 404 Squadron and four flak suppression Beaufighters from 235 and 248 Squadrons, was dispatched to find and sink the ship. Three Beauforts were brought down by enemy fire before they could make their torpedo runs, while the other nine Beauforts were able to drop their torpedoes but failed to hit their target. A second attack force, which consisted of fifteen Beauforts from 86 Squadron, missed the target completely, flying too far north. They were then attacked by Messerschmitt Bf 109s, which brought down a further four Beauforts. During these attacks Bristol Beaufighters were deployed in flak suppression and escort roles, the first time that Coastal Command had used the Beaufighter in this way, which went on to set the pattern for future sorties. In 1942 Beauforts were deployed to the Indian Ocean and the Mediterranean, where the aircraft based at Malta played an important part in attacking Axis shipping during the war in North Africa. The Beaufort was also used as a conventional bomber and for minelaying duties before being redeployed as trainers. The last of the Beauforts were retired from the Fleet Air Arm's 762 Squadron based at Dale in 1946.

The Bristol Beaufighter was a long-range heavy fighter that was a modified Beaufort design. It made its maiden flight on 17 July 1939 and entered service a year later on 27 July 1940. In all, more than 5,500 Beaufighters were manufactured by the Bristol Aeroplane Company, the Fairey Aviation Company and Rootes, but the bulk of the aircraft, around 3,300 machines, were produced by the Ministry of Aircraft Production. The Beaufighter served with a total of fifty-two RAF squadrons in north-west Europe and subsequently in the Middle and Far East. The aircraft was also successfully operated by the Royal Australian Air Force, with the Australian Department of Aircraft Production (DAP) producing its own variant, the Mk XXI attack torpedo bomber, from 1944.

The Coastal Command Beaufighter TF Mk X variant had a crew of two or three, the aircraft was 41 feet 8 inches in length, had a wingspan of 57 feet 10 inches and was 15 feet 10 inches high. It was equipped with two 1,770hp Bristol Hercules XVII 14-cylinder radial engines, which gave it a maximum speed of 318mph at 10,000 feet and an operational ceiling of 15,000 feet. The Coastal Command variant was armed with four 20mm Hispano fixed forward-firing cannons and one trainable rearward-firing machine-gun. The aircraft could carry one torpedo, plus two 500lb bombs and eight rocket projectiles.

In early 1941 the Beaufighter had been fitted with Airborne Intercept (AI) radar sets and had become a formidable night fighter. This role was taken over by the faster and more manoeuvrable de Havilland Mosquito later in 1942, which left the Beaufighter to make its mark in anti-shipping and ground attack sorties. The United States Army Air Force took delivery of 100 Beaufighters in the Mediterranean during the summer of 1943, which saw service with the 414th, 415th, 416th and 417th Night Fighter Squadrons.

The Coastal Command variants were utilized with new tactics created by the North Coates Strike Wing that was based at RAF North Coates in Lincolnshire. Formations of Beaufighters would be deployed as bomber escorts and would suppress enemy flak with their 20mm cannon and rockets. This would clear a path for the torpedo bombers to make their runs and launch their incendiaries. These tactics were introduced in the summer of 1943 and in a ten-month period were responsible for sinking almost 30,000 tons of enemy shipping. The North Coates Strike Wing alone sank half of all tonnage between 1942 and the end of the war, which amounted to 117 vessels or 150,000 tons, with 120 Beaufighters lost and a total of 241 servicemen killed or reported missing. The Australian DAP Beaufighters from RAAF 30 Squadron fought in the Battle of the Bismarck Sea suppressing enemy fire whilst escorting USAAF Boston A20 and B-25 Mitchell bombers. The aircraft was retired from the RAF in 1946 and the remaining aircraft were largely converted to target tug duties with their last ever flight in this capacity on 17 May 1960.

The Bristol Buckingham was a variant of the Beaufighter that first flew on 4 February 1943 and was designed as a medium bomber for the RAF. The Air Ministry had originally requested a design from British manufacturers for an aircraft to replace the Bristol Blenheim in 1940. Bristol proposed the Type 162 Beaumont and an order for three prototypes was placed by the Air Ministry in late 1940. The Buckingham's maiden flight was in 1943 and was not successful. The aircraft had rather poor stability and needed a number of modifications, including increasing the size of the twin-tails. This delayed the aircraft from being able to go into production so much so that by the time Bristol was ready to begin manufacturing the air war over Europe had changed significantly, with daytime bombing raids being undertaken by American forces and night-time medium bomber raids being successfully carried out by the de Havilland Mosquito. Consequently in August 1944 the Air Ministry cancelled the design requirement. A nominal contract for 119 aircraft was placed with Bristol by the Ministry in order to enable the company to retain their workforce ready for the Bristol Brigand and Hawker Tempest that were shortly to go into production. Some sixty-five unfinished Buckinghams were converted to Buckmaster transport aircraft, which also served as trainers well into the 1950s. The Buckingham had a crew of two, whilst the C1 transport variant had gun positions removed to make room for four passengers. The C1 was 46 feet 10 inches in length, had a wingspan of 71 feet 10 inches and stood 17 feet 6 inches high. It was fitted with two 2,520hp Bristol Centaurus VII 18-cylinder radial engines, which gave it a top speed of 336mph at 12,000 feet, a range of over 2,000 miles and an operational ceiling of 28,000 feet.

Bristol's last aircraft of the Second World War was the Bristol Brigand that was intended as a replacement for the Beaufighter. The Brigand was designed by Frise in 1944 and took the wings, tail and undercarriage from the Bristol Buckingham and applied them to a new oval shaped fuselage. The aircraft had a crew of three, was 46 feet 5 inches in length, had a wingspan of 72 feet 4 inches and was 16 feet 4 inches high. It was fitted with two 2,470hp Bristol Centaurus 57 radial piston engines, which gave it a maximum speed of 358mph at 13,700 feet, a range of around 2,000 miles and an operational ceiling of 26,000 feet. The Brigand was armed with four 20mm Hispano cannons and up to 3,000lb of bombs and projectiles. The Beaufighters of 45 Squadron based at RAF Tengah at Singapore were the first to be replaced by the Brigand. From here they flew sorties against communist guerrillas during the Malayan Emergency. The aircraft suffered from numerous technical problems, which ultimately led to it being grounded. RAF 45 Squadron replaced their machines with de Havilland Hornets in January 1952. Later in the same year, when the Brigand's main spars were found to be defective, the remaining aircraft were phased out and replaced with de Havilland Vampires.

The Post-war Era

Following the end of the Second World War the Bristol Aeroplane Company created a new helicopter division with the British helicopter pioneer Raoul Hafner, who was born in 1905 in Austria. He worked with the aero engine manufacturer Pobjoy Short at Rochester in 1938 and was later interned as an enemy alien in 1940 until he became a naturalized citizen. He joined Bristol as chief helicopter designer and was responsible for the Type 171 Sycamore, which first flew on 27 July 1947 and entered service with the RAF in 1953. In 1960 all British helicopter manufacturing was consolidated with Westland Aircraft under pressure from the government to streamline the aircraft industry. Hafner became Westland's technical director until he retired ten years later in 1970. Hafner died in 1980 at the age of seventy-five following a yachting accident.

In 1945 Bristol established the luxury car maker Bristol Cars based at Patchway just outside the city and started by using designs for pre-war BMW motor cars. A director of Bristol, Mr HJ Aldington, visited BMW's bombed factory in Munich in 1945 and brought a number of designs back to Britain, along with BMW's chief engineer, Dr Fritz Fiedler. The Bristol 400 was the first car produced by the new company and was first seen at the Geneva Motor Show in 1947. Following the sale of Bristol to the British Aircraft Corporation in 1960 Sir George White, the son of the founder of the British and Colonial Aeroplane Company, bought the car division with former Formula 1 racing driver Tony Crook and formed Bristol Cars Limited. Following Sir George's retirement in 1973 Crook bought his shares in the company and became the managing director. On 3 March 2011 Bristol Cars Limited went into administration and was subsequently bought by Kamkorp, a Swiss holding company owned by the UK-based Indian businessman Kamal Siddiqi, which also owns the UK company Frazer Nash Research, the world's leading electric and hybrid vehicle technology company. But in the post-war years it was as an aircraft and aero engine manufacturer that Bristol continued to make its mark, in particular in the field of civil aviation.

The Bristol Freighter was a twin-engined freighter and airliner that was designed by Bristol's new post-war designer, Dr Archibald E. Russell. The Bristol Freighter had a crew of two, was 68 feet 4 inches in length, had a wingspan of 98 feet and stood 21 feet 8 inches tall. The Freighter was of an all-metal monoplane construction, with a square-shaped fuselage and with the cockpit positioned high up to ensure maximum stowage space internally. The prototype first flew on 2 December 1945 from the company's aerodrome at Filton. The second prototype made its maiden flight a few months later on 30

April 1946. It began proving flights in the livery of Channel Islands Airways and carried some 10,000 passengers in six months. The third aircraft was the first to be built specifically as a freighter and included a set of nose doors. Military versions of the aircraft were used by air forces from Argentina, Australia, Burma, Canada, Iraq, New Zealand and Pakistan, as well as Britain's Telecommunications Research Establishment and the Aeroplane & Armament Experimental Establishment at Boscombe Down. However, it was as a civil aircraft that it achieved success, with machines exported to operators in North and South America, Europe, the Middle and Far East. In all, some 214 Bristol Freighters were built, the last being delivered in March 1958 to Dan Air. In Britain it was used extensively on short-haul routes, ferrying cars as well as passengers, by operators such as Air Ferry, British European Airways, Dan Air and Silver City Airways. On 14 July 1948 Silver City Airways made the first flight ferrying cars and passengers from Britain to Europe, flying from Lympne Airport on the Kent coast, a few miles west of Folkestone, to Le Touquet Airport, forty miles south of Boulogne-sur-Mer on the north French coast. In 1953 the Mk XXXII variant, known as the Superfreighter, was introduced, which had a longer, broader fuselage that enabled the capacity to increase from twelve passengers to twenty and from two cars to three. Lydd Airport in Kent opened in 1955 with Silver City Airways and British United Air Ferries, which later became British United Airways, operating passenger and car air ferries to France. Today Lydd Air is based at the airport, from where regular flights to Le Touquet are still offered.

Brabazon and Beyond

On 23 December 1942 the British government established a special committee chaired by Lord Brabazon of Tara to investigate the country's post-war civil aviation needs. The Brabazon Committee's report outlined the need for a number of key aircraft to be developed, which included a large long-haul transatlantic airliner, a smaller shorter-haul airliner that could service the Empire routes and a high-speed jet-engined airliner capable of speeds in excess of 500mph.

Bristol introduced the Bristol Brabazon in 1949 in response to the report's requirement for a transatlantic airliner. This cumbersome aircraft was taken out on its 25-minute maiden flight by Bristol's chief test pilot Bill Pegg on 4 September 1949. The Brabazon could have a crew of between six and twelve and could carry 100 passengers in spacious comfort, despite the aircraft being comparable in size to today's Boeing 767-400ER, which can carry up to 375 passengers. The Brabazon was 177 feet in length, had a wingspan of 230 feet and stood 50 feet high. It was fitted with eight 2,650hp Bristol Centaurus radial engines, with paired contra-rotating 3-bladed Rotol propellers 16 feet in diameter and supported by a fuel capacity of 13,650 imperial gallons. The aircraft had a maximum speed of 300mph, a cruise speed of 250mph at 25,000 feet and a range of 5,500 miles.

The Brabazon report stipulated that the aircraft should provide 200 cubic feet for every passenger and 270 cubic feet for premium passengers, which is comparable to the total space within a small hatchback motor car today. In order to provide this amount of space the design included a fuselage that was 25 feet wide, which is around 5 feet more than the Boeing 747. BOAC agreed to an interior layout with a forward area consisting of six compartments for six passengers and a seventh with three passengers. The mid-section, above the wing that was 6 feet deep, had 38 seats laid out in groups of four around small tables, with their own pantry and galley. The rear section was to house a 23-seat cinema, cocktail bar and lounge. It is perhaps little wonder that only one aircraft was ever built and was subsequently scrapped as most airlines decided that it would be too large and costly to operate. Its size is very much in keeping with modern large airliners, but its layout and passenger carrying capacity is a far cry from the economic model of today.

The construction of the Brabazon prototype required an expansion of facilities at Filton and an extension to the runway from 2,000 feet to 8,000 feet, which was laid directly over the village of Charlton, requiring the company to relocate the local residents. The aircraft was flown at the Farnborough Air Show in 1950, at Heathrow Airport in London in the same year and at the Paris Air Show in 1951. The following year, after BOAC had cooled on the project, the British government announced that development work on the second prototype would be halted and on 17 July 1953 Edwin Duncan Sandys, the Minister for Supply, announced that the project was cancelled. In October 1953 the Brabazon, which had flown for only 382 hours was scrapped along with the partially completed second prototype.

Despite the failure of the Brabazon aircraft Bristol was awarded a contract to develop the propeller-driven airliner for the Empire outlined in the Brabazon Committee's report. This became the Bristol Britannia and Bill Pegg took the Britannia out on its maiden flight from Filton on 16 August 1952. By the time the aircraft was introduced in 1957 competing jet-engined airliners from de Havilland and Boeing were already waiting in the wings and quickly superseded the slower Britannia. As a result only eighty-two machines were delivered. The mysterious crashes of three de Havilland Comet aircraft understandably led the Air Ministry in 1953 to demand a further more rigorous set of aircraft tests. This decision inevitably delayed the introduction of the Britannia, a situation that was made worse when on 4 February 1954 the second Britannia prototype was damaged after being forced to land on mudflats on the Severn Estuary. The first eighteen Britannia aircraft to be delivered were received by BOAC from September 1957 and the airline made its first non-stop flight with a Britannia on 19 December 1957 when one of the fleet flew from London to Canada.

The Bristol Britannia 310 Series had a crew of between four and seven and could carry up to 139 passengers. The aircraft was 118 feet 4 inches long, had a wingspan of 142 feet 3 inches and was 37 feet 6 inches high. It was fitted with four 4,450hp Bristol Proteus 755 turboprops, which gave it a maximum speed of 397mph, a range of 4,268 miles and an operational ceiling of 24,000 feet. Of the 85 aircraft that were delivered 14 were lost in air accidents with a total of 365 people killed; over a third of these were as a result of a crash following a missed approach at Nicosia on 20 April 1967.

In the years prior to the company's merger into the British Aircraft Corporation in 1960, Bristol undertook experimental work with supersonic aircraft that later contributed to the design and development of the Concorde. The experimental Bristol 188 research jet was the last aircraft to be built by the company while it was still an independent manufacturer. The 188 was 71 feet long, had a wingspan of 35 feet 1 inch and stood 13 feet 4 inches high. It was fitted with two de Havilland Gyron Junior DGJ10 turbojet engines. The sleek 188 was built as an experiment with stainless steel as a material for construction of aircraft designed to fly at Mach 2 and above, which was work intended to support the development of the Avro 730 reconnaissance bomber. The 188 made its maiden flight on 14 April 1962 and a total of three aircraft were built, one used solely for static testing for long periods to allow the study of kinetic heating and skin temperature of up to 300°C. Additional aircraft were planned but these were cancelled when the Avro 730 was halted in 1957. From its first flight in April 1962 the 188 made 51 flights and reached a maximum speed of Mach 1.88 at 36,000 feet, around 1,300mph; it never reached its intended design speed of Mach 2. Some of the technical information gained from the research undertaken with the 188 was employed in the development of Concorde, which was built from aluminium alloys rather than stainless steel. The project was cancelled and the last flight of the Bristol 188 was on 12 January 1964.

The British government's desire to consolidate the aircraft industry in Britain led to the merger of the Bristol Aeroplane Company with English Electric, Hunting Aircraft and Vickers-Armstrongs (Aircraft), which formed the British Aircraft Corporation (BAC) in 1960. Bristol and English Electric each took a 40 per cent share of the new business and Vickers took 20 per cent. Bristol Cars was sold by the company in 1960 to ensure that it did not form part of BAC and in 1966 the aero engine manufacturer Bristol Siddeley was sold to Rolls-Royce.

Chapter 6

Thomas Sopwith and the Camels of Kingston

T homas Sopwith established the renowned Sopwith Aviation Company when he was just twenty-four years old. The list of individuals that worked with him during those early years and throughout the First World War reads like a who's who of British aviation, including Harry Hawker and Herbert Smith. Yet the company that produced the aircraft that were the mainstay of the RFC during those dark days of war was not to last the test of time and went into liquidation in 1920. Undaunted by the closure, Sopwith co-founded HG Hawker Engineering with his friend and colleague Harry Hawker and served as the company's chairman. A keen yachtsman he also competed in the America's Cup in his aptly named yacht *Endeavour*. Sopwith lived for over forty years at Compton Manor, near Kings Somborne, ten miles north of Southampton in Hampshire. At the church of St Peter and St Paul at Kings Somborne is a stained glass window memorial. The inscription reads: 'In memory of Sir Thomas Sopwith 1888–1989. Twice his foresight saved this nation in time of danger'.

Thomas Octave Murdoch Sopwith was born on 18 January 1888 in Kensington, London; he was the youngest of eight children and had seven sisters. He attended school in Hove and studied engineering at Hill Head, near Portsmouth. Tragedy struck in 1898 when he was only ten years old. The family had taken a holiday in Scotland and was staying on the Isle of Lismore. Sopwith had a gun lying across his lap, when suddenly it accidentally went off and the shot killed his father. The incident haunted Sopwith for the rest of his life.

The American aviator John Bevins Moisant had made a good deal of money from a sugar plantation that he bought with his brother in El Salvador and at the request of the Nicaraguan president he went to France to further investigate the world's growing interest in aviation. Whilst in France he asked Louis Blériot to teach him to fly and soon became an enthusiastic flyer. In 1909 he built the first metal aircraft and the following year, on 23 August 1910, made the first flight across the English Channel with a passenger. He made the flight with his mechanic Albert Fileux and his cat, Mademoiselle Fifi. It was this charismatic aviator and his pioneering flight that captured the imagination of a young twenty-two-year-old Sopwith, who went to Brooklands Aerodrome determined to learn to fly and to take to the air himself. In 1910 Sopwith made his maiden flight with the French aviator Gustav Blondeau in a Farman aircraft. Blondeau graduated from the Farman Aircraft Company based at Mourmelon-le-Grand in northern France on 10 July 1910 and later joined the engine manufacturer Gnôme et Rhône before establishing his own flying school at Brooklands Aerodrome. It was here that he met the aviatrix Hilda Hewlett. She was born in 1864 in London and was the first British aviatrix to earn a pilot's licence. They established the aircraft manufacturer Blondeau and Hewlett together, which produced over 800 aircraft, many under licence. Blondeau and Hewlett was the first British manufacturer of aircraft designed by the Caudron Airplane Company, which was subsequently bought by Renault in 1933.

Sopwith had become totally engrossed by aviation and set about teaching himself to fly with a British Avis monoplane. His first flight of his own was a disappointment. He took off at Brooklands Aerodrome on 22 October 1910 but through his inexperience as a pilot he crashed his aircraft after just 300 yards. However, through sheer perseverance he developed his flying skills sufficiently for the Royal Aero Club to award him Aviation Certificate No. 31 on 22 November 1910.

The following month on 18 December the Royal Aero Club declared Sopwith the winner of the Baron de Forest £4,000 prize, when he flew 169 miles across the English Channel from Eastchurch to Thirimont in Belgium, in 3 hours 40 minutes. Sopwith used his significant prize money from the Baron de Forest to establish the Sopwith School of Flying at Brooklands. Cecil Grace had also taken part in the event but had mysteriously disappeared while flying back from Les Baraques. The number of entrants had been reduced significantly before the event, leaving the actor Robert Loraine, who made the first Marconi wireless transmission from an aeroplane the following year in 1911, Alexander Ogilvie and Clement Greswell. Engine trouble dogged Loraine, who was eventually forced to land on difficult terrain and ran his aircraft into a dyke. Ogilvie attempted the flight from Camber Sands near Rye, East Sussex, but strong winds forced him to land suddenly a short distance into his journey and he severely damaged his aircraft. Greswell also planned to take off from Eastchurch with an aircraft from the Grahame-White Aviation Company, but dense fog crept up the English Channel and he decided to give up his attempt.

The Sopwith Aviation Company
Sopwith established the Sopwith Aviation Company in June 1912 with Fred Sigrist, who had had a tremendous working relationship with Sopwith both as chief engineer and adviser since 1910. Sigrist was in control of the Sopwith business during the First World War and oversaw the development of many

aircraft including the 1½ Strutter, of which the prototype was nicknamed the Sigrist Bus. The former Sopwith Aviation Company factory at 69 Sigrist Square, Kingston-upon-Thames is now a Grade II listed building and is used as furnished office accommodation. After the First World War Sigrist helped Harry Hawker and Sopwith to establish HG Hawker Engineering. Sigrist was also joint managing director of the Gloster Aircraft Company, which was bought by Hawker Aviation in 1934, and in addition to the Sopwith Aviation Company he also became a director of Armstrong-Siddeley, AV Roe, Air Service Training and Armstrong Whitworth Aviation.

The Sopwith Aviation Company produced more than 16,000 aircraft during the First World War, which were operated by many air forces around the world, as well as the Royal Flying Corps, the Royal Naval Air Service and subsequently the Royal Air Force. Perhaps the company's most famous aircraft was the single-seater Sopwith Camel fighter, of which more than 5,400 were built. The Camel was operated by British forces, as well as those from Australia, Belgium, Canada, Estonia, Greece, Latvia, the Netherlands, Poland, Sweden and squadrons of the United States Army Air Service.

The company opened its first factory in December 1912 in a disused ice rink in Kingston-upon-Thames. The company's first truly successful aircraft was the two-seater Sopwith Tabloid, which first flew in November 1913 with the Australian Harry Hawker, the company's chief test pilot, at the controls. The two-seater Tabloid did not have ailerons; instead it relied upon wing warping to achieve lateral rolling. The aircraft was originally equipped with an 80hp Gnôme, Monosoupape rotary engine. During an early flight at Farnborough, with a passenger on-board, it was able to climb to 1,200 feet in only one minute and reached a maximum speed of 92mph.

A float plane variant called the Schneider was also developed. Howard Pixton used this aircraft, powered by a 100hp Gnôme Monosoupape engine, to win the Schneider Trophy in Monaco in 1914, when he achieved an average speed of 86.8mph. A single-seater version of the Tabloid was used extensively by the RFC and the RNAS in the early part of the First World War from 1914. This aircraft was later developed into the single seat, scout and bomber biplane seaplane the Sopwith Baby, which was used extensively by the RNAS from September 1915 after the Tabloid was retired from active service.

When the small and highly manoeuvrable Tabloid first appeared on the Western Front it was a ground-breaking aircraft. Its performance exceeded anything that had gone before, which was not a surprise considering its Schneider Trophy heritage. In all, some forty Tabloid aircraft were built, with a further 160 Schneider machines manufactured. The Tabloid was operated as a scout at the start of the First World War and soon became used as a bomber. The single-seater Tabloid was 23 feet long and stood 10 feet high, with a wingspan of 23 feet 6 inches. It was fitted with a 100hp Gnôme Monosoupape 9-cylinder rotary engine, which gave the aircraft a maximum speed of 92mph, a range of

315 miles and an operational ceiling of 15,000 feet. The armament consisted of a forward-firing .303-inch Lewis machine-gun and two 20lb bombs. It became the first British aircraft to undertake an offensive sortie over Germany on 22 September 1914. However, the Tabloid's most famous raid was on 8 October 1914 when two aircraft took off from Antwerp and attacked the Zeppelin sheds at Cologne and Düsseldorf. The aircraft were unable to find the shed at Cologne and so attacked the railway station, but at Düsseldorf they approached at 600 feet and were able to bomb the shed, destroying Zeppelin LZ 25 ZIX.

The acclaimed aircraft designer Herbert Smith joined Sopwith in 1914 as a draughtsman and soon became the chief engineer. He is credited with designing the 1½ Strutter, which first flew in December 1915. The aircraft was the first British two-seater fighter and the first British aircraft to see active service equipped with a synchronized machine-gun. It was initially equipped with a 110hp Clerget engine and the design was evolved from the Sigrist Bus that had first flown six months earlier. The upper wings were attached to the fuselage with a pair of short struts and a pair of longer struts, which when viewed from the front appeared to form a W shape. The 1½ Strutter and the Sopwith Pup were the first British aircraft with synchronizing gear that allowed an interrupted machine-gun to fire through a moving propeller. During the summer of 1915 it became clear that the Fokker Eindecker monoplane fighters of the German *Fliegertruppen* held the upper hand in the skies over the trenches. The 1½ Strutter, along with the single-seater Airco DH2 biplane, the Royal Aircraft Factory FE2 two-seater pusher biplane and the Nieuport 11, each contributed greatly to putting an end to this Fokker scourge on the Western Front. The 1½ Strutter went into production in April 1916 and in all, over 1,400 machines were built for the RFC and RNAS, with a further 4,500 manufactured in France for the French Armée de l'Air. However, by January 1917 the 1½ Strutter was rapidly falling behind other fighter aircraft and a more powerful 130hp Clerget 9B engine was fitted to production aircraft in a belated attempt to improve its performance. This gave the aircraft a maximum speed of 102mph at 6,500 feet, an operating ceiling of some 13,000 feet and an endurance of over 3 hours. However, the improvements came too late and the aircraft was relegated to long-range reconnaissance duties, but only when fighter escorts could be made available.

The Sopwith Pup was also designed by Herbert Smith and the aircraft made its maiden flight in February 1916, reaching operational units in October 1916. The Pup was operated along the Western Front by the RFC and from British aircraft carriers by the RNAS. Squadron Commander Edwin Dunning became the first person to land an aircraft on a moving ship on 2 August 1917, when he safely landed a Sopwith Pup onto the flight deck of HMS *Furious*. Sadly, Dunning was killed while attempting to make his third landing when his aircraft crashed and went over the side of the ship. Despite his tragic accident Dunning's achievement was heralded and the Pup was pressed into service on-board three aircraft carriers, HMS *Campania*, HMS *Furious* and HMS *Manxman*.

The Pup was well regarded by its pilots and from the autumn of 1916 through to the summer of 1917 the aircraft helped to tip the balance of air power away from the Germans, with RFC 54 Squadron the first to take delivery of the new aircraft in France in December 1916. In all, 1,770 Sopwith Pups were manufactured and they became a formidable aircraft against the German Fokker, Halberstadt and Albatros biplanes. The Pup was 19 feet 4 inches long, had a wingspan of 26 feet 6 inches and was 9 feet 5 inches high. It was equipped with a Le Rhône air-cooled rotary engine, which generated 80hp allowing the aircraft to reach a maximum speed of 112mph at sea level. It was armed with a single Vickers .303-inch machine-gun that with the aid of synchronized gears fired forward through the propeller. Advances in German fighters meant that the Pup soon became outperformed and a shift in the balance of power meant that the aircraft were withdrawn from front-line operations by the end of 1917 and were returned to Britain to undertake home defence and training roles.

The Sopwith Triplane, which was affectionately known as the Tripe, served briefly as a fighter from November 1916 with the Royal Naval Air Service but, despite being well received by its pilots, was withdrawn in the middle of 1917 having been superseded by the now famous Sopwith Camel.

One of the most noted First World War pilots to fly the Triplane was the Canadian Flight Commander Raymond Collishaw, who later became Air Vice Marshal Collishaw. He was the Service's highest-scoring fighter ace and was the second highest scoring Canadian fighter ace of the war. His highly successful wartime sorties culminated on 6 July 1917 when he became the first Commonwealth pilot to score six victories in a single day. During 1917 Collishaw was Flight Commander of B Flight, 10 Naval Squadron, RNAS and although pilots were discouraged from painting their aircraft Collishaw had his flight paint their machines entirely black. B Flight, which was made up entirely of Canadian pilots, became known as Black Flight and over the next three months they scored eighty-seven victories against the *Luftwaffe*, with Collishaw himself achieving thirty-three of these.

Herbert Smith based the design of the Triplane closely on that of the Pup. He changed the biplane design to include three narrow-chord wings that significantly increased the pilot's all-round visibility. The aircraft was 18 feet 10 inches long, had a wingspan of 26 feet 6 inches, stood 10 feet 6 inches tall and was armed with a single .303-inch synchronized Vickers machine-gun. The armaments contributed to the aircraft's short service history as other fighter aircraft, such as the Albatros, were fitted with two guns and as such were more formidable in combat. When the Triplane went into production it was equipped with a 130hp Clerget 9B rotary engine, which allowed the aircraft to reach a maximum speed of 117mph. In all, 147 aircraft were manufactured in a six-month period from July 1916 through to January 1917 by the Sopwith Aviation

Company, Clayton & Shuttleworth Limited and Oakley & Co. Limited. The Triplane finally entered its brief period of service with RNAS 1 Naval Squadron in December 1916, with 8 Naval Squadron in February 1917 and with 9 and 10 Naval Squadrons by May 1917. However, field maintenance for the aircraft was not easy, spare parts were difficult to come by and the wings on some aircraft collapsed when in a steep dive due to inadequate bracing wires on the machines that were manufactured by Clayton & Shuttleworth. The Triplane's days were well and truly numbered with the introduction of the faster, stronger and more heavily armed Sopwith Camel in the summer of 1917. By the end of the year the Triplane had been withdrawn and ended up as an advanced trainer with RNAS 12 Squadron.

The Sopwith Camel

The Camel was a single-seater fighter biplane that first flew on 22 December 1916 at Brooklands with Harry Hawker again in the pilot's seat. It entered service in June 1917 and became the most successful British aircraft of the First World War, during which it destroyed 3,000 enemy aircraft, more than any other Allied fighter. In all, 5,490 were produced and saw service with the RFC, the RNAS and subsequently the RAF, as well as air forces from Australia, Belgium, Canada, Estonia, Greece, Latvia, Netherlands, Poland and Sweden and with the United States Army Air Service.

The Camel F1 was 18 feet 9 inches in length, had a wingspan of 28 feet and stood 8 feet 6 inches tall. It was fitted with a 130hp Clerget 9B 9-cylinder rotary engine that enabled the aircraft to reach a maximum speed of 115mph, to have a range of 300 miles, an operational ceiling of 19,000 feet and an endurance of 2 hours 30 minutes. It was armed with two fixed, forward-facing, synchronized .303-inch Vickers machine-guns and could carry up to four 25lb bombs. The Camel name came from a hump that was created by a metal fairing fitted over the gun breeches at the front of the aircraft.

Although the Camel was a formidable fighting machine, it was cumbersome to fly and was not popular amongst pilots, particularly those new pilots learning to fly. The aircraft could stall at 48mph or less, which would put the machine into a severe spin. In addition, if the fuel mixture was not set accurately the engine could cut out when attempting to take off, which forced the aircraft to crash.

The Camel entered service with RNAS 4 Naval Squadron in June 1917 near Dunkirk and by February 1918 a total of thirteen squadrons operated the Camel on the Western Front. Major William Barker VC, DSO and Bar, MC and two Bars was a Canadian fighter ace, who between September 1917 and September 1918 scored forty-six victories in his Sopwith Camel, making it the most successful fighter in the RAF's history. Barker was awarded the Victoria Cross for his actions on 27 October 1918; when flying a Sopwith Snipe he inadvertently crossed enemy lines near the Forêt de Mormal on the French and Belgian border.

He was first attacked by a Rumpler two-seater aircraft, which he was able to shoot down, and was then attacked by a formation of Fokker DVIIs from *Jagdgruppe* 12, consisting of *Jasta* 24 and *Jasta* 44. In a dramatic dog fight with at least fifteen aircraft he was hit in the legs three times and had his left elbow shot away, yet still managed to shoot down another three enemy aircraft. Barker crash-landed behind Allied lines and was rushed to hospital in Rouen, France, where his life hung in the balance. It was not until 1 March 1919 that he had recovered sufficiently to walk a few steps for his investiture for the Victoria Cross at Buckingham Palace.

The main production variant was the land-based Sopwith Camel F1. The 2F1 was a naval version that was armed with a single Vickers machine-gun that was

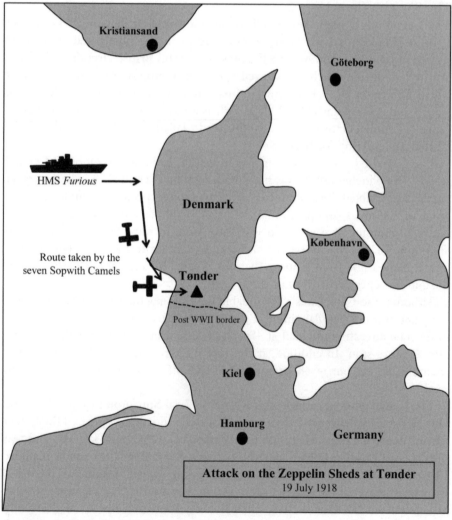

Attack on the Zeppelin sheds at Tønder, 19 July 1918.

located on top of the upper wing and the aircraft was fitted with flotation bags located near the rear of the fuselage. Only 275 of this version were built but they managed to take part in a number of dramatic sorties. Seven aircraft took off from HMS *Furious* on 19 July 1918 in the first successful aircraft carrier air strike, when they attacked the Zeppelins sheds at Tønder and destroyed the airships *L54* and *L60*.

The following month Flight Sub-Lieutenant Stuart D Culley was flying a Camel 2F1 when he famously attacked and brought down Zeppelin *L53* on 11 August 1918. This aircraft is now on display at the Imperial War Museum in London. In the summer of 1918 another Camel 2F1, number N6814, was used in trials as a parasite fighter under the airship *R23*. The Camel remained in service until after the end of the First World War, when the Sopwith Snipe was expected to be the replacement for the Camel, but production delays meant that it did not to see service until after the war had ended.

From Camels to Dolphins

The Sopwith Dolphin two–bay single-seater biplane fighter was a late entrant into the First World War, entering service in early 1918. The Mk I aircraft, which was designed by Herbert Smith, was 22 feet 3 inches in length, had a wingspan of 32 feet 6 inches and stood 8 feet 6 inches tall. It was equipped with a 220hp Hispano Suiza 8E engine, which was significantly more powerful than the 130hp Clerget 9B engine fitted to the Camel. The Hispano Suiza engine allowed the Dolphin to reach a maximum speed of 119mph and to climb to an operational ceiling of 19,000 feet. The aircraft was armed with two fixed .303-inch Vickers synchronized machine-guns.

Harry Hawker took the Dolphin out on its maiden flight on 23 May 1917. Following trials at Martlesham Heath on 28 June 1917 the Ministry of Munitions placed an initial order for 500 aircraft from Sopwith and 200 hundred aircraft from Hooper & Company, which during the war built Sopwith Camels at the rate of three per day. Hooper & Company had built the first royal car, which had a Hooper body fitted onto a Daimler chassis and was delivered to the Royal Family at Sandringham on 28 March 1900. An order for a further 200 aircraft was given to Automobiles Darracq SA, the French automobile manufacturer founded in 1896 by Alexandre Darracq. Production for the Dolphin started in earnest during October 1917 and the first 121 aircraft were delivered by the end of that year, coming operational with RFC 19 and 79 Squadrons in February 1918. The Dolphin was a relatively easy aircraft to fly, it was fast and highly manoeuvrable, which all contributed to the positive way in which it was received by its pilots. The machine's ability to operate at speed at high altitude meant that it was often pitted against German Rumpler CVII reconnaissance aircraft, which were capable of operating for extended periods above 20,000 feet.

Captain Francis Warrington Gillet initially served as an Air Cadet with the US Army Signal Corps but was given a conditional discharge. Determined to play his part in the First World War, he enlisted in the Royal Flying Corps in Canada. After he received his wings he was posted to France on 29 March 1918 and became an acclaimed fighter ace flying a Sopwith Dolphin. He shot down his first aircraft in August and during the next three months until the Armistice he scored a total of seventeen victories against German aircraft, with a further three against observation balloons. His total of twenty victories meant that he was the second highest scoring American ace, with Captain Eddie Rickenbacker in first place.

The New Zealander Lieutenant Ronald Burns Bannerman, who later became Air Commodore Bannerman, flew a Dolphin for RFC 79 Squadron. His first victory was on 4 August 1918, when he brought down a Fokker DVII. He scored a total of seventeen victories while flying a Dolphin and became New Zealand's third most successful ace. This highly successful unit also had three other aces, who were the American Captain Frederic Ives Lord, with nine victories, Canadian Captain John McNeaney with five victories and American Lieutenant Edgar Taylor with five victories. Major Albert Desbrisay Carter, who served with 19 Squadron, achieved thirteen of his nineteen victories while flying a Dolphin. Carter joined the Canadian Air Force after the war and was killed in a flying accident on 22 May 1919 while taking a Fokker DVII on a test flight at Shoreham Aerodrome. He is buried in Old Shoreham Cemetery, Shoreham-by-Sea in West Sussex.

After the end of the First World War the Dolphin, although successful as a fighter, was quickly phased out by July 1919. In all, some 2,072 Sopwith Dolphins were manufactured and around 1,500 machines that were waiting for engines to be fitted were never finished; the unused airframes were scrapped.

The Closing Months of the War

By 1917 Herbert Smith had already started work on the design of an aircraft to replace the Camel, which became the Sopwith Snipe. This was a slower, heavier aircraft compared with the Camel, but was highly manoeuvrable. The Snipe was 19 feet 9 inches in length, had a wingspan of 30 feet 1 inch and stood 8 feet 9 inches tall. The aircraft was powered by a 230hp Bentley BR2 rotary engine, which gave it a maximum speed of 121mph at 10,000 feet and an operational ceiling of some 19,500 feet. The Snipe boasted an armament of two .303-inch Vickers synchronized machine-guns and was able to carry four 25lb bombs on external racks.

The Snipe entered service with RAF 43 Squadron in September 1918 and with the Australian Flying Corps 4 Squadron in October 1918. Machines were also delivered to RAF 208 Squadron in November 1918, which although meant as replacements for the Camel arrived too late to enter active service before the end of the war. However, some aircraft did see action in 1919 as part of the Allied forces intervention in the Russian Civil War in favour of the White Russians. The Snipe became the RAF's main single-seater fighter after the war and remained in service until 1926. Even though over 4,500 Snipes had been ordered from Sopwith, Boulton & Paul Aircraft Limited, the Coventry Ordnance Works, D Napier & Son, Nieuport and Rushton Proctor & Co. Ltd, only 497 were ever manufactured.

Another late entrant in the First World War was the Sopwith Cuckoo, a biplane torpedo bomber that served with the RNAS from late 1918. Of the 350 ordered the first 90 were delivered before the Armistice was signed. The Cuckoo Mk I was 28 feet 6 inches in length, stood 11 feet high and had a wingspan of 46 feet 9 inches. It was eventually equipped with a 200hp Sunbeam Arab V8 engine that gave the aircraft a maximum speed of 103.5mph and an operational ceiling of 12,100 feet. It was armed with an 18-inch Mk IX torpedo. The requirement for a single-seater torpedo bomber aircraft that was capable of carrying a 1,000 lb torpedo and that had an endurance of four hours was laid down by Commodore Murray Sueter, later Sir Murray Sueter, who was appointed as the Navy's superintendent of aircraft construction in 1915. Sueter oversaw the creation of the RNAS and was the first to promote the idea of firing torpedoes from aircraft. Sopwith came up with the Snipe as the answer to Sueter's request for a torpedo bomber and included in its design a split-axle undercarriage so that a 1,000lb torpedo could be carried. Although the aircraft was designed to take off from a flight deck on a ship, it was not able to land on an aircraft carrier as it had no arresting gear installed, which somewhat limited its operational potential. The aircraft first flew in June 1917 and following a series of trials an initial order for 100 aircraft was placed with Fairfield Engineering and Pegler & Company in July 1917. Unfortunately, these contractors had little experience with constructing aircraft and severe delays occurred, a situation that was made worse by the short supply of the Hispano Suiza 8 engines that were initially intended to be fitted. To try and overcome these delays the airframe was adapted to accommodate the much heavier Sunbeam Arab engine, which only exacerbated the production delays. Eventually, the Admiralty saw sense and awarded the contract to the experienced aircraft manufacturer Blackburn Aircraft, which delivered its first machines in May 1918. However, design flaws were quickly uncovered that required further redesign work to the undercarriage, the tailskid and the rudder. Further trials at RAF East Fortune led to the aircraft being passed fit for squadron duties and deliveries to the Torpedo Aeroplane School at East Fortune started in August 1918. Production by Fairfield Engineering eventually got underway in the same month and the company went on to produce a total of fifty machines. Pegler & Company started to manufacture the aircraft in October 1918 and produced twenty machines; more than a year after the original contracts had been awarded. Blackburn produced the bulk of the production and delivered a total of 162 aircraft. The Sopwith Snipe was retired from active duty on 1 April 1923 when 210 Squadron, the last squadron to use the aircraft, was disbanded at Gosport.

The Sopwith Salamander was an armoured ground attack biplane that was a land-based version of the Sopwith Snipe. The Salamander first flew on 27 April 1918, but by the time it entered service the First World War was already over. The aircraft was 19 feet 6 inches in length, had a wingspan of 31 feet 3 inches and was 9 feet 4 inches high. The Salamander was equipped with a 230hp Bentley BR2 rotary engine that enabled it to reach a top speed of 117mph at 10,000 feet, which increased to 125mph at low altitude. It had an operational ceiling of 13,000 feet and had an endurance of 1 hour 30 minutes. The armament consisted of two .303-inch Vickers synchronized machine-guns and it was capable of carrying four bombs. Sopwith had expected that the Salamander would be manufactured in large numbers, but with the end of the war the need for such aircraft was greatly diminished, particularly in volume. The contracts that had been awarded to Sopwith, the Air Navigation Co., Glendower Aircraft and Palladium Motors were cancelled and only 419 machines were eventually produced. The Salamander was retired from the RAF by the middle of the 1920s.

Excess Profits Duty

The end of the First World War not only meant that aircraft contracts were being cancelled but that hundreds of surplus aircraft had come onto the market, which made it difficult for the aviation industry to solicit interest in new machines. Desperate to establish themselves in new markets, the aircraft manufacturers turned away from military production and began to develop new ideas and adapt their existing designs for the growing civil aviation industry. Sopwith attempted to develop a number of new designs but none received the same level of enthusiastic support that their wartime machines had and consequently did not make it into large-scale production. A sport version of the Pup was developed into the two-seater Sopwith Dove in 1919, which had shortened wings that were swept backwards and was powered by an 80hp Le Rhône rotary engine, but only ten aircraft were built. The Sopwith Schneider was a single-seater biplane seaplane designed to compete in the Schneider Trophy air race of 1919. However, the race was called off due to severe fog and the aircraft was subsequently converted to a land-based version called the Sopwith Rainbow. Only one was built, which crashed in 1923.

The Sopwith Atlantic, also of 1919, was a single-engined long-range aircraft designed to enable Harry Hawker to attempt the first transatlantic flight. On 18 May 1919 Hawker and his navigator, Kenneth Mackenzie-Grieve, took off from Newfoundland, but were forced to ditch the aircraft shortly into their journey due to engine trouble. Only one Atlantic was built.

The Sopwith Wallaby was a single-engined long-range transport biplane that was subsequently used by the Australian Aerial Services. The aircraft was devised to enter the Australian government's competition for an England-to-Australia flight, which offered the winner a £10,000 prize. The Sopwith Wallaby

G-EAKS took-off from Hounslow on 21 October 1919 and headed for Australia. Bad weather and technical problems caused severe delays to the flight, which by April 1920 had staggered as far as the Dutch East Indies. On 17 April the Wallaby crashed on the island of Bali. The damaged aircraft was crated up and shipped to Australia and was converted into an eight-seater transport aeroplane that was used by the Australian Aerial Services until it was retired. Only one Wallaby was built.

The Sopwith Antelope was a single-engined, three-seater transport biplane based on the Sopwith Wallaby that first flew in 1920. Only one machine was built, which remained in operation until 1935. Despite the development of these numerous experimental machines and a determination to find a civil footing in post-war Britain, the Sopwith Aviation Company's future was soon to be cut short.

Sir William Pearce was the Liberal Member of Parliament for the east London constituency of Limehouse for sixteen years, from 1906 to 1922. He was appointed chairman of the Parliamentary Select Committee on War Profits in 1919, which was established to investigate ways in which the government could tax the substantial wealth that some individuals and businesses had made during the First World War. After much discussion and behind-the-scenes negotiations a report written by Pearce was produced and accepted by Parliament. The report concluded that a levy should not be applied on individuals and businesses, but a discretionary tax could be imposed that could raise £500 million from 75,000 taxpayers. There was strong opposition to the proposal, which led the Cabinet to decide not to introduce a war profits levy but to use existing excess profits legislation. Consequently, during 1920 the Sopwith Aviation Company was presented with a large claim for Excess Profits Duty by the British government in respect of Sopwith's wartime business. Sopwith asked the authorities whether the duty could be paid over a number of years, but the government refused. As a result of this refusal in September 1920 the Sopwith Aviation Company was faced with a substantial tax demand that it could not afford to pay and consequently decided that it had no alternative but to go into voluntary liquidation.

The following month Thomas Sopwith, Harry Hawker, Fred Sigrist and Bill Eyre established HG Hawker Engineering Limited, which later became Hawker Aviation and more latterly Hawker Siddeley. Sopwith was delighted that the new company was able to take-over the old Sopwith factory in Kingston-upon-Thames in Surrey as well as the staff that were based there and, most importantly of all, the culture and traditions that they had built up together since the company had started eight years earlier. The Hawker Hurricane, Typhoon, Tempest, Sea Fury, Hunter and Harrier were all built at the same Sopwith factory at Kingston-upon-Thames. Thomas Sopwith remained chairman of the new company until he retired and then served as a consultant to Hawker Siddeley until 1980, when he was a mere ninety-two years old.

Sopwith was not just an outstanding aviator, but he also harboured a passion for the open sea and was a keen yachtsman. In 1934 he entered the America's Cup with his 130 feet J class yacht *Endeavour*, which was built by Camper and Nicholson in Gosport, England, and in 1937 he entered a second J class yacht, *Endeavour II*. Sopwith funded the development and construction of both boats, which were designed by the noted British yacht designer Charles E Nicholson. Sopwith was at the helm for both races and came close to winning in 1934. Sopwith commissioned the yacht *Philante* in 1937, which was also built by Camper and Nicholson. The yacht was requisitioned by the Admiralty during the Second World War and became HMS *Philante*. In 1947 Sopwith sold the craft and it became the King of Norway's royal yacht.

Sir Thomas Sopwith was recognized throughout his life for the outstanding contribution that he made to British aviation, which included being made a Commander of the British Empire in 1918 and being knighted by Queen Elizabeth II in 1953. As part of his hundredth birthday celebrations a special flypast of military aircraft was arranged over his home at Compton Manor in Hampshire. He died on 27 January 1989 at the age of 101 and was buried next to his wife, Phyllis Brodie Sopwith, at All Saints Church, Little Somborne near Winchester in Hampshire.

There are numerous examples of original and replica Sopwith aircraft at aviation museums in the UK and around the world, many still airworthy. The most notable include the Shuttleworth Collection at Old Warden Aerodrome near Biggleswade in Bedfordshire, the Fleet Air Arm Museum at Yeovilton in Somerset and the RAF Museum in Hendon, North London.

Chapter 7

Harry Hawker and the Hawker Hurricane

The Hawker Hurricane, the iconic Second World War fighter and backbone of the Britain's air defences during the Battle of Britain, first flew fourteen years after the company's founder, the Australian Harry Hawker, was killed in an air crash at Hendon Aerodrome.

Hawker was born in Moorabbin, south-east of Melbourne in Victoria, Australia, on 22 January 1889. As a boy he was fascinated by motor cars and grew up helping out at local garages. He would help build motor engines at Hall & Warden in Melbourne and later qualified as a mechanic while working at the Tarrant Motor & Engineering Company.

He first came to England in 1912, where he worked briefly with Commer, the commercial vehicle manufacturer based in Luton in Bedfordshire, before later in the same year moving to the Sopwith Aviation Company. His passion for aviation drove him to learn to fly at Brooklands Aerodrome and soon he began instructing other new pilots. He became Sopwith's chief test pilot and in October 1912 won the British Empire Michelin Cup for flight endurance in a Burgess-Wright aeroplane, with a time of 8 hours 23 minutes. Then in 1914 he achieved an altitude record of some 12,900 feet. Apart from a short trip to Australia in 1914 where he demonstrated the Sopwith Tabloid to enthusiastic crowds he remained at Sopwith throughout the First World War and played a pivotal role in designing and testing many of the company's new aircraft.

In 1918 the *Daily Mail* newspaper had put up a prize of £10,000 for the first person to fly across the Atlantic within seventy-two consecutive hours and it was Hawker's adventurous personality that led him to make an ill-fated attempt on the prize. Together with Kenneth Mackenzie-Grieve as his navigator he set off from Mount Pearl, Newfoundland, on 18 May 1919 in a Sopwith Atlantic biplane. However, engine trouble fourteen hours into the flight forced Hawker and Mackenzie-Grieve to deviate from their planned route and attempt to find a suitable vessel in the busy North Atlantic shipping lanes from which to seek assistance. A freighter, the *Danish Mary*, managed to pick them up but the absence of a wireless set meant that their rescue could not be reported until they had made port at Butt of Lewis, the most northerly point of the Isle of Lewis in the Outer Hebrides, Scotland. Although their heroic flight had failed the *Daily Mail* still awarded them a consolation prize of £5,000.

The following year in September 1920 the Sopwith Aviation Company went into voluntary liquidation following a claim for Excess Profits Duty by the British government, which was levied on a number of companies that were deemed to have made excess profits from their contribution to the war effort. Harry Hawker, Thomas Sopwith, Fred Sigrist and Bill Eyre bought the assets of the now defunct Sopwith Aviation Company and formed HG Hawker Engineering Limited, the original name for the business that in 1933 became Hawker Aircraft and then Hawker Siddeley in 1935. Sopwith was appointed chairman of the new company and remained in the role until his retirement. Hawker, on the other hand, was not to live to see the success that the company that bore his name would achieve. On 12 July 1921, while practising for an air display at Hendon Aerodrome, his Nieuport Goshawk biplane, a civil version of the Sparrowhawk that was specifically built as an air racer, crashed and he was killed. His last resting place is at St Paul's Church, Chessington in Surrey.

The period following the Depression in the late 1920s and early 1930s saw a great deal of expansion at HG Hawker Engineering, which began with a change of name in 1933 to Hawker Aircraft Limited and then in 1934 the company acquired the Gloster Aircraft Company. In 1935 the company merged with the engine manufacturer Armstrong-Siddeley, which included Armstrong Whitworth Aircraft and AV Roe and Co. The new company became Hawker Siddeley Aircraft Limited and that is how it stayed until 1960, when the British government encouraged the consolidation of the aircraft industry in Great Britain.

The Influence of Sydney Camm

One of the most important people to the success of Hawker Siddeley was its chief designer Sydney Camm, who joined the company in 1923 and stayed for forty-three years. Camm was born in 1893 and showed an interest in aviation from an early age. He worked as a carpenter at Martynside, the aircraft and motorcycle manufacturer based at Brooklands Aerodrome, and later assisted the noted aircraft designer George Handasyde. Martynside collapsed as a business following a fire at its factory in 1922. The next year Camm joined Hawker as a senior draughtsman and within two years had become chief designer.

Thomas Sopwith described Camm as the greatest aircraft designer in the world, a view that many of his peers agreed with. Camm received the British Gold Medal for Aeronautics in 1949, served as President of the Royal Aeronautical Society in 1954, received the Society's Gold Medal in 1958 and was knighted by Queen Elizabeth II in 1953. Shortly before his death in 1966 Camm was informed that he was to be awarded the Daniel Guggenheim Medal, which is presented each year to an individual who has made an outstanding contribution to the advancement of aeronautics. Camm's exceptional range of aircraft designs for Hawker included the Cygnet biplane in 1924, the Tempest, Hunter and Harrier. But the most memorable aeroplane to emerge from his drawing board was the Hawker Hurricane, not because it was the most technically advanced aircraft, even of its day, but for the role that it played in the Battle of Britain and the defence of Britain in its hour of need. In all, some 14,533 Hurricanes were delivered, which outnumbered all other fighter aircraft during the Second World War. Hurricane production also included over 1,000 Sea Hurricanes and 1,400 machines manufactured in Canada by the Canada Car and Foundry. The Supermarine Spitfire held a more glamorous position in the public's eyes and often overshadowed the contribution of the Hurricane, despite the latter being responsible for more than half of all RAF victories during the battle.

In 1934 the Air Ministry issued specification F36/34 for a fighter built around the experimental Rolls-Royce PV-12 aero engine, later named the Merlin. Camm's first proposal was rejected by the Air Ministry and so he set about a new monoplane design based on the Hawker Fury that was developed by Hawker Siddeley as a private venture. On 6 November 1935 the Hurricane prototype made its maiden flight from Brooklands Aerodrome, where Hawker Siddeley had an assembly plant, with Flight Lieutenant Paul Bulman at the controls.

One of the advantages of the Hurricane design was that it was already becoming out-dated, having incorporated construction techniques employed in the building of the older biplanes, including mechanical rather than welded joints. This meant that aircraft could easily be assembled, using basic tools and machinery. It also meant that field repairs could easily be affected, enabling a fast turnaround for damaged aircraft repaired by ground crew. Camm's design employed a steel tube construction for the fuselage, which supported a doped linen covering mounted on frames and longerons. This allowed bullets and shells to pass through the aircraft, again enabling fast repairs in the field. Eventually, an all metal stressed skin wing was fitted, replacing the former fabric-covered wing in April 1939. A high mounted cockpit gave the aircraft a humpbacked appearance, but more importantly allowed the pilot excellent all-round visibility. The Hurricane Mk IID anti-tank aircraft was 32 feet 2 inches long, had a wingspan of 40 feet and stood 13 feet 1 inch high. This variant was fitted with a Rolls-Royce Merlin XX 12-cylinder liquid-cooled engine that generated 1,460hp. The aircraft was capable of a top speed of 322mph, had a range of 900 miles and an operational ceiling of 32,100 feet. The armament consisted of two fixed 40mm Vickers 'S' guns below each wing and two .303 Browning machine-guns in each wing. The first Hurricanes to be delivered were the first monoplane fighter aircraft to become operational with the RAF and were the first operational fighters to have a maximum speed in excess of 300mph. The first operational aircraft were delivered to 111 Squadron based at RAF Northolt in November 1937 and almost 500 Hurricanes were in service with eighteen squadrons by the start of the Second World War. The Hurricane first saw action on 21 October 1939, when A Flight from 46 Squadron took off from North Coates on the Lincolnshire coast and attacked a formation of nine Heinkel He 115B floatplanes over the North Sea, bringing down four of the aircraft.

Air Chief Marshal Sir Hugh Dowding, Commander-in-Chief of RAF Fighter Command, initially agreed to four squadrons of Hurricanes being relocated to assist with the defence of France. RAF 73 Squadron arrived on 10 September 1939, followed soon afterwards by 1, 85, 87, 607 and 615 Squadrons, which on 30 October 1939 first saw action ten miles west of Toul, when Pilot Officer PWO Mould of 1 Squadron in Hurricane L1842 brought down a Dornier Do 17P and became the first RAF pilot to bring down an enemy aircraft over mainland Europe during the Second World War. By May 1940 reinforcements were required as the German *Blitzkrieg* gathered momentum. The Battle of France began on 10 May 1940 and 3, 79 and 504 Squadrons joined their RAF colleagues in France. However, heavy losses on the ground and in the air mounted in the face of the unstoppable German forces. On 14 May alone twenty-seven Hurricanes were shot down and fifteen pilots killed. A week later on 20 May all Hurricane units in Northern France were ordered to return to Britain and abandon their bases. The full withdrawal was completed by 21 June and of the 452 fighters deployed only 66 returned home. Some 178 machines were abandoned at a number of airfields in northern France, including Merville, Abbeville and Lille.

Hurricanes based in Britain served during Operation *Dynamo*, the evacuation of the defeated and stranded British, French and Belgian forces pursued by German troops during the Battle of Dunkirk. Some 14 Hurricane units brought down 108 enemy aircraft during the operation between 26 May and 4 June 1940, with 22 pilots killed and three taken prisoner.

With German forces positioned directly across the English Channel, the Battle of Britain began on 10 July 1940 and officially lasted until 31 October, however, the worst of the air conflict took place between 8 August and 21 September. During the battle the Germans lost 2,739 aircraft, with 55 per cent of the losses accredited to the highly manoeuvrable Hurricanes that would seek out the slower bombers, whilst the faster Spitfires attacked the German fighters and were officially accredited with 42 per cent of the victories.

The only Victoria Cross awarded to a member of Fighter Command during the Second World War was earned during the Battle of Britain by Flight Lieutenant Eric Nicolson of 249 Squadron. On 16 August 1940 he was flying with two other Hurricanes near Southampton when they were attacked from above by Messerschmitt Bf 110 fighters. All three aircraft were hit, Nicolson was wounded and his aircraft became engulfed in flames. He hurriedly attempted to bale out, but in leaving the aircraft saw that one of the Bf 110s had overshot his aircraft, so he climbed back into his cockpit, by then an inferno, and engaged the enemy aircraft.

The Hurricane went on to provide invaluable service in the air during the Blitz of 1941 and a version was sent to Egypt to replace the outdated Gladiators and support the North Africa campaign, which experienced heavy losses against the Bf 109E and F variants. From November 1941 the Hurricane also found itself up against the new more agile and more powerful Italian *Regia Aeronautica* Macchi C202 Folgore and during the five-day artillery barrage against El Alamein that started on 23 October 1942 six squadrons of Hurricanes flew a total of 842 sorties with the loss of 11 pilots.

Malta's air defences consisted mostly of Gloster Gladiator biplane fighters and when Italy entered the war on 10 June 1940, Malta's air defence rested with only a handful of Gladiators. Reinforcements were sent and four Hurricane aircraft arrived on the island at the end of June. Over 200 enemy aircraft flew from bases in Sicily to attack the island throughout the whole of July. During this time only one Gladiator and one Hurricane were lost. Fortunately additional reinforcements were able to get through and on 2 August 1940 a further twelve Hurricanes and two Blackburn B-24 Skua aircraft, the carrier-based two-seater combined dive-bomber and fighter, arrived on Malta. Despite repeated attacks by Italian and German aircraft they were not able to break the Maltese spirit. A further twenty-three Hurricanes in southern Italy landed on Malta at the end of April 1941 and in May, but fortunately much of the *Luftwaffe* were redeployed to the Russian front and left their bases on Sicily in June 1941. A further assault by the Germans on the island in early 1942 was again met with stiff opposition. In March fifteen Spitfires were sent to Malta from the aircraft carrier HMS *Eagle* but it was the Hurricanes that had the greatest success protecting the island and the vital shipping lanes that supplied the North Africa campaign.

The Hurricane also operated with distinction further afield. Nearly 3,000 aircraft were delivered to Russia to assist with its defence against the German invasion. Many were shipped in crates as part of the perilous northern convoys that were in easy reach of the *Luftwaffe* aircraft based in Finland. Some fifty-two Hurricanes were sent to Singapore, also in crates, which as a testament to the simplicity of the design and the method of construction, were all assembled in under forty-eight hours. The aircraft attempted to support the ill-fated defence of Singapore and Malaya, where British forces had completely underestimated the might of the Japanese Imperial Naval Air Service.

A number of important variants of the Hurricane were developed throughout the Second World War, including the Hurribomber, which came into service in October 1941 and could carry up to 500lb of bombs. From September 1943 the Hurricane Mk IV, which was adapted to carry four rocket-propelled missiles, saw action in the Middle and Far East, as well as in Europe. The Sea Hurricane was developed from the land-based Hurricane that operated as Catapult Aircraft Merchantmen and with the Fleet Air Arm. Initially the aircraft served in the Baltic and the Mediterranean, where the aircraft were launched by catapult, with the pilot having to ditch into the sea and be recovered. These Hurricat 'catafighters' were soon developed to work from aircraft carriers and were fitted with an arrestor hook and catapult spools. Most of the 440 aircraft of this variant that served with the Fleet Air Arm were converted RAF versions, some dating back to 1938, and only sixty were newly built. The first Fleet Air Arm Mk I Sea Hurricanes joined 880 Squadron on 15 March 1941 and were joined by a further 300 Mk IB machines that were equipped with catapult spools and a V-frame arrestor hook, as well as a further twenty-five Mk IIA Hurricanes converted to Sea Hurricane IB or hooked Hurricane II fighters. From October 1941 they commenced active duty on-board MAC-ships, merchant ships that had a short flight deck installed. The last Sea Hurricane variant was the Mk XIIA, which served in the North Atlantic. The Sea Hurricane made an important contribution during the Second World War, including involvement in the 1942 Operations *Harpoon* and *Pedestal* to Malta, the amphibious assault on Madagascar Operation *Ironclad*, as well as the early CAM ship Hurricats. Although the Sea Hurricane last saw service in 1945, by 1943 it had largely been withdrawn from front-line duties.

Typhoons and Tempests

Sydney Camm's prolific design output at Hawker Siddeley extended well beyond that of the Hurricane. He was responsible for a wide range of other aircraft both during and after the Second World War. The Hawker Typhoon was a single-seater fighter bomber designed by Camm that made its maiden flight on 24 February 1940. In all, some 3,300 machines were built and they served with the RAF between 1941 and 1945. Numerous ongoing design problems prevented the Typhoon from taking up the role as a replacement for the Hurricane as had been intended. Instead the aircraft became a low-altitude interceptor and with the addition of bombs and ground attack rockets in 1943 it became one of the RAF's most accomplished ground attack aircraft. The Typhoon Mk IB, with a 2,100hp four-bladed Napier Sabre IIB engine, could achieve a maximum speed of 412mph at 19,000 feet.

Camm sought to improve the design for the Typhoon and in doing so developed the Hawker Tempest, a formidable fighter aircraft that made its maiden flight on 2 September 1942. The Tempest came into service in April 1944 and in all a total of 1,702 aircraft were built. In September 1944 the Tempest flew from forward airfields in England and played an important role in support of Operation *Market Garden*. The Tempest Mk V was equipped with either a Napier Sabre IIA, B or C liquid-cooled sleeve valve engine, which produced 2,260hp and allowed it to attain maximum speed of 435mph at 18,000 feet.

The Hawker Sea Fury was the last prop fighter to serve with the Royal Navy and was a direct descendent of the Typhoon and the Tempest. The aircraft made its maiden flight on 21 February 1945 and the first production Sea Fury came into operational use in September 1946, after the Second World War had finished. The FB11 variant was equipped with a Bristol Centaurus XVIII 18-cylinder radial engine, which generated 2,480hp, allowing it to achieve a top speed of 460mph at 18,000 feet. Originally Camm envisaged the Hawker Fury as a replacement for the Tempest and had designed the aircraft as early as 1942. The first prototype for the land-based Fury took off on 1 September 1944. Development work for the Fury and Sea Fury was by then closely aligned, but with the end of the Second World War in Europe the contract for the Fury was cancelled and all development work was concentrated on the Sea Fury variant. Aircraft LA610 was fitted with a Napier Sabre VII engine, which generated up to 4,000hp and allowed a maximum speed of 485mph, which made it the fastest prop aircraft developed by Hawker. In total 565 Hawker Sea Fury machines were built and they served with the Fleet Air Arm for ten years between 1945 and 1955, although the Burmese Air Force was apparently still operating the aircraft in 1966.

The Gloucestershire Aircraft Company

In 1934 the Gloucestershire Aircraft Company was acquired by Hawker Aircraft and became a wholly owned subsidiary, although it continued to develop aircraft under its own name. The following year in 1935 Hawker Aircraft merged with JD Siddeley, which comprised Armstrong-Siddeley and Armstrong Whitworth Aircraft, to form Hawker Siddeley Aircraft Limited.

The Gloucestershire Aircraft Company's origins date back to the outbreak of the First World War in August 1914 when manufacturing capacity was urgently needed for the production of aircraft essential for the Royal Flying Corps in France. The Aircraft Manufacturing Company (Airco), which was established in 1912 at Hendon Aerodrome by George Thomas Holt, was urgently seeking additional factory space as the company struggled to meet its orders for the DH2 pusher fighter designed by Geoffrey de Havilland. Airco's Hugh Burroughes was recommended to approach HH Martyn and Company at Sunningend near Cheltenham, a noted manufacturer with well-respected carpentry and woodworking production skills. Initially Airco awarded contracts to HH Martyn for the manufacture of components for Farman Aircraft. The quality of the work led to Airco awarding further contracts for components for the DH2 and BE2C. In the spring of 1917 the two companies decided to enter into a joint venture and created a new business called the Gloucestershire Aircraft Company, specifically to handle all of Airco's sub-contract work.

Following the end of the First World War the Gloucestershire Aircraft Company acquired components for the Nighthawk fighter biplane that was produced by Nieuport & General Aircraft. Nieuport & General closed down in August 1920, along with the other aircraft companies owned by Samuel Waring, which included British Aerial Transport and the Alliance Aeroplane Company. The Gloucestershire Aircraft Company continued to develop the Nighthawk after Nieuport had closed, renaming the aircraft the Sparrowhawk, with an initial order for fifty aircraft placed by the Japanese Imperial Naval Air Service. The Mars I racing biplane was developed from the Sparrowhawk and with pilot Mr JH James at the controls the aircraft won the Aerial Derby in 1921 with a speed of 163.3mph, then again in 1922 with a maximum speed of 177.9mph. In 1923 the aircraft was reconstructed and renamed the Gloster I, which had a wingspan of 20 feet and a wing area of 165 square feet. This time the aircraft was flown by Larry Carter and the aircraft won its third consecutive Aerial Derby in 1923 at a speed of 192.4mph. The Air Ministry had announced that it would buy the winner of the 1923 Derby and as a result the Mars I / Gloster I entered service with the number J7234. The aircraft was later fitted with floats and became the Gloster I Seaplane, with a wingspan of 21 feet and capable of a top speed of 185mph. This variant was used as a trainer for the pilots that were to compete in the 1925 Schneider Trophy. The following year the company decided to shorten its name to the Gloster Aircraft Company, in part to help foreign customers who found the spelling of the original name difficult to pronounce.

Henry Philip Folland was born in Cambridge in 1889 and was the son of a stonemason. Like his contemporary Harry Hawker his early working life centred on the flourishing motor trade. He served an apprenticeship with the Lanchester Motor Company in Coventry from 1905. He moved to the Daimler Motor Company as a draughtsman three years later and by 1912 he was working at the Royal Aircraft Factory at Farnborough in Hampshire. In November 1916 the Nieuport & General Aircraft Company was established to build French Nieuport 11 fighters under licence by Samuel Waring, who owned the furniture manufacturing business Waring & Gillow. By 1917 Folland had joined Nieuport & General as chief designer and was later joined by Howard Preston. Folland had worked on the design of the ill-fated Nieuport Nighthawk fighter and in August 1918 the Air Ministry had placed an initial order for the aircraft. However, persistent engine problems delayed production and then, with the end of the First World War and a sharp drop in demand for new aircraft, the order for the Nighthawk was cancelled and Nieuport & General was wound-up. Folland then transferred to the Gloucestershire Aircraft Company and became responsible for a number of the company's classic aircraft, including the Gloster Grebe, the RAF's first post-First World War fighter that entered service in 1923 and the Gloster Gauntlet fighter biplane that first flew in January 1929 and entered service in 1933. The Gauntlet was the last RAF fighter aircraft to have an open cockpit and was the basis of the highly successful Gloster Gladiator that entered service in 1934, the same year that Gloster was acquired by Hawker Aircraft. Following the sale of Gloster to Hawker, Folland felt that Hawker's design team would overshadow his own contributions and decided to leave and establish his own aircraft manufacturing company. On 24 December 1937 Folland acquired the British Marine Aircraft Company based at Hample, near Southampton in Hampshire, and renamed the business Folland Aircraft Limited. In 1959 Hawker Siddeley bought Folland Aircraft as part of the British government's consolidation of the UK aircraft industry and in 1963 the Folland name was dropped altogether.

The Gloster Gladiator was the RAF's last biplane fighter. It made its maiden flight on 12 September 1934 and was introduced three years later in January 1937. The Gladiator was a highly successful aircraft in the air and on the balance of payments, with numerous machines sold to air forces around the world, including in Belgium, China, Egypt, Finland, France, Greece, Iraq, Norway and South Africa. During the Second World War the Gladiator served with the RAF and although already superseded by more capable monoplane designs such as the Supermarine Spitfire and the Hawker Hurricane, the aircraft performed well, seeing action on many fronts including over France, Norway, Greece and the heroic defence of the island of Malta.

The Gloster Gladiator was initially designed with an open cockpit and first flew in September 1934. By the time operational evaluations were being undertaken by the RAF on 3 April 1935 the Gladiator prototype aircraft had a fully enclosed cockpit and was equipped with an 830hp Bristol Mercury IX engine that gave it a top speed of just over 250mph. The Gladiator Mk II variant was fitted with a Bristol Mercury VIIIA 9-cylinder radial engine that produced 830hp and gave the aircraft a maximum speed of 257mph. The aircraft was 27 feet 5 inches in length, had a wingspan of 32 feet 3 inches and stood 11 feet 7 inches tall. It was armed with four fixed forward-firing .303-inch Colt-Browning machine-guns. By August 1935 an initial order for twenty-three aircraft had been placed, with a further 180 ordered in September of that year. The Sea Gladiator was developed for use by the Royal Navy's Fleet Air Arm and had a stronger airframe, a lifeboat and catapult points as well as an arrestor hook to enable the aircraft to be slowed when landing on the deck of an aircraft carrier. A total of ninety-eight Sea Gladiators were built and more than half were still in operational use at the outbreak of the Second World War. Gloster also manufactured aircraft for Hawker Siddeley during the war, delivering some 2,750 Hurricanes by 1942, when production was changed to the new Hawker Typhoon. However, Gloster's most significant landmark contribution to the development of British military aviation was the Gloster Meteor, the only jet-engined aircraft to be used by Allied forces during the Second World War. The Gloster E28/39 was built to an Air Ministry specification issued in 1939 to provide an aircraft that could test Frank Whittle's new turbojet engine in flight. The E28/39 was a single-engined experimental aircraft that first flew on 15 May 1941 when it took off from RAF Cranwell. The Gloster Meteor was a twin-engined jet fighter that first flew on 5 March 1943. Later versions of the Meteor set a number of world airspeed records when they reached 606mph in 1945 and 616mph in 1946. A total of 3,947 Meteors were built and remained in service until the late 1950s.

Post-war Aircraft

Following the end of the Second World War Hawker Siddeley, like many other aircraft manufacturers, was keen to develop new designs that could attract lucrative government contracts. It was clear to many, including Hawker Siddeley's chief designer Sydney Camm, that with the rapid development of the jet engine the prop fighter would soon be obsolete. Camm's response was to develop the Hawker Sea Hawk, the company's first jet fighter which made its maiden flight on 2 September 1947. The Sea Hawk was 39 feet 8 inches long, had a wingspan of 39 feet and was 8 feet 8 inches high. It was powered by a 5,400lbf Rolls-Royce Nene 103 turbojet that gave it a top speed of 602mph at sea level, a range of 800 miles with external fuel tanks and an operational ceiling of 44,500 feet. In all, 542 machines were delivered and first entered service in 1953 with 806 Squadron and remained with the Fleet Air Arm until 1983. Hawker Siddeley produced the first thirty units before production was switched to Armstrong Whitworth Aircraft to allow the former to concentrate on the Hawker Hunter.

The single-seater Hunter jet fighter first flew on 20 July 1951 and in all 1,972 aircraft were built. The Hunter F Mk I was 45 feet 10 inches long, had a wingspan of 33 feet 8 inches and stood 13 feet 2 inches tall. It was fitted with a 6,500lbf Rolls-Royce Avon 100 turbojet engine that gave it a maximum speed of Mach 0.96, around 710mph, at sea level. The Hunter broke the world airspeed record on 7 September 1953, when Squadron Leader Neville Duke reached 727.6mph flying over Littlehampton in West Sussex. Duke was a noted fighter ace during the Second World War with twenty-seven accredited victories. After the war he joined Hawker as assistant chief test pilot in 1948 and became the company's chief test pilot in 1951. He was awarded the Order of the British Empire in 1953 for his achievements with Hawker and in particular with supersonic flight. The Hawker Hunter was chosen to equip two RAF display teams, the Black Arrows that flew twenty-two Hunters in a record-breaking full loop in formation and the Blue Diamonds that flew sixteen of the aircraft.

The Hunter was superseded by the Hawker Siddeley Harrier, the world's first operational vertical / short take-off and landing ground-attack aircraft that first flew on 28 December 1967. The aircraft became known as the Harrier Jump Jet and was based upon the design of the Kestrel, Hawker Siddeley's early vertical and short take-off experimental aircraft, again designed by Sydney Camm. The Harrier GR1 was 47 feet 1 inch long, had a wingspan of 30 feet 4 inches and stood 11 feet 7 inches tall. It was fitted with a 21,500lbf Rolls-Royce Pegasus 103 turbofan engine that had four swivelling nozzles. Four vertical flight puffer jets located in the nose, tail and wing tips used engine bleed air. The Harrier GR1 could reach a maximum speed of 661mph at sea level. It had a combat radius of 172 miles with a 6,000lb bomb payload and an operational ceiling of 50,000 feet. The Harrier came into service on 1 April 1969 and in all 718 aircraft were built. The Harrier was used by the RAF and the Royal Navy in close air support, reconnaissance and ground-attack roles. The aircraft played a prominent role in the Falklands War in 1982 flying from HMS *Hermes* and from the converted merchant ships *Atlantic Conveyor* and *Atlantic Causeway*. The last production aircraft were delivered to the RAF in 1986. The Harrier also saw service with the Thai Navy, the Indian Navy, the Spanish Navy and the United States Marine Corps. With the consolidation of British aircraft manufacturers in 1960 and the eventual nationalization of the industry in 1977, it is no surprise that the Hawker Harrier became the British Aerospace Harrier. The aircraft was redesigned to become the BAe Harrier II and the AV-8B Harrier II that was built by British Aerospace and the American aircraft manufacturer McDonnell Douglas.

In 1960 Hawker Siddeley acquired the de Havilland Aircraft Company that was responsible for the de Havilland DH106 Comet, the world's first jet airliner. The Comet first flew in 1949 and entered service with BOAC on 2 May 1952. The Hawker Siddeley Nimrod was based on the Comet and served with the RAF for over forty years in a number of roles, including maritime patrol, anti-submarine and electronic intelligence gathering. A total of 51 Nimrod aircraft were built and they entered service in October 1969. The last remaining signals intelligence Nimrod R1 aircraft made their final flight at RAF Waddington at the end of June 2011, their out-of-service date was put back to allow them time to support NATO operations in Libya. The MR MK2 aircraft had a crew of 13, was 129 feet 1 inch long, had a wingspan of 114 feet 10 inches and stood 29 feet 9 inches high. It was fitted with four 12,140lbf Rolls-Royce Spey 250 turbofan jet engines that allowed a maximum speed of 575mph, a range of 5,755 miles and an operational ceiling of 42,000 feet. The Nimrods replaced the RAF's ageing fleet of Avro Shackletons and provided essential support during the 'Cod Wars' of the 1970s. In 1972 Iceland sought to protect its own fishing industry and unilaterally declared an Exclusive Economic Zone that reached well beyond its own territorial waters. The aircraft also offered support during the Falklands War, Britain's Operation *Granby* during the first Gulf War between October 1990 and March 1991, with NATO's operations over Serbia in 1999 and more recently with operations in Afghanistan. The aircraft has also played an invaluable role in numerous air-sea rescue operations in the North Sea.

The Hawker Siddeley Hawk first flew on 21 August 1974 and entered service with the RAF in 1976 as a trainer aircraft. Following the nationalization of the aircraft industry in the UK the Hawk continued as the BAe Hawk and is still produced by British Aerospace. Over 900 aircraft have been manufactured and it has become a highly successful British export, serving with air forces and navies in Australia, Bahrain, Canada, Finland, India, Indonesia, Kenya, Kuwait, Malaysia, Oman, Saudi Arabia, South Africa, South Korea, Switzerland, the United Arab Emirates and Zimbabwe. The Hawk Advanced Jet Trainer is a two-seater aircraft, with accommodation for a student and an instructor. It is 36 feet 7 inches in length, with a wingspan of 30 feet 9 inches and stands 13 feet 1 inch tall. It is fitted with a single 5,200lbf Rolls-Royce/Turbomeca Adour 151 turbofan engine that gives the aircraft a maximum speed of 645mph, an endurance of four hours and an operational ceiling of 50,000 feet.

Reorganization and Amalgamation

A number of internal reorganizations took place at Hawker Siddeley following the end of the Second World War. The company changed its name in 1948 to the Hawker Siddeley Group. It comprised Hawker Siddeley Aviation and Hawker Siddeley Dynamics, which focussed on the development of missiles and space technologies. In 1948 the Hawker Siddeley Group purchased the Canadian aircraft manufacturer Victory Aircraft from the Canadian government and renamed the business AV Roe Canada. By 1958 it it had become Canada's third largest company and had expanded into engine manufacturing, mining, steel production and railway locomotives. It was also responsible for 45 per cent of Hawker Siddeley's total revenue. By 1962 AV Roe Canada was dissolved and its assets were transferred to Hawker Siddeley Canada. In 1959 the aero engine manufacturer Armstrong-Siddeley had merged with the Bristol Engine Company to become Bristol Siddeley. By the late 1950s the tide had started to turn for the UK aircraft industry as the British government coerced manufacturers to amalgamate, stating that contracts would only be awarded to a smaller number of merged businesses. Consequently, in 1959 the Hawker Siddeley Group acquired Folland Aircraft and then in 1960 bought the de Havilland Aircraft Company and Blackburn Aircraft. Three years later the Hawker Siddeley Group restructured itself and decided that all new aircraft development would use the HS (Hawker Siddeley) naming convention, which put an end to many glorious names in British aviation.

On 29 April 1977 the Aircraft and Shipbuilding Industries Act brought into State ownership the country's aircraft and shipbuilding concerns and in doing so created British Aerospace and British Shipbuilders. Hawker Siddeley Aviation and Hawker Siddeley Dynamics, which represented only around a quarter of the total Hawker Siddeley business, were nationalized. These two divisions merged with the British Aircraft Corporation and Scottish Aviation to become British Aerospace. The company's business interests in other sectors and in other countries were retained by a separate holding company and focussed on railway engineering, signalling and industrial electronics. During the 1980s Hawker Siddeley Group plc rationalized further, selling off many of its North American manufacturing assets and in 1992 was bought by BTR plc for £1.5 billion.

However, today Harry Hawker's name still lives on in the world of aviation. In August 1993 British Aerospace sold off its private jet business, British Aerospace Corporate Jets, to the Raytheon Company, which renamed the business Raytheon Corporate Jets. The Beech Aircraft Corporation and Raytheon Corporate Jets merged in September 1994 and became Raytheon Aircraft. In July 2006 Raytheon announced that it planned to sell off its aircraft manufacturing business, which on 26 March 2007 was acquired for $3.3 billion USD and became Hawker Beechcraft.

Today there are ample opportunities to see Hawker and Gloster aircraft on the ground and in the air, including at the Tangmere Military Aviation Museum in

West Sussex, the Science Museum in London, the RAF Museum in Hendon, the Fleet Air Arm Museum at Yeovilton in Somerset, the Brooklands Museum at Weybridge in Surrey, the Imperial War Museum at Duxford in Cambridgeshire and the Shuttleworth Collection at Old Warden Aerodrome in Bedfordshire. One of the best loved participants at air displays around the UK is the Battle of Britain Memorial Flight, which has been delighting crowds since it was founded in 1957. The Flight maintains five Supermarine Spitfires, one of only two airworthy Lancasters in the world, a Chipmunk, a C-47 Dakota and two Hawker Hurricanes, Mk IIC number LF363 and Mk IIC number PZ865, the last of 14,533 Hurricanes to be built.

Chapter 8

RJ Mitchell and the Birth of the Spitfire

Like many great artists Reginald Joseph Mitchell's fame grew exponentially after his death. The designer of the Spitfire, which played such a vital role in Britain's defence during the Second World War, died two years before the aircraft flew in active service and did not see the success that the aircraft was to have and the esteem in which the nation would regard him. During his short yet highly productive life he did not receive the public recognition that many thought he deserved. He was, however, awarded the CBE in 1932 for his achievements in high-speed aviation and for the success that he and Supermarine had had with winning the prestigious Schneider Trophy air races five times, in particular the three successive victories between 1927 and 1931 that enabled Britain to win the cup outright.

Schneider Trophy
The Coupe d'Aviation Maritime Jacques Schneider was established in 1911 as a racing competition principally for seaplanes by the financier, accomplished balloonist and aviation enthusiast Jacques Schneider. The *Fédération Aéronautique Internationale* oversaw the races along with the relevant aero club from the host country. The winning club would host the next race. Each aero club could enter three aircraft. The rules also stated that if an aero club won three races within five years then that club could keep the trophy and a prize of 75,000 francs would be awarded to the pilot.

Between 1913 and 1931 the Schneider Trophy race was run eleven times. The first competition was held at Monaco on 16 April 1913. It was won by French pilot Maurice Prevost in a Deperdussin at an average speed of 45.71mph. Howard Pixton won for Great Britain in 1914 flying a Sopwith Tabloid at an average speed of 86.83mph. Following the First World War the race was resumed and was held at Bournemouth. The foggy weather conditions were not conducive for air racing and eventually the Italian team was deemed to have won, but was later disqualified and the race results were void.

In 1920 and 1921 the race was held at Venice and the Italians, not surprisingly, won on both occasions. Not surprisingly because in 1920 they were the only nation that entered and Luigi Bologna won flying a Savoia S.12 at an average speed of 43.83mph. The following year the only non-Italian entrant failed to start, consequently Giovanni de Briganti won in a Macchi M.7bis at an average speed of 117.85mph.

The 1922 race was held in Naples. Supermarine entered the Sea Lion II, piloted by Henri Biard, and won at an average speed of 145.72mph. The 1923 race was held at Cowes and the American team won in a Curtiss CR-3, flown by US Navy Lieutenant David Rittenhouse at an average speed of 177.27mph. The race was not held in 1924 because apart from the Americans no other nations made it to the start line. The Italian and French entrants withdrew and both of the British team's aircraft crashed in pre-race trials.

The Americans hosted the 1925 race at Baltimore, but Mitchell's Supermarine S4 crashed during a test flight and could not take part. The race was won by the American pilot James Doolittle in a Curtiss R3C-2 that reached an average speed of 232.57mph. Doolittle went on to become General James Doolittle and commanded the infamous Doolittle Raid on 18 April 1942, when four months after the Japanese attack on Pearl Harbor sixteen B-25 bombers took off from the aircraft carrier USS *Hornet* and flew 620 miles to bomb a number of high-profile targets in Japan.

In 1926 the Italians won at Hampton Roads, Virginia, with a Macchi M.39 piloted by Mario de Bernardi at an average speed of 246.50mph. Following the crash of the S4 the previous year Mitchell and his team at Supermarine did not have sufficient time to develop a replacement aircraft and did not compete in the 1926 race either. Determined not to lose out for a third time Mitchell set about developing a new aircraft, the S5, which took to the air for the first time on 7 June 1927. The Supermarine S5 N220 was a single-seater that was 24 feet 3½ inches long, had a wingspan of 26 feet 9 inches and stood 11 feet and 1 inch tall. The S5 was powered by a 900hp Napier Lion VIIA water-cooled broad arrow engine that gave it a maximum speed of 319.57mph. It was widely regarded in aviation circles that Britain's disappointing performance in the 1925 race was due not only to the superiority of the other competitors' aircraft but also to the poor way in which the team had been managed. When the Air Ministry agreed to fund a British entry to the 1927 race Hugh Montague Trenchard, Marshal of the Royal Air Force, intervened and established the RAF High Speed Flight specifically to pilot and maintain the aircraft.

The 1927 Schneider Trophy race was held on Monday 26 September at Venice, a day later than planned due to bad weather. A 50km triangular course was laid out around the Lido, with pilots required to make a total of seven laps. The Italian team entered three Macchi M.52s, while the British, the only other nation to enter, put up two S5s and a Gloster IVB. The Gloster completed the first lap of the race with an average speed of 266.5mph. The first of the Macchi aircraft to fly immediately posted an average speed of 275mph and it became clear that only the S5s would have a chance of winning the race. After an impressive start two of the Italian Macchi aircraft ran into trouble, one crash-landed and a second pulled out with engine trouble. Shortly after, one of the three S5s also developed engine trouble and was out of the race. The final Macchi punctured a fuel tank and crashed into the Venetian lagoon. Flight Lieutenant Sydney Webster roared into the lead and took the race with an average speed of 281.66mph, breaking the world records for both seaplanes and landplanes. Immediately the pilots were heralded by an eager press and became heroes the length and breadth of the country, but Mitchell, who was happy to keep out of the public eye, found his contribution broadly overlooked.

The organizers of the Schneider Trophy decided to change the rules in 1928 and changed the race from an annual event to a bi-annual event to allow the competing nations adequate time to develop their aircraft. It was announced that the next race would be in 1929 and would be hosted by Great Britain and held over the Solent.

While working on the development of the Supermarine S6 Mitchell concluded that the 900hp water-cooled Napier Lion VII A engines had reached the limit of their performance. In need of a suitable replacement Mitchell approached Sir Henry Royce. This marked the beginning of a highly successful relationship between Supermarine and Rolls-Royce that led to the creation of the Merlin and Griffon engines. Sir Henry agreed to develop a motor for the Schneider Trophy that could produce 1,500hp, with the potential to go to 1,900hp with further development work. In just six months Rolls-Royce delivered its first R engine. The design of the S6 was based upon the S5, with fuel tanks fitted in the floats to allow for the extra fuel required by the thirsty R engine. The additional heat generated by the engine was dissipated across the surfaces of the wings and floats, which were used as radiators. The S6 was 25 feet 10 inches long, had a wingspan of 30 feet and was 12 feet 3 inches high. Fitted with the new 1,900hp Rolls-Royce R inline engine the aircraft could reach a top speed of 328mph.

The next race was held on 7 September 1929 and consisted of seven laps of a 50km circuit over the Solent near Southampton. Over one and a half million spectators squeezed onto a fleet of small ships along the route and into every vantage point around the Solent. Two countries entered teams, Great Britain and Italy. The Italians entered two Macchi M.67s and a Macchi M.52R. The British team entered two S6 aircraft and an S5. Britain flew first and set an average speed of 324mph after their first lap. The Italians were again frustrated by engine trouble and both of their Macchi M.67s pulled out on their second lap. The remaining Macchi M.52R was not able to compete with the superior S6 and Flight Lieutenant Henry Waghorn finished first, having set an average speed of 328.65mph. The Macchi M.52R came in second with an average speed of 284.2mph and the S5 came in third place having achieved a creditworthy average speed of 282.11mph.

By 1930 the great Depression was taking its toll around the world and the British government, which had previously funded Britain's Schneider Trophy entry, decided that the expected £100,000 cost could not be justified. Efforts were made to persuade the government otherwise, pointing out the positive effects on exports that had been achieved from previous wins, but the government remained steadfast in their thinking. Supermarine gave up hope of entering the race, which was made worse in the knowledge that Britain, along with the Americans and Italians, had won the trophy twice before and all three nations were in a position to win it outright if they could secure a third victory.

Assistance came from quite an unusual quarter. In early 1931 the colourful Lady Lucy Houston, widow of Sir Robert Houston, her third husband, gave £100,000 to Supermarine in order to allow them to compete. This left Mitchell barely enough time to prepare a suitable aircraft for the race. Rather than develop a new S7 he chose to improve the existing aircraft and created the S6B. The main difference with the S6 was a more powerful Rolls-Royce R engine that produced a much superior 2,350hp, an increase of 450hp compared with the 1929 version. This necessitated further cooling in the floats to help dissipate the extra heat from the new engine. Overall the new aircraft was 28 feet 10 inches long, 3 feet longer than the S6. The wingspan remained the same at 30 feet and the height was consistent at 12 feet 3 inches. In total two S6Bs were built for the race, along with two S6s fitted with the new floats and designated S6As. The first S6B was delivered to the High Speed Flight at Calshot Spit on the on 21 July 1931. The RAF's High Speed Flight for the race had been set up in May 1931 with Squadron Leader Augustus Orlebar in command. Orlebar later became Air Vice Marshal and Deputy Chief of Combined Operations in 1943. The Flight was made up of pilots Flight Lieutenant John Boothman, Flight Lieutenant George Stainforth, Flight Lieutenant Freddy Long, Flight Lieutenant EJL Hope, Flying Officer Leonard Snaith, Lieutenant RL Brinton of the Fleet Air Arm and Flight Lieutenant WF Dry as Engineering Officer.

The 1931 Schneider Trophy race was set to be run on 12 September; however by the time the race day had come along all of the other competing nations had pulled out, leaving Britain to compete alone. Nine days before the race the Royal Aero Club had refused a request from the Italian and French teams for a postponement. Flight Lieutenant John Boothman was declared the winner with an average speed of 340.08mph and the British team had won the Schneider Trophy outright in perpetuity. Later on race day Flight Lieutenant George Stainforth flew a Supermarine S6B and set a new world speed record of 379mph. Over the coming days the S6B would go on to break the world speed record twice more, and on 29 September Mitchell's aircraft became the first to break the 400mph barrier with an average speed of 407.5mph.

The Schneider Trophy itself was designed by Monsieur E Gabard and shows a silver-plated Spirit of Flight kissing the waves and is mounted on a marble base. The Royal Aero Club had become the outright owners of the trophy

Schneider Trophy Winners and Speeds 1913–1931

Year	Location	Aircraft	Pilot	mph	Nation
1913	Monaco	Deperdussin	Maurice Prevost	45.71	France
1914	Monaco	Sopwith Tabloid	Howard Pixton	86.83	UK
1919	Bournemouth, UK	Race voided after Italian team disqualified			
1920	Venice, Italy	Savoia S.12	Luigi Bologna	43.83	Italy
1921	Venice, Italy	Macchi M.7bis	Giovanni de Briganti	117.85	Italy
1922	Naples, Italy	Supermarine Sea Lion II	Henri Biard	145.72	UK
1923	Cowes, UK	Curtiss CR-3	David Rittenhouse	177.27	USA
1925	Baltimore USA	Curtiss R3C-2	James Doolittle	232.57	USA
1926	Hampton Roads, USA	Macchi M.39	Mario de Bernardi	246.50	Italy
1927	Venice, Italy	Supermarine S5	Sydney Webster	281.66	UK
1929	Calshot Spit UK	Supermarine S6	Henry Waghorn	328.65	UK
1931	Calshot Spit UK	Supermarine S6B	John Boothman	340.08	UK

following Britain's third victory and in 1977 they donated it to the Science Museum in London.

The Royal Aero Club of Great Britain revived the race in 1981 and it is open to any propeller land-based aeroplane that can maintain a speed of 100mph in a straight line. Although the venue has changed from time to time the race is invariably run in the Solent area. On 4 September 2010 tragedy struck when two light aircraft that were taking part in the race for the Rolls-Royce Merlin Trophy were involved in a mid-air collision. One of the aircraft crashed into woods near Ryde on the Isle of Wight killing both on-board, whilst the second aircraft was able to make a crash-landing at Bembridge Airport

RJ

Reginald Joseph Mitchell was born at 115 Congleton Road, Butt Lane in Staffordshire, on 20 May 1895, the eldest of three boys to Herbert and Eliza Jane Mitchell. Mitchell's father spent much of his life as headmaster at a number of different schools in the area before establishing his own printing company in Hanley, Stoke-on-Trent. Mitchell developed an interest in aviation while he was at Hanley High School where he would design, build and fly his own model aircraft. At the age of sixteen Mitchell secured an apprenticeship at the Kerr Stuart & Company locomotive engineering works in Fenton. Although he started in the workshop he later moved to the drawing office, attending evening classes to study engineering and mathematics. In 1917, at the age of twenty-two, Mitchell was offered a position with Supermarine Aviation Works Limited at Woolston in Southampton. The following year he married Florence Dayson and together they had one son, Gordon.

Mitchell's career blossomed at Supermarine. He became chief designer in 1919, chief engineer in 1920 and technical director by 1927. The following year in 1928 Supermarine was taken over by Vickers-Armstrongs and became Supermarine Aviation Works (Vickers) Limited. Part of the contract with Vickers-Armstrongs was that Mitchell should stay in his position for a period of five years following the sale. From 1920 to 1936 Mitchell achieved a number of significant landmarks with Supermarine. He designed and developed twenty-four aircraft, including the Swan, Walrus, Stranraer and the Southampton. He strengthened his reputation with his unparalleled success with the Schneider Trophy, which culminated in Britain winning the trophy outright in 1931 with the Supermarine S6B.

The Spitfire
In 1930 the Air Ministry issued specification F7/30 for a new fighter with a range of requirements, including the need for a maximum speed in excess of 250mph. At the time Mitchell had been toying with ideas for a new fighter and Vickers-Armstrongs authorized the development of his Type 224 as a submission to the Air Ministry. The Supermarine Type 224 first flew in February 1934 and was an open cockpit monoplane, with gull wings, fixed spatted undercarriage and was powered by a 600hp evaporative-cooled Rolls-Royce Goshawk engine. In all, eight designs were submitted to the Air Ministry in response to F7/30. These were the Blackburn F3, the Bristol Type 123, the Bristol Type 133, the Gloster Gladiator, the Gloster SS19, the Hawker PV3, the Supermarine Type 224 and the Westland F7/30. The Air Ministry selected the Gloster Gladiator biplane, which went into production in 1934.

Mitchell had already been working on improvements to the designs of the Type 224 and developed the Type 300, which had a retractable undercarriage and a wingspan reduced by 6 feet. The initial design of the Type 300 was submitted to the Air Ministry in July 1934 and was also rejected. Mitchell again made refinements that incorporated a faired, enclosed cockpit, breathing apparatus and smaller, thinner wings. This revision was powered by the new and much more powerful Rolls-Royce PV-XII V-12 engine that was later given the name Merlin. By November 1934 Mitchell had got the support of Vickers-Armstrongs to begin detailed design work on this new version of the Type 300. In December the Air Ministry issued contract AM 361140/34 and £10,000 for the construction of a prototype that was designated K5054 and on 3 January 1935 the Ministry created a new specification F10/35, which was specifically drafted around the Type 300, and they formalized their contract with Supermarine.

On 5 March 1936, four months after the Hurricane's maiden flight, K5054 took to the air for the first time from Eastleigh Aerodrome, later to become Southampton Airport. Vickers-Armstrongs' chief test pilot, Captain Joseph Summers, made the flight, which lasted for a mere eight minutes. Upon landing he is reputed to have said 'don't touch anything'. A second test flight was made on 10 March after a new propeller had been fitted and during which the retractable undercarriage was wound up for the first time. By the middle of May 1936 K5054 had reached 330mph, which outstripped the maximum speed of Sydney Camm's Hurricane. It then reached 348mph while Captain Summers was transporting the aircraft to Squadron Leader Anderson at the Aeroplane & Armament Experimental Establishment (A&AEE) at RAF Martlesham Heath. The following month on 3 June 1936 the Air Ministry placed its first order for 310 Spitfires before the prototype had completed its formal appraisal at the A&AEE. The public had their introduction to the aircraft later that month when the Spitfire flew at the RAF air display at Hendon Aerodrome on Saturday 27 June 1936.

Production for the RAF's order was expected to start straightaway, but Supermarine found that its plant at Woolston, Southampton, was already running at capacity fulfilling orders for Walrus and Stranraer flying boats. Understandably Vickers-Armstrongs was reluctant to entrust its new charge to too many outside contractors and was slow to release design drawings and components. Consequently, delivery was delayed and the Air Ministry took the view that it should restrict its orders to the initial 310 and have Supermarine build Bristol Beaufighters at Woolston once the order had been completed. After some considerable lobbying by Vickers-Armstrongs and Supermarine the Air Ministry was persuaded that it was able to meet demand and as a result the Ministry ordered a further 200 aircraft on 24 March 1938. The Spitfire Mk VB was powered by a 1,440hp Merlin V-12 engine that gave the aircraft a maximum speed of 374mph at 13,000 feet. This variant had an operational ceiling of 37,000 feet and a maximum range of 470 miles. It was 29 feet 11 inches in length, had a wingspan of 36 feet 10 inches and stood 11 feet 5 inches tall. The Mk VB was armed with two 20mm cannons and four .30-inch machine-guns in the wings.

The revolutionary design of the Spitfire was not unique when Mitchell proposed the Type 300. He was able to bring together a combination of new ideas into a single aeroplane that had a singular impact on aviation design thereafter. The Type 300 had design similarities with the Heinkel He 70 Blitz, which was designed as a mail plane for Deutsche Lufthansa in the early 1930s. The RAE was the first to develop under-wing radiators and monocoque construction had first appeared in the United States of America. One of the most memorable design features of the Spitfire was the use of elliptical-shaped wings. Mitchell and his design team had as early as 1934 opted to go for this type of design to overcome the conflicting requirements that the wing had to be thin to minimize drag and thick enough to house the armament and the retractable undercarriage. The idea for the elliptical wing was provided by Canadian Beverley Shenstone, Mitchell's aerodynamicist at Supermarine. The excellent aerodynamic properties of the elliptical shape also lent themselves well to the design requirements of the fin and tailplane assembly, which enabled the centre of mass for the elevators and rudder to be pulled forward so that surface flutter could be reduced.

The first production Spitfire that was completed at the Woolston plant was K9787, which flew for the first time on 14 May 1938, a year after Mitchell's death. The Spitfire remained in production for ten years and, in all, some 20,351 aircraft were manufactured, with a further 2,334 examples of the Seafire. The last to have been retired is thought to have left active service from the Irish Air Corps in 1961.

A Brilliant Career Cut Short

Mitchell was not comfortable in the limelight and apart from the immense admiration of his aviation peers he was generally unknown by the public. At Supermarine his colleagues regarded him with warmth and affection. He was an inspiring, charismatic leader who through instinct was able to get the best out of those who worked around him. It is not surprising therefore that his staff were devoted to him.

Mitchell's brilliant career was to be tragically cut short at an early age. In August 1933 he was diagnosed with rectal cancer. Despite major surgery he continued to work, not only on the Type 317 four-engined bomber but also on the Spitfire. The plans and an early model mock-up of the Type 317 were destroyed during a German air raid on the Supermarine plant and the aircraft never reached production. Remarkably, Mitchell refused to allow his illness to curtail him. In July 1934, a year after his surgery, he gained his pilot's licence. Unfortunately, in 1936 his cancer returned and he was finally forced to give up work early in 1937. From his garden in Russell Place, Southampton, he was able to watch test flights for the Spitfire. He died at home on 11 June 1937, having never seen any of the Spitfires in active service. Following his death the development work for the Spitfire continued under the stewardship of Supermarine draughtsman Joseph Smith, who oversaw all future variants as well as the Seafire and the Spitfire's replacement, the Spiteful.

Mitchell's achievements with the Schneider Trophy and then his race against time to complete the development of the Spitfire knowing that he was dying of cancer were the subject of the 1942 British propaganda film *The First of the Few*, entitled *Spitfire* in the United States of America. The film was produced and directed by Leslie Howard for British Aviation Pictures and starred Howard as RJ Mitchell, with David Niven as the fictional test pilot Geoffrey Crisp and Rosamund John as Mrs Mitchell. Mitchell's widow, Florence, and their son, Gordon, were frequent visitors to the set at Denham Studios during filming, despite the fact that the film contained numerous obvious inaccuracies. It went on to be a tremendous success at the box office in the UK and in the United States of America, which did much to lift morale.

The following year Howard was killed in suspicious circumstances when a KLM Royal Dutch Airlines Douglas DC-3, Flight 777, travelling from Lisbon, Portugal, to Bristol, was attacked by *Luftwaffe* Junkers Ju 88 C6 fighters over the Bay of Biscay and all seventeen people on-board were killed. It has been suggested that the Germans thought that the British Prime Minister Winston Churchill was on-board. Churchill was in Algiers around that time and later wrote in his autobiography that a mistake made about his movements may have cost Howard his life.

Supermarine Aviation Works Limited
Supermarine Aviation Works Limited began life in 1913 when Noel Pemberton-Billing established Pemberton-Billing Ltd to design and manufacture flying boats. Over the next three years the company built prototypes for the Supermarine PB29 and Supermarine Nighthawk, both of quadruplane design where four fixed-width wings were mounted one above the other. They were intended as an answer to the Zeppelin threat during the First World War and were equipped with recoilless Davis guns.

Pemberton-Billing was eager to develop a political career. In 1916 he won a by-election for the Hertford constituency and was elected as a Member of Parliament. He sold Pemberton-Billing Ltd to Hubert Scott-Paine, the factory manager, who changed the company's name to Supermarine Aviation Works Ltd.

The company was later sold to Vickers-Armstrongs in 1928, which renamed the company Supermarine Aviation Works (Vickers) Ltd. Ten years later Vickers-Armstrongs reorganized all of its aircraft design and manufacturing under the name Vickers-Armstrongs (Aircraft) Ltd. Supermarine, however, retained a degree of independence with its aircraft known as Vickers-Armstrongs Supermarine. For most of its early years Supermarine had concentrated on the design and development of floatplanes. The company's first landplane was the Spitfire. During the Second World War the company produced the Seafire, a version of the Spitfire for the Royal Navy. Work on the company's first heavy bomber, the four-engined Supermarine B12/36, was cut short by the *Luftwaffe*'s persistent bombing of the Woolston plant in Southampton. The Supermarine Spiteful was designed by Joseph Smith and was developed from the Spitfire. The Spiteful first flew on 30 June 1944. A total of nineteen, including two prototypes, were built. The Seafang followed in 1946, with just eighteen built.

Following the Second World War Supermarine developed the Attacker, the Royal Navy's first jet fighter, which first flew in its naval form on 17 June 1947 and entered active service in August 1951. A total of 185 Attackers were built, including three prototypes. The Attacker was 37 feet 6 inches in length, had a wingspan of 36 feet 11 inches and stood 9 feet 11 inches tall. It was fitted with a 5,100lbf Rolls-Royce Nene 3 turbojet that gave the aircraft a maximum speed of

590mph at sea level and an operational ceiling of 45,000 feet. It was armed with four 20mm Hispano cannons. The Supermarine Swift was designed by Joseph Smith and was the successor to the Attacker. A total of 197 were built and they entered active service in 1954. The Swift was 42 feet 3 inches in length, with a wingspan of 32 feet 4 inches and stood 12 feet 6 inches tall. It was powered by a 9,450lbf Rolls-Royce Avon 114 turbojet that gave it a maximum speed of 685mph at sea level and an operational ceiling of 45,800 feet. The armament consisted of two 30mm Aden cannons. The Supermarine Scimitar followed and was a naval strike fighter that was introduced in 1957. A total of 76 were built and it became the last Supermarine aircraft. The Scimitar was 55 feet 4 inches in length, with a wingspan of 37 feet 2 inches and stood 15 feet 3 inches tall. It was powered by two 11,250lbf Rolls-Royce Avon 202 turbojets that gave it a maximum speed of 710mph and an operational ceiling of 50,000 feet.

In 1960, under enormous government pressure the British aviation industry was shaken up and Vickers-Armstrongs (Aircraft) Limited merged with English Electric Aviation Ltd, the Bristol Aeroplane Company and Hunting Aircraft to form the British Aircraft Corporation (BAC).

Recognition
Although Mitchell received little public recognition for his contribution to British aviation in his lifetime, there have been many efforts to right that wrong and recognize his many landmarks. A statue was erected outside the Potteries Museum in Hanley, Stoke-on-Trent near his birthplace. The Mitchell Memorial Theatre in the town was built just after the Second World War by public subscription. A bust of Mitchell can be found at Southampton University and at the RAF Club in London. A memorial can also be visited on the site of the Supermarine factory in Hazel Road, Woolston at Southampton.

A replica of the Spitfire prototype, K5054, was erected on the roundabout outside the entrance to Southampton Airport in 2004 to commemorate the anniversary of the first test flight of the aircraft. The statue caused controversy locally when it was confirmed that it was to be made by a German company. In 2006 five Spitfires took off from the airport to mark the seventieth anniversary of the first test flight on 5 March 1936. RJ Mitchell Memorial Lectures are held in Stoke-on-Trent and at Southampton University, which also offers a special Mitchell Scholarship in Aeronautical Engineering. In 2006 the Ministry of Defence threw down their Grand Challenge for inventors to put forward ideas that could lead to a Ministry of Defence contract. The winner would also receive the RJ Mitchell Trophy for Innovation, which is made from the wing spars of Spitfire MK356, the metal donated by the RAF Battle of Britain Memorial Flight. In September 2005 English Heritage commemorated Mitchell with a Blue Plaque at his former home in Russell Place, Portswood in Southampton. The house was built in 1927 to Mitchell's own design and it was while he lived there that he finalized the design for the Spitfire. He stayed at Russell Place until his death in 1937. An astonishing new statue of Mitchell by artist Stephen Kettle was unveiled in September 2005 in the Flight Gallery at The Science Museum, London. The statue is made of around 400,000 individual pieces of Welsh slate and took more than 2,000 hours for Kettle to complete. The statue portrays Mitchell at a drawing board with his shirt sleeves rolled up. In July 2010 *The Daily Telegraph* newspaper reported that a rare trophy that had been awarded to Mitchell by the Hampshire Aero Club in October 1936 had come to light on the seventieth anniversary of the Battle of Britain and had been donated to the Solent Sky Museum by Owen Hill, a part-owner of the original club. The trophy, which is in the shape of a replica de Havilland DH60 Moth, was awarded to Mitchell for his success with landing competitions and demonstrates his ability as a pilot in his own right, an achievement made more remarkable as it came when he was terminally ill with cancer and just seven months before he died.

Today there are over seventy Spitfires around the world, as far afield as USA, India, Brazil, Australia, New Zealand, Canada, Netherlands, Germany, France and Sweden. Amazingly, forty-five are still in flying condition, with eighteen of them still thrilling crowds at air shows across the UK. A testament indeed, if one was needed, of the enduring charm of the Spitfire and the continued admiration for RJ Mitchell, his invaluable contribution to British aviation and the nation's morale in time of war.

Chapter 9

Herbert Smith and the Development of the Fighter

The aviation designer Herbert Smith made a singular contribution to the development of the fighter in Great Britain and Japan. Smith took charge of new aircraft design at the Sopwith Aviation Company in November 1914 and in an illustrious yet short career with Sopwith that lasted until the company went into liquidation in 1920 he was responsible for a prolific range of fighter aircraft. He began development work on the Sopwith Triplane in April 1916 and the aircraft flew for the first time just six weeks later on 28 May. Smith was also responsible for two other single-seater versions of the Triplane, the Snark that was fitted with a 360hp ABC Dragonfly engine, the twin-engined Cobham triplane bomber, the Snipe that was powered by a 230hp Bentley BR2 motor, the single-seater armoured trench fighter the Salamander, the two-seater trench fighter the Buffalo and the Dolphin with its 200hp Hispano Suiza 8B engine. Most prominently Smith is credited as the designer of the Sopwith Camel that was based on a concept by Thomas Sopwith, Harry Hawker and Fred Sigrist as well as the Mitsubishi 1MF Type 10 carrier fighter that was operated by the Japanese Imperial Navy from 1923. A key feature of Smith's designs was that the pilot, engine and armament were all brought close together within the aircraft so that the weight was concentrated to ensure the maximum possible manoeuvrability. The practicality of this design concept was shared by Thomas Sopwith and Harry Hawker and helped to ensure the supremacy of the Sopwith fighters in combat during the First World War.

Following the collapse of the Sopwith Aviation Company in 1920 Smith was invited by the Mitsubishi Internal Combustion Engine Manufacturing Co. Ltd, based in Nagoya, Japan, to assist them with the development of a new aircraft manufacturing division. During his time with the company he developed a number of leading aircraft designs, including the 1MF carrier fighter, the 2MR reconnaissance aircraft and the B1M torpedo bomber.

Smith returned to Britain in 1924 and despite being offered a position with Hawker Engineering as its chief designer and another offer from Vickers-

Armstrongs of a post with its new Canadian division, he chose to have nothing more to do with the aviation industry and retired at the age of thirty-four. In 1975 Smith was awarded Honorary Companionship of the Royal Aeronautical Society in recognition of his singular contribution to aircraft design and development. Three years later in 1978, at the age of eighty-eight, he died at his home in Skipton in Yorkshire.

The Rise of the Fighter

The birth of the fighter aeroplane took place when a small aircraft engine spluttered, coughed and stopped. All was silence save for the wind singing through the bracing wires. A little French Morane monoplane had gently glided down behind the German lines with a malfunctioned motor. It was April 1915 and the pilot, a French air force officer by the name of Roland Garros, realized that he was about to become a prisoner of war. He had touched down amongst the shell-pocked landscape and the vivid flashes of the furious artillery duels could be seen on the horizon accompanied by the continual crump of the field gun reports.

Sometime in the previous March of 1915 Garros had shot down five German observation planes, achieved by using a light machine-gun fixed along the top of the engine cowling and firing through the whirling propeller, which was lined with steel plates to protect the wooden blades. This inspiration had been prompted by the destruction of an enemy reconnaissance plane in late 1914 that had been shot down by the use of a handheld machine-gun in a plane flown by Lieutenant Emile Stribick and Marcel David. Garros, a pre-war stunt pilot and the first man to fly across the Mediterranean Sea, had been unable to overcome the problem of protecting the propeller when in combat other than using steel plates. Then a tenet of German infantry ran at the double across the barren field and took Garros into captivity.

The Morane monoplane was carefully examined by German aviation experts who quickly realized the significance of the armament layout. The problem was handed to Anthony Fokker, a Dutch aviation designer building aircraft for the German Army Air Service, and it became clear that a mechanical interrupter gear had to be perfected and manufactured as the Germans used steel-jacketed parabellum ammunition. The result was the manufacture of the Fokker E Type single-seater monoplane, with forward-firing armament and the mechanical interrupter-gear based on the designs of Franz Schneider of 1913 for the LVG Company.

By the autumn of 1915 the so-called Fokker scourge had commenced and would last until the spring of 1916, when Allied aircraft with a superior performance and comparable armament went into squadron service. Since the early part of the year the C category observation two-seater biplanes of the German Army Air Service had been armed with a moveable machine-gun in the observer's cockpit. Conversion courses for pilots trained to fly the new E Type monoplane were organized at the *Flieger* station near Mannheim in August 1915 under the control of the *Kampfeinsitzer-Abteilung Ein*. Four months later in December 1915 some forty Fokker E Type machines were in active service. Eventually, four E Type monoplanes were attached to each *Feldflieger-Abteilung* to defend the six C Type observation biplanes of each respective unit.

In the following summer of 1916 the C type observation aeroplanes had been equipped with an additional machine-gun firing forward through the whirling propeller disc and operated by the pilot. The E Type monoplanes were organized into *Kommandos* for special operations on detachment and later in the year the *Kommandos* were re-organized into *Jagdstaffel* on a permanent basis to be associated with such famous names as Max Immelmann, Oswald Boelcke, Ernst Udet, Erich Löwenhardt and Manfred von Richthofen. Clearly, Allied air superiority had been lost and could only be re-established by the introduction of new and superior designs.

Sopwith's Response

It is thought that the first British fighter was the Sopwith Scout, subsequently affectionately christened the Sopwith Pup, which made its maiden flight in February 1916. It was the first British aircraft to be armed with a single Vickers rifle-calibre machine-gun of .303-inch bore, equipped with 500 rounds of ammunition and installed with a Sopwith-Kauper interrupter gear. On successfully completing prototype trials the new machine was ordered into quantity production on 31 July 1916 for both the Royal Flying Corps and the Royal Naval Air Service. It was to remain in production until November 1918, by which time 1,770 machines of this type had been delivered.

The Pup was a small aeroplane. The design had a wing span of 26 feet 6 inches, an overall length of 19 feet 4 inches and was 9 feet 5 inches high. The machine was of an all-wooden construction, with a simple design both structurally and aerodynamically that consisted of a wire-braced box girder fuselage and a two-spar single bay main plane. Power was provided by a Le Rhône 9C 9-cylinder air-cooled radial motor that developed 80hp at 1,200rpm for take-off and used a wooden two-bladed fixed pitch propeller. The aircraft was able to achieve a maximum speed of 112 mph and had a range of 310 miles. The Pup had a rate of climb of 5.16 minutes to 5,000 feet, 13.16 minutes to 10,000 feet and had an operational ceiling of 17,500 feet. An 18-gallon fuel tank was located in-between the radial engine and the cockpit that gave the fighter an endurance of three hours. The Sopwith Pup was a very popular machine with its pilots. It was easy to fly and had a small turning circle that made it an excellent opponent to the German Albatros D.I and D.II fighter planes of September 1916, despite these having twin machine-guns that fired through the propeller disc. By the July of 1917 the Sopwith Pup had become outclassed in every respect except for its great manoeuvrability and although it was obsolete it was retained as a trainer. In August 1917 the Sopwith Pup became the first land-based aeroplane to fly from the flight deck of an aircraft carrier, HMS *Furious*, and heralded a new concept of air–sea warfare philosophy.

The Sopwith Camel was the successor to the Pup and was first flight tested during December 1916. This new machine was highly aerobatic and extremely manoeuvrable, an almost 'Sopwith' aeronautical characteristic that gave an immediate response to the operation of the control surfaces, no doubt because all of the weight had been placed within a small area at the forward end of the aircraft. Unhappily the upward vision of the pilot was somewhat obscured, whilst it seemed tail heavy when given full throttle and at no time did the Camel obtain a comparable performance with the German fighters. However, it was the first British fighter to be equipped with twin rifle calibre .303-inch Vickers machine-guns that fired forward through the propeller disc with the aid of an interrupter-gear.

Smith's design work meant that the Camel was constructed with a wire-braced wooden box girder fuselage, with single bay fabric-covered wings and was of an orthodox form of construction. It stood some 8 feet 6 inches high, with a wing span of 28 feet and a fuselage length of 18 feet 9 inches. The aircraft was powered by a 130hp Clerget 9B 9-cylinder rotary engine that gave it a maximum speed of 115mph at 6,500 feet, along with an endurance of 2 hours 30 minutes and an operational ceiling of 19,000 feet. Besides an offensive armament of two Vickers synchronized machine-guns the Camel was armed with four 25lb high-explosive bombs that were located on a bomb rack below the centre section of the fuselage. The armament allowed the Camel to operate as a fighter as well as with ground attack missions against the German trenches and dug outs. The Camels, however, lacked adequate armour plate for the protection of the pilot and the engine. As a result the aircraft suffered very high losses on the Western Front. Following successful flight tests during December 1916 the new aircraft was ordered into full production with deliveries to the Royal Flying Corps and Royal Naval Air Service commencing in May 1917. Eventually, the Camel accounted for the destruction of some 2,790 enemy aircraft over northern France and elsewhere, a higher rate of destruction than any other comparable machine. In all, there were some 2,500 Camels in France and Belgium by November 1918 and although 5,140 were built in total the aircraft was rarely used by the RAF after the First World War.

The last important aircraft designed by Smith during the war was the Sopwith Snipe, which was an evolution of the Sopwith Camel. The aircraft first flew in October 1917 and came into operational service in 1918. The Snipe was 19 feet 9 inches long, had a wingspan of 30 feet 1 inch and a height of 8 feet 9 inches. The aircraft was powered by a 230hp Bentley BR2 rotary engine that enabled it to climb higher and fly faster than the Camel. The Snipe had an endurance of 3 hours, could achieve a top speed of 121mph at 10,000 feet and had an operational ceiling of 19,500 feet. The armament consisted of two

303-inch Vickers machine-guns and four 25lb bombs. The Snipe was well regarded on the Western Front and remained in service with the RAF until 1926.

The Designer

Herbert Smith was a fair haired, steel blue eyed Yorkshireman who was born in Bradley near Skipton on 1 May 1889, the son of the chief accounts clerk to the London North Eastern Railway in Bradford. He was educated at the local primary school and the Bradley and Keighley Grammar School before he completed a mechanical engineering diploma at Bradford Technical College. He gained valuable working experience in the field of machine tools with Messrs Dean Smith & Grace Ltd of Keighley and later worked in the drawing office of Smith Major and Stephens Ltd, which manufactured lifts and cranes. Before the outbreak of the First World War he worked at the British and Colonial Aeroplane Company and developed his knowledge of aviation under Captain Frank Barnwell and Henri Coandă. In 1914 he was appointed as leading draughtsman to the Sopwith Aviation Company and was quickly promoted to the position of chief designer.

When Smith joined Sopwith it did not have an official designer. At that time the chief draughtsman was Mr Ashfield, a former school teacher, who would be given detailed design instructions from Sopwith, Sigrist and Hawker before laying out the drawings. They developed the 1½-Strutter, as well as the Pup and Camel, both of which were based upon the design of the Tabloid. Smith later recalled seeing a Tabloid at the Hendon Aerodrome, in 1913. He believed that most of Sopwith's aircraft produced before the First World War were manufactured from full-size chalk drawings, one of the earliest known uses of the aviation lofting process. On the 11 November 1918 the Armistice was signed and war operations ceased. Immediately the government cancelled all outstanding war contracts and many technicians, engineers and scientists were quickly walking the streets looking for work. Some minor attempts were made to organize commercial airline services but these could hardly absorb the vast number of people who had hitherto been employed in the aircraft industry. It was claimed by some government sources that aeroplanes would never be required again. In September 1920 the Sopwith Aviation Company Limited went into voluntary liquidation and by November the same year the HG Hawker Engineering company had been established and had taken over most of Sopwith's assets.

The Magic of the Orient

Japan was the leading naval power in the Orient and had established a Naval Air Corps during 1916 on a budget of 35,000 yen. In 1917 the Imperial Navy had provided three squadrons of warships for Great Britain to operate in the Indian Ocean, Australian waters and the Mediterranean Sea. This was at the height of the German U-boat campaign in European waters and the Royal Navy was hard pressed to provide sufficient escort vessels for convoy duty. In return Great

Britain was called upon to agree to support the Japanese claims at the peace conference to the Shandong province of China and the former German possessions in the Pacific Ocean area. On 13 February 1917 Great Britain agreed. Following the negotiations of the 1918 Treaty of Versailles, both China and America had refused to ratify the new treaty. Japan in self-defence felt obliged to initiate a warship building programme to obtain parity with the US and Great Britain by constructing eight new battleships and eight new cruisers, despite the opinion of several Japanese industrialists at the time that such a rearmament programme was beyond Japan's economic ability.

In 1917 the Naval Air Corps had established a central administrative organization in the aeronautical section of the Naval Affairs Bureau. The Imperial Naval General Staff were already highly impressed with the organization and operation of the British Royal Naval Air Service. At that time six Sopwith Cuckoo torpedo bomber biplanes had been exported to Japan and became the basis of all future Japanese naval torpedo bomber developments. In 1919 Japan purchased a further forty aircraft including one and two–seater Sopwith designs. The Imperial Naval Air Service and the Imperial Army Air Corps also shared five Sopwith Pups for experience and evaluation purposes. About this time Mitsubishi Heavy Industries commenced the manufacture of aircraft at the Mitsubishi Internal Combustion Engine Manufacturing Co. Ltd in the dockyard at Kobe. Assistance was given in building and flying large flying boats by members of a French aviation mission that was originally invited to Japan at the request of the Imperial Army Air Corps.

In April 1920 a launch platform was built on the *Wakamiya Maru*, which was originally the Russian freighter the *Lethington* that was captured by the Japanese in 1905 during the Russo–Japanese war. In June 1920 Lieutenant Kuwabara made the first successful take-off from the deck of the *Wakamiya Maru* using a Sopwith Pup. The ship played a vital role in the development of Japan's aircraft carrier techniques that were later employed on HIJMS *Hosho*, the world's first purpose-built aircraft carrier that was commissioned in December 1922.

The Air Missions

Herbert Smith and a team of aeronautical engineers were invited to Japan by Mitsubishi in 1920, together with other engineers from Junkers and Rohrback of Germany, to initially create the Mitsubishi Aircraft Company and eventually to promote engineering design expertise within that company.

During 1920 Admiral Kato HIJMN, former Japanese chief delegate to the Washington Naval Conference, at the behest of the Imperial Naval General Staff approached the British government with a request for an official aviation mission to go out to Japan. The British government delayed its reply and later informed Tokyo that the request could not be complied with owing to a shortage of personnel. A second approach was made that suggested a private mission may be despatched along with a request for the name of a suitable air force officer to direct the operation as the Imperial Navy wished to model the Aviation Corps along the lines of the former Royal Naval Air Service.

In January 1921 Colonel the Master of Semphill, a distinguished air force officer, was chosen to lead the mission. He drew up an agreement with Rear Admiral Kobayashi HIJMN, the Japanese London Naval Attaché, as to the organization and terms of reference for the mission's operations. During February 1921 Semphill worked out the details of his equipment and organization requirements, which included eighteen officers and twelve warrant officers, all of whom had been granted acting ranks in the Imperial Navy. The mission was to be sub-divided into six sections; flying, technical, armament, photographic, administration and medical. Herbert Smith and his aeronautical team arrived in Nagoya, Japan, during February 1921 and oversaw the construction of the aircraft department. It is alleged that Major Winder, chief of the Vickers branch office in Nagoya, headed the development scheme for the Mitsubishi Aircraft Company. This particular project was not completed until late in 1922.

The Semphill mission sent out an advance party to Japan in March 1921 under the control of Commander Mears RN, second in command to Colonel Semphill. Mears was accompanied by three flying officers and two engineering warrant officers. This advance guard was located at NAS Kasumigaura, an aerodrome one mile from the lagoon shore of Lake Kasumi on a raised platform of land of some 700 acres in extent. Future expansion of the airfield facilities could have been undertaken in the surrounding countryside so that expansion could have extended up to 1,400 acres if need be. The seaplane station and flying boat anchorage was on the shoreline of a non-tidal lake of an approximate 60-square mile area, being some 30 miles long by ¾ mile wide. This facility offered quite unrivalled opportunities for amphibious aircraft training and operations. The main railway line was connected to the airbase by means of a light railway track for supplying freight and fuel. The advance party of the mission considered the quarters to be of an extremely high standard, offering comfortable facilities for relaxation and good catering standards.

By July 1921 all personnel of the Semphill mission had arrived in Japan except one officer who remained in England to purchase the required equipment and to inspect and supervise the despatch of the goods to Japan. The remaining members of the mission in Kasumigaura were engaged on aerodrome preparation duties that cleared, levelled and drained ground where necessary. Meanwhile, at the extensive manufacturing facilities in Nagoya the installation of machinery, machine tools and jigs was well on the way to completion. By 1922 the Mitsubishi Aircraft Company would possess the largest aviation design and manufacturing facilities in the Orient, with additional production capacity available at Kobe and Shibaura, Tokyo. Eventually, Herbert Smith and his design team were in a position to commence designing four different types of aircraft for the Imperial Naval Air Service. In this work as chief designer Smith was assisted by John Brewsher and Ernest Comfort as designers and an embryonic works staff. Headed by Jack Hyland, chief engineer, the works staff comprised Mr RA Lipscombe and Mr BW Walters, (tinsmiths), Mr JA Salter (fitter) and Mr AE Venn (rigger). The new Mitsubishi prototype aircraft were tested by Captain WR Jordan DSC DFC, who was the company test pilot. During July 1921 most of the members of the Semphill mission had arrived in Kasumigaura and at the end of that month a Shinto ceremony was held on the station. Watched by some 30,000 people, many of whom had walked great distances to be present at the ceremony and to inspect the aircraft, the new station was commissioned. A wooden propeller was placed on the altar of the Shinto shrine and the priest consecrated the ground for the exclusive use of the Imperial forces.

By September 1921 instructional courses were underway with flying training that used the Gosport system of tuition. The Gosport system of flying had been developed by Major Smith Barry RFC during the First World War owing to his dissatisfaction with the methods of training at that time. As the Commanding Officer of No. 1 Reserve Squadron in France he had seen the results of poor pilot training. Determined to correct this situation he was subsequently appointed to the advanced school of flying at Gosport, Hampshire, with some of the best pilots withdrawn from France and Avro 504a aircraft for instructional purposes. These machines, unlike previous training planes, were equipped with dual controls in which the pupil sat in the front cockpit and the instructor behind. However, what was new was the use of a speaking tube by the instructor that was connected to two ear pieces that were worn by the pupil so that instructions could be given once airborne. Flying instruction took on a new dimension and proved so successful that the Gosport system has been used ever since. The initial training course at Kasumigaura was organized for flying officers, one of whom came from the Imperial Army Air Corps, whilst other courses were held for officers concerned with armaments, engineering and photography. Separate courses were organized but along similar lines for warrant officers, petty officers and ratings. In the meantime the Imperial Navy had awarded contracts to the Mitsubishi Aircraft Company for the design, development and manufacture of carrier-borne aircraft. These machines were designed by Herbert Smith and flight tested by Captain WR Jordan.

The New Designs

The Mitsubishi 1MF was a single-engined, single-seater, single-bay biplane similar in outline to the Martinsyde F4 machine, but with a Sopwith outlined tail. The 1MF3 was powered by a 300hp Mitsubishi Hi V-8 water-cooled engine that gave it a maximum speed of 132mph. The aircraft was 22 feet 8 inches long, had a wingspan of 27 feet 11 inches and stood 10 feet 2 inches tall. The machine was equipped with two .303-inch Vickers machine-guns. The Mitsubishi 1MT was a single-seater triplane torpedo bomber powered by the British-built Napier Lion engine that developed 450hp. With a divided undercarriage a torpedo could be carried for attack operations. The 1MT1N was 32 feet 1 inch long, had a wingspan of 43 feet 6 inches and stood 14 feet 8 inches tall. The Mitsubishi 2MR was a two-bay biplane that accommodated a pilot and a gunner for reconnaissance operations and was powered by the 300hp Mitsubishi Hi V-8 water-cooled Hispano Suiza licence-built motor. The B1M was a two-seater biplane torpedo bomber equipped with the 500hp British Napier Lion 12-cylinder engine. It was 32 feet 1 inch in length, had a wingspan of 48 feet 5½ inches and was 11 feet 6 inches high. The aircraft had a maximum speed of 130mph and an operational ceiling in excess of 14,500 feet.

As a result of all this design and development work the Imperial Naval Air Service accepted the Mitsubishi 1MF biplane fighter and designated the machine as Type 10 carrier fighter of which 138 machines were built. The single-seater triplane the Mitsubishi 1MT proved too heavy for carrier operations and although some 20 models were built the aircraft was never adopted. The 2MR was adopted as Navy Type 10 carrier reconnaisance aircraft and 159 were built. The Mitsubishi B1M was put into production as the Type 13 carrier attack plane with some 443 examples manufactured by 1933.

Successful carrier flight trials had been undertaken as far back as June 1916, when Commander Rutland RN flew a Sopwith Pup from a platform 20 feet long that was located above the forward gun turret of HMS *Yarmouth*, however the aircraft could only be landed by ditching in the sea as near to the mother ship as possible. It was not until 1917 that Squadron Commander Edwin Dunning RN took off and landed back on to the 220 feet long flush flight deck of HMS *Furious*. Similar trials were conducted by the Imperial Naval Air Service with a Type 10 fighter designed by Herbert Smith, a Parnell Panther and a Gloster Sparrowhawk, which flew from platforms mounted over gun turrets on battleships and cruisers. Since the aircraft could not re-land aboard the mother ship the projects were discontinued.

On 27 December 1922 the newly designed and purpose-built aircraft carrier HIJMS *Hosho* was commissioned. She displaced 7,470 tones, was 542 feet in overall length, 59 feet wide and 30¾ feet from deck to keel. She was propelled by two shaft geared steam turbines developing 30,000 shaft horsepower, which gave her a maximum speed of 25 knots. The *Hosho* was armed with four 5.5-inch guns and two 3.1 inch guns. The latter were subsequently replaced with around twenty 25mm anti-aircraft weapons. She accommodated seven fighter planes, ten attack bombers and four reconnaissance aircraft, with a total complement of 550 officers and men. Built at the Tsurumi shipyard between 1920 and 1922 the *Hosho* was finally scrapped in 1946. Facilities aboard the carrier included two deck lifts as well as mirrors and landing lights to assist carrier pilots descending and landing. Both Captain WR Jordan of the Mitsubishi Aircraft Company and Major Buckley of the Semphill mission demonstrated landings on the *Hosho*, with aircraft that included the Supermarine Seal and the Vickers Viking. The test flight of Captain Jordan took place in February 1923 and in the following March

1st Lieutenant Toshiichi Kira HIJMN carried out a similar operation. In December 1923 the Imperial Naval General Staff took the decision that the Imperial Navy would initiate a programme to train aircraft carrier pilots. HIJMS *Hosho* was relegated to training operations and after a refit steamed out of the shipyard as a flush deck carrier, with the funnels and bridge structure removed. The ship was no longer in front line operational use.

Two Blackburn Swift Mk II aircraft had accompanied the British aviation mission to Japan and were based at Kasumigaura Naval Air Station forty miles north-east of Tokyo. They were used as instructional aeroplanes for training pilots in deck landing and torpedo-dropping techniques. This part of the training programme was under the control of Major Brackley, who at that time held the rank of Lieutenant Commander in the Imperial Navy. Brackley found that the British Napier Lion engines did not function efficiently when used for low-flying operations over the Pacific Ocean. A number of experimental flights were undertaken and it was discovered that the compression ratio of the engines had to be reduced to 5.1 for successful low-flying operations. During February 1923 Major Brackley was appointed Aviation Adviser to the Imperial Navy and in July 1923 he advised Colonel Semphill that the Blackburn Swift Mk II should no longer be used for torpedo-dropping operations.

On 1 September 1923 a devastating earthquake in the Kanto district destroyed a large area of eastern Japan. The ships in one port sank when fuel tanks were burst open by the earthquake and ships' fuel oil poured into the waters of the harbour. As a result an uncontrollable fire swept across the water when the oil was ignited by sparks from the fires around the port area. In Tokyo the Naval Air Service laboratory wind tunnel and the entire establishment were destroyed. The new aircraft carrier HIJMS *Amagi* was so severely damaged that the ship had to be scrapped. The *Amagi*'s replacement was the *Kaga* aircraft carrier that had been converted from a battleship during 1924. Under the terms of The Washington Naval Treaty the *Kaga* had to be scrapped. However, reinstatement took place when the battleship re-entered the shipyard to be converted to an aircraft carrier of the same name.

In 1924 the Semphill mission had completed its three-year contract. Colonel Semphill had already suggested to the Imperial Navy that they should develop land-based long-range aircraft that could be used for offensive maritime operations. During the term of contract the mission had spent 70 per cent of its time in an executive capacity and 30 per cent in an advisory position. It had been decided that during the final period of the mission's work Japanese personnel would run the service, with a small percentage of instructors operating in the background. During April 1924 His Imperial Highness the Prince Regent returned from his European tour. An aerial escort was provided that was led by the aviation mission and comprised four formations of five aircraft each. An escort was also provided for HRH the Prince of Wales, who was aboard HMS *Renown*, when the ship was two hours' sailing from Yokohama. His Imperial

Majesty the Emperor conferred decorations on all the personnel of the aviation mission in grateful thanks for all the hard work they had put in to make the mission such a success. Even the Prince of Wales was honoured. He was made an honorary General of the Imperial Japanese Army.

Herbert Smith had also completed his contract and later accompanied by the embryonic staff from Mitsubishi returned home to England. Both Ernest Comfort and John Brewsher joined Vickers-Armstrongs in England as senior designers and worked on the design and development of metal-skinned wing constructions. They were also responsible for designing the Vickers Type 151 Jockey low-wing monoplane interceptor fighter, the Westland Coventry Ordinance Works Gun fighter and the Vickers Venom fighter aeroplanes. It is suggested that the Vickers Venom fighter in some way inspired the concept of the German Focke Wulf Fw 190 and the Mitsubishi A6M1 Zero fighters, which played such a devastating role in the Second World War. Herbert Smith chose not to have any more involvement with the aviation industry and retired to his home in Yorkshire.

There are many examples of Smith's aircraft that can still be seen today, both as static exhibits and in flying condition at air museums around the world. The enduring popularity of these aircraft at air shows is a testament to Herbert Smith's capability and diversity as an aircraft designer. Perhaps one of the most poignant memorials is at St Michael and All Angel's church in Lyneham in Wiltshire. In 2007 a special stained glass window was donated by 47 Squadron, stationed at RAF Lyneham, in recognition of the squadron's home in the town. The window is installed in the church's northern aisle and features three aircraft, the Hercules XV179, the Bristol Beaufighter and Herbert Smith's Sopwith Camel. The window was designed by Trevor Wifin and constructed by Salisbury Stained Glass. It was formally blessed on the 9 September 2007 by the Rt. Rev. John Kirkham and Rev. Anthony Fletcher. In a small way the window not only acts as a reminder of the achievements of those that have designed and flown notable aircraft, but also of those that have paid the ultimate price in more recent conflicts and have returned home from foreign battlefields through RAF Lyneham.

Chapter 10

Charles Rolls, Henry Royce and the Magic of Merlin

The names of Rolls and Royce are revered around the world for their connection with luxurious cars and aero engines. Yet Charles Rolls did not live to see the heights to which his name would travel. He was the first Briton to be killed in an air crash when the tail of his Wright Flyer broke off during an air display over Bournemouth on 12 July 1910. Henry Royce, the technical designer of the pair, died in 1933 and left a legacy that would preserve the name of Rolls-Royce for the future. It was a Rolls-Royce engine that powered Alcock and Brown during the first west to east Atlantic crossing, another that powered Britain's victory with the Schneider Trophy and the most famous of all, the Merlin, that provided the power behind the iconic Second World War fighter, the Supermarine Spitfire.

Charles Stewart Rolls

Charles Rolls was born on 27 August 1877 at the family's home in Berkeley Square in London. He was the third son of John Allan Rolls, who served as Member of Parliament for the Welsh constituency of Monmouthshire and who was raised to the peerage in 1892. The family's home was the expansive Victorian mansion *The Hendre* near Monmouth. It was here that Rolls spent much of his youth. He was educated at Eton, where his passion for engineering and motors led to his nickname Dirty Rolls. He studied Mechanical and Applied Science at Trinity College, Cambridge University, in 1894. Two years later he visited Paris, bought a Peugeot Phaeton motor car and became a member of the French Automobile Club. At that time the Peugeot was the first car in Cambridge and was one of only three in Wales.

Rolls became a member of the Self-Propelled Traffic Association, which was established at a meeting at the Cannon Street Hotel in London to lobby against the restrictive measures of the various Locomotive Acts in the late nineteenth century. The Acts, which were also known as the Red Flag Acts, placed controls on mechanically propelled vehicles on Britain's roads. The 1865 Act imposed a speed limit of 4mph in the country and 2mph within towns. The Act also required all vehicles to have a crew of three, one of which had to walk sixty yards in front of the vehicle carrying a red flag. The 1896 Act removed the requirement for a crew of three and increased the speed limit to 14mph. The Association merged with the Automobile Club of Great Britain in 1897.

Following his graduation from Cambridge University in 1898 it became evident that Rolls' skills lay more with business management than with engineering. In January 1903, with an initial capital investment of £6,600 provided by his father, he established CS Rolls & Company, a motor car dealership in Fulham, London, to sell imported Peugeot and Minerva vehicles from France and Belgium.

Henry Edmunds, a shareholder of Royce Limited, met Rolls through the Automobile Club and suggested that he look at Royce's two-cylinder Royce 10 motor cars. Initially, Rolls was not interested, assuming that the vehicles were likely to be as noisy and cumbersome as the foreign cars he had experienced. Edmunds persisted and eventually managed to persuade Rolls to travel to Manchester to meet Royce for what would become a fateful meeting. Charles Rolls and Henry Royce met for the first time with Edmunds at the Midland Hotel in Manchester on 4 May 1904. The meeting was a great success and led to a formal agreement on 23 December 1904 where CS Rolls would sell all of the vehicles that Royce could produce. The vehicles would include two, three, four and six-cylinder models and would all bear the name Rolls-Royce. Two years later on 15 February 1906 the partnership was formalized and Rolls-Royce Limited was registered. Rolls became the technical managing director and was granted an annual salary of £750, with a 4 per cent share of all profits over £10,000. The following year the new company acquired CS Rolls & Co.

Rolls put a great deal of energy into promoting the company and its elegant, quiet and stylish vehicles, including travelling extensively through Europe and the United States of America. However, his passions lay not just with motoring but also with aviation. He was a keen early pioneer and after a number of years found that Rolls-Royce was becoming a distraction. In 1909 Rolls resigned as managing director and took a non-executive directorship, leaving Henry Royce to oversee the development of the business.

Rolls helped establish the Aero Club in Great Britain in 1903; the club acquired its Royal status some years later, and he was only the second person in Britain to gain a pilot's licence. In 1903 he won the Gordon Bennett Gold Medal for making the longest single flight that year. He attempted unsuccessfully to persuade Royce to design an aero engine in 1907 and two years later in 1909 he was one of the first customers for a Wright Flyer manufactured by Short Brothers at Rochester. On 2 July 1910 Rolls made it into the record books by becoming the first person to make a double-crossing of the English Channel. The flight took a total of ninety-five minutes and was also the first eastbound over the Channel. He was awarded the Royal Aero Club's Gold Medal for his achievement and statues commemorating the event are to be found in Dover and in Rolls' home town of Monmouth.

Ten days later on 12 July 1910 tragedy struck. Rolls had taken off from Hengistbury Airfield adjacent to Hengistbury Head, a scenic headland on the south coast near Bournemouth in Dorset. During the flight the tail section of his Wright Flyer broke off and the aircraft crashed to the ground killing Rolls. He became the first Briton and only the eleventh person in the world to be killed in a flying accident. A large statue of Rolls was erected in Agincourt Square in Monmouth just below a statue of Henry V, where Rolls is seen in sporting attire holding a model biplane. The Royal Aeronautical Society erected a plaque commemorating Rolls in the grounds of St Peter's School in Bournemouth near the spot where he was killed. The inscription reads; 'This stone commemorates Hon. Charles Stewart Rolls who was killed in a flying accident near this spot on the 12 July 1910, the first Briton to die in powered flight.' Rolls was interred at St Cadoc's Church, Llangattock, Monmouth, Monmouthshire in Wales, where on 12 July 2010 special celebrations were held to mark the one hundredth anniversary of Charles Rolls' untimely death.

Sir Frederick Henry Royce

Henry Royce, one half of the twentieth century's most iconic motor car and aero engine name, and the brilliant engineer behind the Merlin engine, had only one year's formal schooling before his father's death forced him to go out to sell newspapers for WH Smith in London in order to help keep his family.

He was born, Frederick Henry Royce on 27 March 1863 in Alwalton on the outskirts of Peterborough, the youngest of five children. The family had run a small flour mill but after that business failed they moved to London, where his father died when Royce was just nine years old. With the financial help of an aunt he was able to begin an apprenticeship with the Great Northern Railway back in Peterborough when he was fifteen, but left after three years due to financial difficulties. Back in London he took a position with the Electric Light and Power Company and then in 1882 took advantage of an opportunity to move to its Liverpool office.

Royce established FH Royce & Co., an electrical and mechanical-engineering company in 1884 at Blake Street in Manchester. Not long after Royce had started the company, he took on a business partner, Ernest Claremont, who invested £50 in the venture, along with £20 by Royce. Expansion meant that the business could move to new premises at Cooke Street in December 1888. The business was registered as a limited company in 1899 and became Royce Limited. In the same year Claremont became a director of the Salford cable maker WT Glover. Henry Edmunds had become managing director of Glover's in 1893 following the death of the company's founder. In 1901 Royce purchased land in Trafford Park next to Glover's, with plans to develop further workshop facilities. In March 1903 Edmunds became chairman of Glover's and Claremont was appointed managing director, and then arranged with Edmunds to exchange shares in Royce Limited for shares in Glover's. This gave Edmunds an active interest in the company.

In 1902 Royce's health began to fail due to the immense pressure of work and he was convinced to travel to South Africa, with his wife Minnie, for a ten-week holiday to visit his wife's sister. It is claimed that a copy of Gérard Lavergne's book *The Automobile – its construction and management*, that was signed 'FH Royce' and dated 'September 1902' was found amongst Royce's papers and may have been read by Royce during this holiday. Upon his return he stopped using his quadricycle and bought a 10hp two-cylinder Decauville motor car. Royce was pleased with many aspects of the car but had concerns over the attention to detail. He had the car stripped down, the components measured, drawn and then had the vehicle reassembled at his factory, with a number of modifications. In May 1903 Royce set about developing three prototype motor cars. The first Royce engine was a 10hp petrol motor that was run for the first time on 16 September 1903. With bodywork manufactured by John Roberts of Hulme, the car was assembled at the company's Cooke Street works and was taken out for its first drive on 1 April 1904, when it travelled the twenty miles from the workshop to Royce's home at Brae Cottage.

Henry Edmunds was a keen motor car enthusiast who had purchased his first vehicle in 1898. The following year he had joined the Automobile Club and became a committee member in December 1900. In 1903 Edmunds sponsored the Automobile Club Hill Climbing Trophy and in 1904 convinced the board at Royce Limited to enter their car in to the Automobile Club's Sideslip Trials in London. The trials were to be held between April and May and it was hoped that Rolls might drive the car. Edmunds was aware that his fellow Automobile Club member was anxiously seeking a British-made motor car to sell through his new dealership in Fulham and so persuaded Rolls to travel to Manchester to meet Henry Royce. Following that meeting Rolls-Royce was born. Royce was appointed the chief engineer and the works director. He was awarded an annual salary of £1,250 with a 4 per cent share of the profits over £10,000. Thus Royce complemented Rolls' business acumen and financial investment with his outstanding technical expertise.

In 1908 the company built a new plant at Derby and Royce took a close interest in all aspects of the business. His attention to detail was legendary amongst his engineers, who had to take all new designs to him to be inspected before they could proceed. Overwork and poor diet, combined with the death of his fellow director Charles Rolls the previous year, led to Royce's health failing him again in 1911. The following year he underwent major surgery. His doctors had given him only a few months to live and had ordered him to stay away from the factory in Derby. In 1917, at the age of 54, he moved to West Wittering on the south coast in West Sussex, where he led a quieter, more sedate life.

It was while walking along the beach at West Wittering talking to one of his engineers in October 1928 that Royce first came up with the idea for his R aero engine. The following year the first engine had been manufactured and set a world speed record when it powered the Supermarine seaplane to victory in the 1929 Schneider Trophy with a speed of 328.65mph. An improved R engine powered the Supermarine S6B when it won the next Schneider Trophy on 13 September 1931 with a top speed of 340.08mph. Later in September 1931 the same aircraft, with an improved R engine, became the first aeroplane to fly at more than 400mph, when it broke the world speed record flying at 407.5mph.

During the years of the Depression the luxury sports car manufacturer Bentley Motors Limited found itself struggling. On 10 July 1931 the courts decided in favour of an application by one of Bentley's mortgagees to call in the receiver. The British car maker D Napier & Son had moved away from automobile manufacturing in 1925 and had concentrated on aero engines instead. However, Napier had entered negotiations to buy Bentley, with plans to once again become a car maker. At almost the final moment before a deal was reached with the receiver Rolls-Royce made a higher bid and acquired Bentley Motors Limited on 20 November 1931. Rolls-Royce retained the Bentley name, established a new subsidiary, Bentley Motors (1931) Limited, and moved all production from Cricklewood to Derby.

Following the acquisition a 20/25 engine was fitted to a Rolls-Royce chassis; it had a distinctive Bentley radiator and an open four-seater body. The car was taken to West Wittering for Royce to approve. He felt that such a fast vehicle should have springs with variable stiffness and later that day he sketched out a design for an adjustable shock absorber, which he gave to his housekeeper to pass on to the factory. That night, on 22 April 1933, Frederick Henry Royce died.

In October 1932, six months before his death, Royce launched a private venture to develop the R engine into something that would be of greater use to the RAF, which was given the working title of PV-12. The prototype engine completed initial flight tests in 1934 and was later renamed the Rolls-Royce Merlin. The idea was to produce an engine of about the same performance as the R, albeit with a much longer life. Royce did not live to see the Merlin in the air, but it became a most singular and iconic legacy.

Royce was recognized for his outstanding contribution to the nation during the First World War when he was awarded the Order of the British Empire (OBE) and on 26 June 1930 he was created Baronet of Seaton in the County of Rutland for his services to British aviation. A memorial window for Sir Frederick Henry Royce was unveiled on 23 October 1962 in the north aisle of the nave of Westminster Abbey. The window depicts figures of King Edgar and St Dunstan, with Sir Henry's coat of arms and those of the city of Derby below. Royce was greatly respected for his engineering brilliance, yet at heart remained a well-loved and humble man. On one occasion, whilst visiting the seaplane base at RAF Calshot he signed the visitors' book simply as 'FH Royce, mechanic.'

The First Rolls-Royce Aero Engines

Shortly after the start of the First World War the Royal Aircraft Factory approached Rolls-Royce and asked it to design a new 200hp piston engine. Initially, the company was reluctant to divert away from motor car manufacturing as it had expected the war to be short and that the status quo would be re-established quickly. However, it soon changed its mind and developed the company's first aero engine, the twelve-cylinder Eagle. On 3 January 1915 the Admiralty ordered twenty-five of the new Eagle engines, a month before they had been run for the first time. In all, 4,681 of the liquid-cooled engines were built, with variants ranging from the 250hp Mk I to a 360hp civilian version Mk IX in 1922. During the First World War the Eagle was fitted to a number of military aircraft, including to the Airco DH4 and Vickers Vimy bombers. The six-cylinder Rolls-Royce Falcon was developed from the Eagle and was also first run in 1915, with production beginning in September 1916. The Falcon was fitted to a wide range of aircraft, including the Bristol F2 fighter, the de Havilland DH37, the Fairey F2, the Blackburn Kangaroo and the Vickers Viking. A total of 2,185 motors were built, across three variations, all 190hp. The Hawk was a smaller 75hp engine that was developed from a straight line of six cylinders. It was first run in 1914 and went into production under licence by Brazil Straker in Bristol between 1915 and 1918 during which 205 were built. The Condor I was a 600hp V-12 piston engine developed from the Eagle that first ran in 1918. Variants of the Condor were developed as late as 1932, including the C.I 480hp compression ignition diesel version, of which two were tested and flown. The Condor was fitted to numerous aircraft including the three-engined Blackburn Iris and the twin-engined Short Singapore seaplanes. Despite initial reluctance to enter into the aero engine marketplace, by the end of the First World War Rolls-Royce was firmly established as one of Britain's leading aircraft engine manufacturers.

The Kestrel was a 700hp V-12 engine that was first run in 1926 and was the first cast-block motor made by Rolls-Royce. A total of 4,750 Kestrel engines were built and appeared in some forty variants, which were aspirated, medium supercharged or fully supercharged. A 1935 Hawker Hind with a 640hp Rolls Royce Kestrel V, V-12 engine, with a maximum speed of 186mph is operated by the Shuttleworth Collection at Old Warden Aerodrome in Bedfordshire and still flies at their regular flying days.

The Rolls-Royce Buzzard was an 800hp V-12 piston engine that was fitted to the Blackburn Perth, Handley Page HP46, Kawanishi H3K and the Vickers Type 207. Only 100 examples were built between 1927 and 1933. The Buzzard was the basis for the R racing engine and the infamous Merlin. The Rolls-Royce R was the engine that helped Supermarine win the Schneider Trophy in 1929 and 1931. It was a 2,800hp, 37-litre, V-12, supercharged piston racing engine that was used in the Supermarine S6B aircraft. The R engine also powered numerous land and water speed record attempts by Sir Henry Segrave and Sir Malcolm

Campbell, who used the engine in his Blue Bird car as well as the K3 and K4 power boats.

The Magic of Merlin

The Merlin became Rolls-Royce's most produced engine during the Second World War with nearly 150,000 examples built at the company's plants in Derby, Crewe and Glasgow. Ford of Britain also built the engines at Trafford Park, near Manchester, and the Packard V-1650 variant was built in the United States of America. The Merlin was in production for fourteen years from 1936 until 1950. The engine is perhaps mostly associated with the Spitfire, but more engines were fitted to the four-engined Avro Lancaster than any other machine, closely followed by the twin-engined de Havilland Mosquito. The Merlin 61 that was produced from March 1942 was a V-12 liquid-cooled piston engine that could generate 1,290hp at 3,000rpm at take-off, increasing to 1,565hp at 3,000rpm at 12,250 feet and 1,390hp at 3,000rpm at 23,500 feet. The engine was 88.7 inches long, 30.8 inches wide, 40 inches high and weighed 1,640lb dry weight. It had an overhead camshaft with two in take valves and two exhaust valves per cylinder. A two-speed, two-stage supercharger would automatically boost pressure in line with the throttle and a coolant-air aftercooler operated between the second stage and the engine. The fuel was provided by two independent fuel pumps and a twin-choke up-draught Rolls-Royce SU carburettor with automatic mixture control. The liquid-cooling system was pressurized and used a 70 per cent water and 30 per cent ethylene glycol coolant mixture.

The engine started life as the 740hp PV-12 private venture that first ran in October 1933 and first flew in the Hawker Hart biplane K3036 on 21 February 1935. The first operational aircraft to be fitted with the new Merlin engines were the Fairey Battle and Hawker Hurricane from 1937, followed by the Supermarine Spitfire from August 1938. The engine was developed as a result of the Air Ministry's Specification F10/35, which called for a fighter aircraft that could achieve 310mph. The Supermarine Spitfire and the Hawker Hurricane, which was designed to the earlier specification F36/34, were both developed around the PV-12 engine. Contracts for the two fighters were issued in 1936 and production of the PV-12, which was then renamed the Merlin, was given the go-ahead with government funding. During the engine's long period of production a number of technical enhancements were made, mostly improving the performance of the superchargers designed by Stanley Hooker, who had been with Rolls-Royce since 1938. He would go on to become Sir Stanley Hooker and contributed greatly to the development of the Derwent and Welland jet engines, before moving to the Bristol Engine Company. Hooker's supercharger developments greatly improved the performance of the engine and went into the Merlin 45 variant that saw service with the Spitfire V from October 1940 as well as the Merlin 61 variant that went into the Spitfire IX from July 1942.

The Avro Tutor single-engined biplane K3215 entered service with the RAF in 1933.

Felixstowe Porte Baby flying boat biplane, with a Bristol Scout biplane on the upper wing to form the first parasite aircraft arrangement in May 1916.

De Havilland DH88 Grosvenor House G-ACSS won the 1934 MacRobertson England to Australia Air Race and was flown by CWA Scott and T Campbell-Black. It is seen here restored to its original scarlet paintwork colour at the Shuttleworth Collection.

A Handley Page O-400 twin-engined biplane bomber in 1918.

A Gloster Gladiator I, the last biplane fighter used by the RAF. L8032 seen here at the Shuttleworth collection was built in 1937.

R100 airship moored at Cardington with the Graf Zeppelin airship in the background in April 1930.

Seven Sopwith Camels on the deck of HMS *Furious* on their way to attack the Zeppelin sheds at Tønder in Germany in July 1918.

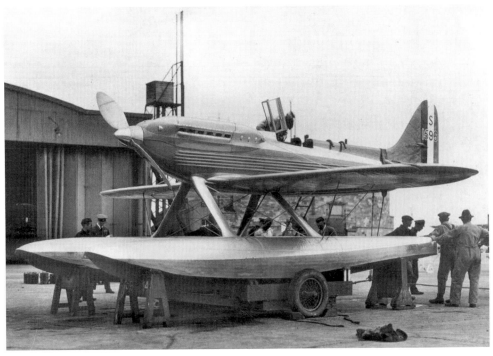

Supermarine S6B seaplane being prepared for the 1931 Schneider Trophy Air Race.

RAF Avro Lancaster Mk I four-engined bomber.

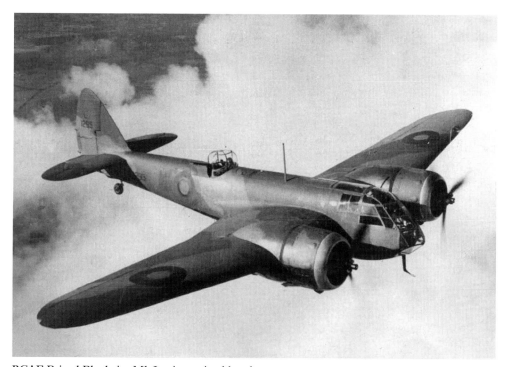

RCAF Bristol Blenheim Mk I twin-engined bomber.

HMS *Ark Royal* with a flight of Fairey Swordfish biplane torpedo bombers flying overhead in 1939.

The RAF Gloster E28 39 first prototype, W4041, taking off in 1941 with the first Whittle jet engine.

Four-engined RAF Handley Page Halifax Mk III bomber.

Fleet Air Arm Hawker Sea Hurricane Mk Ib Z7015 was built in Canada in 1940 and appeared in the 1969 film *Battle of Britain*, seen here at the Shuttleworth Collection.

Supermarine Spitfire Mk V AR501 seen here at the Shuttleworth Collection.

RAF twin-engined Vickers Wellington Mk IA bomber, N2887, in November 1939.

RAF Handley Page HP 80 Victor being serviced in May 1993.

Captain John Alcock and Lieutenant AW Brown prepare their Vickers Vimy for their trans-Atlantic flight at Lester's Field, St John's, Newfoundland, on 14 June 1919.

The British RAF High Speed Flight 1931 Schneider Trophy Team standing in front of a Supermarine S6B (L–R): Flight Lieutenant EJL Hope, Lieutenant RL Brinton, Flight Lieutenant Freddy Long, Flight Lieutenant George Stainforth, Squadron Leader AH Orlebar, Flight Lieutenant John Boothman, Flying Officer Leonard Snaith and Flight Lieutenant WF Dry.

Noted aviators Amy Johnson and her husband Jim Mollison in 1932.

Dr Barnes Wallis, designer of the Bouncing Bomb.

Charles Stewart Rolls, co-founder of Rolls-Royce and the first Briton to die in an air accident.

Sir Henry Royce, co-founder of Rolls-Royce and designer of the Merlin engine.

Flight Lieutenant Charles WA Scott, who with co-pilot Thomas Campbell–Black won the 1934 England to Australia MacRobertson Air Race.

Air Vice-Marshal Ralph Cochrane, Wing Commander Guy Gibson, King George VI and Group Captain John Whitworth examining plans for the Dambuster raid in May 1943.

Geoffrey de Havilland in Perth, Western Australia, having just won the Western Australian Centenary Air Race in 1929.

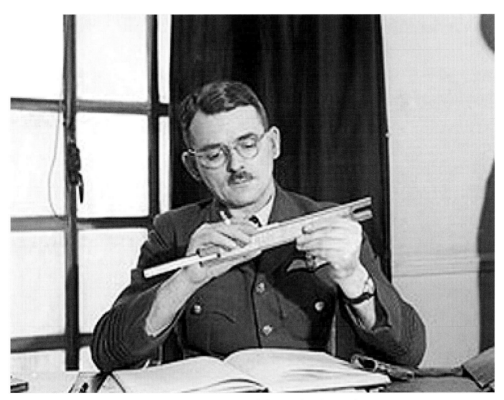

Air Commodore Sir Frank Whittle, the inventor of the modern jet engine.

Douglas Bader with 23 Squadron's 1931 Hendon Display Team shortly before the accident that led to both of his legs being amputated (L–R): Flight Lieutenant Douglas Bader, Flight Lieutenant Harry Day and Flying Officer Geoffrey Stephenson.

Squadron Commander EH Dunning in a Sopwith Pup landing on HMS *Furious* at Scapa Flow on 7 August 1917.

Harry Hawker at St John, Newfoundland, on 10 May 1919 before making his trans-Atlantic attempt.

Reginald Mitchell, the designer of the Supermarine Spitfire.

Robert Watson-Watt, the inventor of Britain's first operational radar system.

Sidney Camm at the Windsor Model Aeroplane Club in 1915 with his wife and two sons. Camm went on to design the Hawker Hurricane and many other important British aircraft.

Aviation pioneer Thomas Sopwith, founder of the Sopwith Aircraft Company.

Ernest Hives had become the Rolls-Royce general works manager in 1936 and was elected to the board in 1937. He was responsible for splitting the engineering and production divisions that enabled the company to be ready for a massive increase in output, particularly of the Merlin engine. Hives was appointed managing director of Rolls-Royce in 1946 and was chairman in 1950, the same year that he was raised to the peerage as Baron Hives of Duffield in the County of Derby. He remained chairman until his retirement in 1956. By the end of the Merlin's production run in 1950 over 112,000 motors had been built in Britain and a further 37,000 had been manufactured under licence in the United States of America. Henry Ford was approached to manufacture the engines in July 1940, but chose not to proceed. An agreement was later reached with the Packard Motor Car Company in September 1940 that was ultimately worth $130 million. The first Packard engine ran in August 1941.

The 700hp Rolls-Royce Peregrine was a revised version of the V-12 Kestrel and was first run in 1938. Development did not progress very far during the Second World War, with the company's efforts being focussed on the Merlin. In all, 301 units were manufactured and it saw some limited service fitted to the Westland Whirlwind and the Gloster F9/37. The 1,700hp Vulture was an X-24 configuration engine that used four-cylinder blocks driving a common crankshaft. The Vulture was fitted to the Avro Manchester and the Hawker Tornado. Both engines were cancelled in 1943.

Rolls-Royce started work on the Griffon in 1938 following a request from the Fleet Air Arm for a new larger engine to power their carrier-borne fighter and anti-submarine aircraft, including the Fairey Firefly. Development of the engine was delayed to allow the company time to focus on the Merlin and as a result the Griffon did not run for the first time until 30 November 1939. The Griffon was a 37-litre, 60-degree V-12, liquid-cooled piston engine that was produced in over 50 different variants and was fitted to the Spitfire and the Avro Shackleton. On 8 November 1939 Mr NE Rowe of the Air Ministry proposed using the engine in the Spitfire, which required a number of modifications to the Griffon. The new variant ran for the first time on 26 June 1940 and entered production as the Griffon II. The Griffon 65 was fitted to the Spitfire F Mk XIV and was 81 inches long, 30.3 inches wide, 46 inches high and weighed 1,980 lb. It had two in take vales and two exhaust valves per cylinder with sodium-cooled exhaust valve stems, actuated via an overhead camshaft. The two-speed, two-stage centrifugal supercharger would boost pressure automatically in line with the throttle and the engine had a water-air intercooler installed between the second stage and the engine. The fuel was provided with automatic mixture control through a triple choke Bendix-Stromberg up-draught, pressure-injection carburettor. The pressurized liquid-cooling system used a 70 per cent water and 30 per cent ethylene glycol coolant mixture. At 2,750rpm it could generate 2,035hp at 7,000 feet, 2,220hp at 11,000 feet and 1,820hp at 21,000 feet. The Griffon ceased production in 1955 after some 8,108 units had been built. It was, in fact, the last V–12 engine produced by Rolls-Royce. Today Griffons are still used to power aircraft in the Battle of Britain Memorial Flight and the last airworthy Avro Shackleton.

Into the Jet Age

Rolls-Royce took over Rover's jet engine development work in 1943 and in doing so inherited the Rover W.2B/26 turbojet developed from Frank Whittle's original design that was built by Power Jets. The W.2B/26 was improved by Rolls-Royce and became the Derwent centrifugal compressor turbojet engine that powered the Gloster Meteor, the world's first operational jet fighter.

In 1941 Rover was selected to begin production of Whittle's revolutionary turbojet engine and established a factory at Barnoldswick near Blackburn in Lancashire. Rover also set up a parallel development facility at Waterloo Mill in Clitheroe, where Adrian Lombard, an aeronautical engineer who had joined Rover at the age of fifteen in the drawing room, made a number of design improvements without the knowledge or input of Whittle himself. Lombard felt that the improvements, which included a new combustion system, were necessary if the engine was to move successfully into mass production. Lombard joined Rolls-Royce in 1943 when the company agreed to take over Rover's interests in the jet engine.

In 1941 Whittle became increasingly frustrated with Rover's work on the engine and its ability to produce satisfactory components. The previous year Whittle had met with Ernest Hives at Rolls-Royce, who had agreed to help the production of the engine by producing key components. By 1943 Rover was cooling on the idea of producing the jet engine and an agreement was reached between Spencer Wilkes of Rover and Hives at Rolls-Royce that Rover would swap its factory at Barnoldswick for Rolls-Royce's Meteor tank engine factory in Nottingham. The technical problems that Rover had experienced were resolved and the renamed Derwent I turbojet engine went into production. The first variant would produce 1,200lbf at 6,000rpm, increasing to 2,000lbf at 16,600rpm at take-off and 1,550lbf at 15,000rpm when at cruising altitude. The engine used a single-stage dual-entry centrifugal compressor with a two-sided impeller. It had ten flow combustors with ignite plugs in chambers three and ten and used a single-stage axial flow turbine with 54 blades. Successive improvements eventually led to the Derwent V, which increased the thrust capability at take-off from 2,000lbf to 3,500lbf. On 27 October 1944 the Rolls-Royce Nene engine that was developed from the Derwent, was run for the first time and was capable of producing 5,000lbf of thrust. The Derwent was fitted to the Avro 707, the Avro Canada C102 Jetliner, the Fairey Delta 1, the Fokker S14 Machtrainer, the Nord 1601 and the highly successful Gloster Meteor. On 7 November 1945 a Gloster Meteor fitted with a Derwent V turbojet engine set a world airspeed record of 606mph. Rolls-Royce had already been established as a leading aero engine manufacturer in Britain, but the success of the Derwent cemented its position and demonstrated its ability to take on the challenges of the new jet age.

The Post-war Era

In the years following the end of the Second World War many aircraft manufacturers desperately sought new markets, particularly within the growing civil aviation sector. With the development of so many airfields around the world during the war the civil airlines were able to make a relatively straightforward transformation from the pre-war seaplanes and flying boats to land-based airliners. Rolls-Royce was ideally placed to bring its wartime expertise into play in the development of new turboprop and turbojet engines for both the civil and military aircraft manufacturers.

The Rolls-Royce RB53 Dart was a popular 1,500hp turboprop engine that was first run in July 1946 and powered the Vickers Viscount on its maiden flight on 16 July 1948. The RB stood for Rolls Barnoldswick, after the factory the company acquired from Rover in 1943. In all, over 7,000 units were built and the engine was fitted to a wide range of small airliners, including the Armstrong Whitworth AW600 Argosy, the Avro 748, the Fokker F27, the Handley Page Dart Herald and the Hawker Siddeley Andover.

The Rolls Royce RB109 Tyne was a twin-shaft turboprop that was first run in April 1955 and test flown in the nose of a specially modified Avro Lincoln the following year. The engine was developed for the four-engined Vickers Vanguard airliner that first flew on 20 January 1959. Later that year engines were delivered for forty-three Vanguards that were ordered by British European Airways and Trans-Canada Airlines. Further variants were fitted to the twin-engined Dassault-Breguet Atlantique long-range reconnaissance aircraft, as well as the Saunders-Roe SR.N4 hovercraft. The SR.N4 ferried passengers and up to thirty cars from Dover to Calais from 1968 to 2000. It was built by the British Hovercraft Corporation, created by the merger of Saunders-Roe and Vickers Supermarine in 1966.

The Rolls-Royce RB163 Spey was a low-bypass turbofan engine that was first run in 1964. The first turbofan engine developed by the company was the 21,000lbf Conway that was introduced ten years earlier in 1954. This engine was too large for many commercial and military applications and consequently Rolls-Royce developed a new smaller design, the RB163 Spey. The engine was fitted to the Hawker Siddeley Trident that made its maiden flight on 9 January 1962 and the British Aircraft Corporation One-Eleven that first flew on 20 August 1963. In the late 1950s the Blackburn Buccaneer became the RAF's primary low-level strike aircraft, with the capability of delivering a nuclear weapon. During the design phase it became clear that an engine would be needed that could optimize fuel consumption while flying at low altitudes. Rolls-Royce solved this problem with the development of the RB168 Spey turbofan engine that was subsequently fitted to the Blackburn Buccaneer, while other variants were fitted to the Hawker Siddeley Nimrod.

In 1966 Rolls-Royce acquired Bristol Siddeley, which was manufacturing the Olympus, Viper, Orpheus and Pegasus engines at its Filton plant outside Bristol. At that time Bristol Siddeley was also producing, in association with the French engine manufacturer Société Nationale d'Étude et de Construction de Moteurs d'Aviation (SNECMA), the Olympus 593 Mk 610 that was used in the supersonic airliner Concorde.

By the late 1960s Rolls-Royce had started to develop its family of RB211 high-bypass turbofan engines that produced up to 60,000lbf. The engines have been fitted to the Lockheed L-1011 TriStar as well as Boeing's 747, 757 and 767 aircraft. The engine was first run in 1969 and subsequently remained in production until 1990, when it was replaced by the Rolls-Royce Trent engines. Rolls-Royce won the contract to be the sole supplier of engines for the TriStar and as a result invested heavily in research and development. The company received a number of subsidies from the British government in order to keep the project going, but eventually the financial commitments were too great and Rolls Royce was forced into bankruptcy on 4 February 1971. In order to save Rolls Royce the Conservative government under Prime Minister Edward Heath decided to nationalize the company and take it into State ownership. In 1973 the motor car division was sold to Vickers-Armstrongs and became Rolls-Royce Motors. As a result of the failure of Rolls-Royce accounting rules were changed and the cost of research could no longer be capitalized. By doing so Rolls-Royce was overstating the value of its assets. The financial problems at Rolls-Royce caused a delay in the production of the RB211 engine and as a result a delay in the introduction of the TriStar. This delay allowed Lockheed's competitor McDonnell Douglas to introduce the DC-10 on 5 August 1971 with American Airlines, several months before the TriStar was introduced on 26 April 1972. In the two decades that the aircraft were produced Lockheed sold 250 TriStars, while McDonnell Douglas sold 446 DC-10s.

The Rolls-Royce aero and marine engine businesses remained a State-owned corporation until 1987, when the Conservative government under Prime Minister Margaret Thatcher privatized the company and created Rolls-Royce plc. Today Rolls-Royce employs nearly 40,000 people in 50 countries and describes itself as 'a world-leading provider of power systems and services for use on land, at sea and in the air, (that) has established a strong position in global markets – civil aerospace, defence aerospace, marine and energy.' The Rolls-Royce customer base extends to 600 airlines and 4,000 operators of corporate and utility aircraft and helicopters. It supplies 160 armed forces around the world and has over 2,000 marine customers, including 70 navies.

In 2009 the company invested £864 million in research and development; of which two-thirds sought to make further environmental improvements to its product range, in particular the reduction of emissions. In the same year the company had underlying revenues of £10.1 billion and on 31 December 2010 Rolls-Royce had an order book worth £59.2 billion. A far cry from CS Rolls & Company, Charles Rolls' single car dealership in Fulham, and Royce Limited, Henry Royce's partnership with Ernest Claremont at Cooke Street in Manchester, that came together on 15 February 1906 to form Rolls-Royce Limited.

Chapter 11

Reginald Pierson and the Wellington Saga

Reginald Kirshaw 'Rex' Pierson CBE, chief designer at Vickers Limited, was born on 9 February 1891 at Little Fransham in Norfolk. His father was the local rector and had always intended for his son to start his career with a position at the Bank of England, however, Pierson's passion for engineering was too strong and in 1908 he was allowed to join Vickers Limited at Erith as an apprentice.

The Vickers Story

Vickers was established as a steelmaker by Edward Vickers and his father-in-law George Naylor in Sheffield in 1828. The business became a public company in 1867 and changed its name to Vickers, Sons & Company. Vickers then set about a period of rapid expansion and acquired a number of businesses. It produced its first piece of armour plate in 1888 and its first artillery weapon two years later in 1890. In 1911 Vickers changed their name again to Vickers Limited and made its first move into the burgeoning world of aviation when it established Vickers Limited (Aviation Department). In 1927 Vickers Limited merged with the engineering company Armstrong Whitworth that was founded by William George Armstrong in 1847 and became Vickers-Armstrongs Limited. Armstrong Whitworth had first moved into aviation in 1912 when it established an aerial department that subsequently became Sir WG Armstrong Whitworth Aircraft Company. Following the merger with Vickers the Sir WG Armstrong Whitworth Aircraft Company was bought by JD Siddeley. Seven years later in 1934 JD Siddeley was acquired by Hawker Aircraft and became the Hawker Siddeley Aircraft Company.

In 1928 Vickers acquired Supermarine Aviation Works Limited, which became Supermarine Aviation Works (Vickers) Ltd. Ten years later in 1938 the two businesses were restructured into one organization and became Vickers-Armstrongs (Aircraft) Limited. The next major change to the company's organization came in 1960, when the British government pushed through its desire for the aviation industry to consolidate. This led Vickers to merge with Bristol, English Electric Company and Hunting Aircraft to form the British

Aircraft Corporation (BAC). Under the new structure Supermarine was shut down in 1963 and the Vickers name ceased to be used on new aircraft two years later in 1965. The Aircraft and Shipbuilding Industries Act 1977 nationalized BAC and Hawker Siddeley Group, which became the State-owned corporation British Aerospace. Vickers' shipbuilding interests were also nationalized under the same act. The remaining parts of Vickers were renamed Vickers plc, which later made a number of acquisitions including the arms manufacturer Royal Ordnance Factory. Vickers also acquired British car manufacturers Cosworth and Rolls-Royce, which were subsequently sold to Volkswagen in 1998. Interestingly, the following year the aero engine manufacturer Rolls-Royce plc bought Vickers plc and sold off the defence divisions to Alvis plc, which became Alvis Vickers. In March 2003 Rolls-Royce renamed its Vickers assets as Vinters. Consequently, the Vickers name only remained with Alvis Vickers until that company was bought by BAE Systems in 2004 and became BAE Systems Land Systems, which extinguished the proud Vickers name for a final time.

Vickers Limited (Aviation Department)

Vickers launched its aircraft division in 1911 and Reginald Pierson immediately asked to transfer to it, where he then worked as a technician under Mr AR Lowe. At the same time he started to learn to fly and gained his aviator's certificate from the Royal Aero Club at Brooklands Aerodrome on 14 October 1913. Pierson's career flourished at Vickers and by 1917, just nine years after joining the company as an apprentice, he was appointed its chief aircraft designer.

As chief designer Pierson was responsible for the twin-engined biplane bomber the Vickers Vimy. The prototype first flew on 30 November 1917 and was originally powered by two 200hp Hispano Suiza engines. This aircraft was Vickers' response to the Air Ministry's First World War requirement for a night bomber that could attack targets deep behind enemy lines in Germany. The Vimy, which was named after the Battle of Vimy Ridge, remained in service with the RAF until 1933. The aircraft was 43 feet 6 inches long, had a wingspan of 68 feet 1 inch and was 15 feet 7 inches high. Engine supply difficulties at that time meant that the Vimy was tested with a number of different engines. The Vimy Mk II variant was was fitted with two 360hp Rolls-Royce Eagle VIII 12-cylinder piston engines, which gave it a top speed of 103mph, a range of 910 miles and an operational ceiling of 7,000 feet. It was armed with a .303-inch Lewis machine-gun mounted in a Scarff ring in the nose, a second machine-gun in a Scarff ring in the mid-fuselage and it could carry a 4,804lb bomb payload. However, the end of the First World War came before the Vimy could be deployed with the RAF. The first aircraft to be delivered went into service with 58 Squadron in Egypt during July 1919. The Vimy served in the Middle East and in the United Kingdom until 1925, when the Vickers Virginia, which was based on the Vimy, was introduced. The Vimy continued in service with the RAF as a training aircraft until 1938.

A number of record-breaking flights and record attempts were made using the Vimy, most notably when John Alcock and Arthur Whitten Brown flew a converted Vimy from St John's, Newfoundland, to Clifden in Ireland in June 1919 and became the first people to fly non-stop across the Atlantic Ocean. In the same year Keith and Ross Macpherson Smith became part of the first all-Australian crew to fly from England to Australia. They took off in a Vimy from Hounslow Heath Aerodrome on 19 November 1919 and landed in Darwin on 10 December 1919, having achieved a total flying time of just 135 hours. Ross Macpherson Smith was killed three years later as a test pilot for a Vickers Viking.

Lieutenant Colonel Pierre van Ryneveld and Major Quintin Brand flew a commercial version of the Vimy in an attempt on the South Africa record. They took off from Brooklands Aerodrome on 4 February 1920 in G-UABA *Silver Queen*. However, engine trouble forced them to land before they could reach Wadi Halfa. The RAF at Heliopolis lent them a replacement Vimy, but that was damaged in Bulawayo while they were attempting to take off. They completed their journey in an Airco DH9, but were disqualified from the record attempt. In recognition of their endeavour the South African government awarded them £5,000 each.

The Birth of the Wellington

During 1928 Lord Trenchard wrote his famous memorandum to the government outlining the doctrine of strategic air power as a policy for the RAF in an offensive role. His comments included:

> The aim of the Air Force is to break down the enemy's means of resistance by attacks on objectives selected as most likely to achieve this end. It is not necessary for an air force, in order to defeat the enemy nation, to defeat its armed forces first. Is an air offensive of this kind contrary to International Law or the dictates of humanity? It is an entirely different matter (from the discriminate bombing of a city for the sole purpose of terrorising the civilian population) to terrorise munitions workers, men and women into absenting themselves from work, through fear of air attack upon the factory. Such destruction is imperatively demanded by the necessities of war. Is the object one which will lead to victory and a correct employment of air power? This form of warfare is inevitable.

Thus the policies that were to be pursued during the Second World War had been laid down and agreed, but a problem now arose finding a suitable aircraft design team to turn the policy into reality. Vickers-Armstrongs had decided to move Dr Barnes Wallis to its aviation division following a visit by Pierson to Howden, Yorkshire, where the airship *R100* was being built by the Airship

Guarantee Company. Wallis's design for the *R100* incorporated his geodetic method of construction. At once Pierson recognized genius in Wallis and in November 1928 he was called to Weybridge to be shown around by the managing director Mr McLean. Eventually, Wallis was to become one of the company's three chief aircraft designers, along with Pierson and RJ Mitchell at Supermarine.

Unfortunately, the Vickers Type 224 that was being built to Air Ministry specification F7/30 was not a success, it was declared useless by the chief test pilot Wing Commander Maurice Summers owing to excessive tail flutter experienced during power dives. On taking up his appointment at Weybridge Wallis investigated the design of the machine and after some time formulated the principles of the geodetic method of construction for aircraft structures that embraced the use of light alloys to achieve the required saving of weight and the necessary strength in the structure of the machine.

In July 1931 the Air Ministry drew up specification G4/31 for a new general-purpose biplane bomber. The Vickers-Armstrongs board of directors was approached by Wallis to opt for a monoplane design embodying the geodetic form of construction. Eventually designs were drawn up, but later in October of the same year the Air Ministry changed the aircraft's role to that of a torpedo bomber and coastal reconnaissance machine. Finally, on 25 April 1932 the Vickers-Armstrongs board decided to go ahead with a private venture to the Air Ministry's original specification G4/31. On 19 June 1935 the new Type 287 Wellesley made its maiden flight from the Brooklands plant in Surrey. The new monoplane was designed by Pierson and embodied all the geodetic principles formulated by Wallis. The Air Ministry was frustrated that the monoplane concept had been proved successful against all its traditionally held ideals. Nevertheless, the Wellesley structural concept had been born.

In the course of September 1932 the Air Ministry issued specification B9/32 for a medium bomber. This initiated design studies for the subsequent Vickers Wellington at a time when Hitler had dissolved the German *Reichstag* and decreed that the National Socialist German Workers Party was to be identified with the German State. Vickers-Armstrongs studied the new requirements and used the test bed figures from the Wellesley project as well as the vast experience and expertise of Wallis and Pierson in its design. New types of guns, engines and structure were to be conceived. By December 1933 the Air Ministry had decided to accept the design principles for the new twin-engined bomber and a contract was awarded for one prototype of the Vickers Type 271 to be built. When the new prototype eventually appeared it was quite different from the Wellington bombers that became so well known during the period of the early 1940s. With a manually operated gun position in the bow and the stern, and with provision for a similar position at the top of the fuselage half way down the aircraft, it was consequently a rather portly looking twin-engined machine with a single fin, rudder and tail. The Type 271 eventually made its maiden flight on the 15 June 1936.

During this period Dr Barnes Wallis had given some lectures on the theory and practical application of the geodetic form of construction. This allowed for flexibility of structure and greater strength, whilst permitting the internal space to be utilized for maximum equipment use and fuel stowage. These lectures were reputed to have taken place at Barrow-in-Furness and among the members of the aviation fraternity attending was a delegation of Japanese aviation officers, who had travelled up especially from London for the occasion. Later it transpired that having acquired the necessary technical knowhow Imperial naval aviation engineers in Japan had endeavoured to reconstruct the system and incorporate it in the new aircraft designs that were then initiated by the Imperial Naval Air Service. However, success eluded the Japanese engineers who had to use the more traditional form of structural layout for aircraft design. It is less than a coincidence that the Mitsubishi G4M1 attack bomber used extensively in the Pacific during the Second World War bore more than just a passing resemblance to the early Wellington.

During January 1935 Group Captain AT Harris, Director of Plans at the Air Ministry, declared light bombers to be obsolete and outmoded. He advocated the use of aircraft flying at maximum range with a maximum offensive payload. This lesson had been learnt during the Abyssinian Campaign when RAF airbases had been located ridiculously near to the Libyan frontier due to the very short range of the Bristol light bombers. It was with ease that the Italian Air Force was able to conduct aerial reconnaissance operations and gauge the strength of the RAF in Egypt. As a result a Long-Range Development Flight was created in England and equipped with Vickers Wellesley bombers. Intensive training commenced immediately and with the early development success achieved by this aircraft the RAF had been sufficiently impressed with the new monoplane for the Air Ministry to place a production contract for 96 Wellesley Mk I aircraft. The Wellesley was 39 feet 3 inches long, had a wingspan of 74 feet 7 inches and stood 15 feet 3 inches tall. It was fitted with an 835hp Bristol Pegasus XX 9-cylinder engine that gave it a maximum speed of 228mph, a range of 2,880 miles and an operational ceiling of 25,500 feet.

It is said that one of the early types of Wellesley bombers was on a flight test over the English Channel when it was lost and disappeared. The matter was reported to the Air Ministry and eventually Lord Vansittart of Denham, chief of the British secret service, was asked to initiate a search of Europe to ascertain the location of the lost machine. Part of the wreckage was supposedly found by British secret agents in a garage in the city of Kiel and it transpired in the course of the investigation that the ill-fated plane had been shot down by a German U-boat in the English Channel. Regrettably the bodies of the two flying officers were never recovered. Attempts were thought to have been made to unravel the secrets of the geodetic system of construction.

To warn the *Luftwaffe* that the British secret service knew of the incident and the fate of the aircraft, it is alleged that secret service funds were used to finance a film that told the story of an aircraft going missing over the English Channel. Lord Vansittart of Denham was a friend of Sir Alexander Korda, who had founded London Films at Denham Studios. In 1939 London Films released *Q Planes*, which starred Ralph Richardson, Laurence Olivier and Valerie Hobson. In the United States of America the film was called *Clouds over Europe*. In the film several British planes carrying secret equipment disappeared over the English Channel. The aircraft were brought down by a mysterious ray that was beamed from a salvage ship that was presumed, but never stated, to be German.

In 1938 the three Wellesley bombers and their crews of the Long-Range Development Flight were readied for an attempt on the world record to Australia. The planes were three-seater machines that were fitted with extra long-range fuel tanks and had their engines fitted with long cowls as extra streamlining. They took off from RAF Ismailia in Egypt on 5 November 1938 and headed east-south-east; one plane landed in Koepang, whilst the two remaining machines landed at Port Darwin Airport having flown 7,162 miles nonstop within 48 hours to achieve the world record. The first service version of the Wellesley bomber was delivered during April 1937 and deliveries continued until May 1938. When war was declared in 1939 Wellesley bombers successfully took part in the British campaigns in Somaliland and Abyssinia against the Italian Colonial Armies and units of the *Regia Aeronautica*.

The Wellington was designed to specification B9/32 and the Type 271 prototype first flew on 15 June 1936. It was later lost at sea on 19 April 1937. A series of prototype developments then took place and the Wellington Mk I bomber was finally completed. It flew for the first time on the 23 December 1937. Service deliveries commenced during October 1938. The Wellington Mk III medium bomber had a crew of six and was 64 feet 7 inches long. It had a wingspan of 86 feet 2 inches and stood 16 feet 5 inches high. It was powered by two 1,500hp Bristol Pegasus XI radial engines, which gave it a maximum speed of 255mph at 12,500 feet, a range of 1,540 miles with its 4,500lb maximum bomb payload and an operational ceiling of 19,000 feet. The armament consisted of eight .303 Browning machine-guns, with two mounted in the nose turret, four in the tail turret and a further two in waist positions.

By September 1939 it was obvious to aviation experts that the Vickers Wellington bomber was Great Britain's most formidable bombing aircraft. Unfortunately, the Weybridge factory could only build one machine per day and it soon became apparent that many more Wellington bombers would have to be built to sustain an air offensive during hostile conditions. It was therefore decided that production of this machine should commence at Squires Gate, Blackpool, where thirty bombers per month could be manufactured, and at Chester where a further fifty machines could be constructed each month.

The most numerous of the early variants was the Wellington IC of which 2,685 were produced out of a total production more than 11,400 machines. Of the early versions the Mk III was the Bomber Command type, of which a total of 1,519 aircraft were manufacted. It was powered by two Bristol Hercules bombers, rated at 1,500hp each, and was armed with a four-gun rear turret. Two Polish Bomber Squadrons were equipped with the Mk IV powered by two 1,200hp Pratt & Whitney engines, whilst a high-altitude turbo-charged version became the Mk V. Later the Mk VI was equipped with a long-range pressurized cabin but no armament. The Mk VII was a research aircraft housing an experimental 40mm gun turret and twin rudders. The Mk VIII was a converted Mk I used by Coastal Command equipped with ASV search radar, a Leigh Light and in some instances a degaussing hoop for the detonation of magnetic mines. The Mk IX was a troop-carrying version and the Mk X became a standard bomber type with Bristol Hercules motors rated at 1,675hp, of which a total of 3,804 machines were constructed. In mid-1942 peak monthly production included 70 aircraft at Weybridge, 130 at Chester and 102 at Blackpool. The Coastal Command version of the Bomber Command type was the Mk XII, which housed a chin radar installation, Leigh Light ventral and was armed with torpedoes. The following Mk XIII had an ASV Mk II radar set with mast antennas and an armed turret. A Coastal Command version, the Mk XIV, was fitted with an ASV Mk III chin radome, wing rockets and a Leigh Light installed in the weapons bay. Two variants were developed as unarmed transport planes for Transport Command duties and two special navigational trainers were produced, the T10 and T19, which were delivered by October 1945 and served until 1953.

The period of intensive development of the Wellington bomber saw a new design being formulated in parallel as a replacement that was named the Warwick. This machine first flew on 13 August 1939 and production of the BI variant commenced in January 1942. Only sixteen Mk I B bomber variants were delivered and the Warwick was quickly adapted to fulfil others roles. General reconnaissance (GR), air sea rescue (ASR) and civil (C) variants were developed and indeed entered service, but problems dogged the aircraft's design from the start. Production of the Vickers Warwick was marred by authoritative indecision because of the unavailability of suitable engines to power the new aeroplane. The Vulture engines that were intended to be installed were deemed to be unsatisfactory. Double Wasp engines were installed in sixteen of the BI type bombers that were eventually used for research and trials. As a result 369 of the ASR type were fitted with the same motors and were fitted with Lindholme parachutes and survival gear including a Mk I lifeboat. Later, Mk II lifeboats were installed along with ASV radar and each plane was armed with eight machine-guns in three separate turrets. The CI model was an unarmed transport followed by the CIII, which had a freight pannier located in the bomb bay necessitating a revised rudder and fin design. A total of 133 aircraft in the GRII version were manufactured for reconnaissance and general duties in the United Kingdom and Mediterranean theatres of operation. However, the ASR model was the chief land plane used on overseas search and rescue. Nevertheless, in the post-war era Coastal Command was equipped with the GRV model armed with .50-inch calibre machine-guns as well as the Leigh Light. When the contract for the Warwick was completed over 800 planes had been manufactured. In the main they were relegated to carriers of mail and as utility transports. They were second only in importance to the Douglas Dakota aircraft of Transport Command during the war years.

With the declaration of war in 1939 the RAF possessed only seventeen squadrons of Whitley, Hampden and Wellington bombers. Of these the Wellington was considered the more formidable, whilst the Whitley proved too slow and the Hampden was ill-armed for daylight operations and thus the latter two were withdrawn and used in secondary roles in the course of the air war. The Blenheim bombers had insufficient range to be able to operate over north-west Germany, whilst the Fairey Battle aircraft were quite inadequate for offensive operations. The air war in China should have taught the British experts the folly of operating day bombers without fighter escorts, but such tactical reports, if they had existed at the Air Ministry from Air Attachés in the Far East or secret service agents, were either pigeon holed, never filed or just ignored.

The first British bombing raid of the war took place on 4 September 1939 with an attack on German warships at Brunsbüttel and Wilhelmshaven by fourteen Wellingtons and fifteen Blenheims. Further attacks took place on 3 December 1939 when twenty-four Wellingtons flew out of RAF Marham and RAF Mildenhall under the command of Wing Commander R Kellet and again attacked German warships in the area of Heligoland. Further attacks were made on shipping in the Schillig Roads, Wilhelmshaven and Jade River area by formations of twelve and twenty-four Wellington bombers on 14 and 18 December. But without long-range fighter escorts the lessons learnt from the bombing raids conducted by the Japanese Navy's long-range Mitsubishi G3M2 bombers over the cities of north and central China during the late 1930s had been completely ignored by British politicians and air experts.

The German Battle Report of 18 December recorded that the *Luftwaffe Kommandeur* was located on the island of Wangerooge in the Friesian group of islands and operated a Freya type radar station. From there, for the first time in recorded history, the *Kommandeur* was able to control and direct from the cathode-ray tube of the apparatus the Messerschmitt Bf 109s onto the formation of British bombers, whose presence had been detected at a range of seventy miles. Thus the German pilots were able to choose the place and time of their attacks, which came from a beam, rear and underneath, or exclusively the rear, in which the tail gunner would be shot dead so that the Bf 109s could approach close in for the kill. The German fighters possessed the advantages of an early warning radar system, superior aircraft speeds and fighter planes equipped with long-range 20mm Rheinmetall-Borsig cannons, which enabled the German pilots to open up an attack as far away as 600 to 900 yards.

The ability of the Wellington bomber to return its crew to England despite harrowing and crippling air battles became legion among the squadrons of Bomber Command, where the aircraft was viewed with affection. Numerous examples existed of machines returning dead and wounded crewmen back to base, with shot away rudder surfaces, burned out cabins, wings half off and little or no fabric on the aircraft surfaces, resulting in the expression 'coming home on a wing and a prayer'. Awards for gallantry were earned not only for pressing on home an attack against overwhelming odds, but also for sheer dogged resolution and determination to fly a mere wreck home to England. But the air war continued unabated with increasing ferocity as tactics changed from daylight attacks to night raids in which the Wellington bomber dropped the first 4,000lb bomb. The machine was still on inventory and in operational use in the Pathfinder Force of Air Vice-Marshal Bennett, as well as in the standard bombing squadrons of Bomber Command. The aircraft was used in the first 1,000 bomber raid, flew in the Middle East as well as in India and against the Imperial Japanese Army and Navy installations in Burma.

From Two to Four, the Vickers Windsor

It was natural that four engines would be fitted to the Wellington design sooner or later. The idea was logical and resulted in the birth of the Vickers Windsor bomber. The prototype DW 506 was first flown by Wing Commander Maurice Summers on 23 October 1943. Using the geodetic form of construction the machine was covered in fabric backed with wire mesh in such a way that any battle damage caused by bullets could be patched up using an electric iron. The cockpit was narrow and accommodated one pilot who possessed a good all-round view with very easy access to the controls. The plane possessed few vices and only limited modifications were necessary to the original design. However, ballooning of the wing fabric had been experienced during the maiden flight caused by the stretching of the material on the upper wing surface known as 'quilting'. The diamond shapes over the surfaces of the aircraft were due to the geodetic structures upon which the fabric was mounted.

Further problems with the fabric were experienced in the course of a test flight with a second prototype, DW 512, when it was struck by a bird and ten square feet of fabric was lost on the starboard wing between the two engines. Although Wing Commander Summers landed safely the accident had increased the stalling speed of the machine. As a result of the accident the cloth was tested further and was improved by backing it with layers of glass cloth. Even this improvement was changed when the fabric was eventually backed by wire mesh, an innovation that was introduced on all subsequent Windsor bombers. The Windsor Type 447, the first of only three prototypes built, had a crew of six to seven, was 76 feet 10 inches long, with a wingspan of 117 feet 2 inches and a height of 23 feet. It was fitted with four 1,6315hp Rolls-Royce Merlin 65 V-12 liquid-cooled engines that enabled the Windsor to achieve a top speed of 317mph at 23,000 feet, a range of 2,890 miles when carrying a bomb payload of 8,000lb and an operational ceiling of 27,250 feet. It was armed with four 20mm cannon in remote controlled barbettes that fired to the rear and could carry a total bomb payload of 15,000lb. The new machine was characterized by the high aspect ratio wings and by the installation of gun barbettes in the aft end of the outer engine nacelles, each of which housed two 20mm cannon guns remotely sighted and controlled by the tail-end gunner. The prototype system had been fitted experimentally to a Vickers Warwick bomber, L9704, but a fourth longeron had to be added to the fuselage to reduce the effects of twisting caused by the firing of the guns and possible defective gun laying.

Parked on the perimeter track the new Windsor bomber appeared to possess a legged undercarriage, with each wheel retracting into its own engine nacelle. This arrangement was considered to produce too much drag on take-off and landing. However, little or no effect on performance was measured during test flights. Nevertheless, difficulty was experienced on the perimeter track whilst turning since the outer wheels tended to dig into soft ground. This was overcome by rolling the machine from the static position. Curiously enough the anhedral of the wings on take-off took on a dihedral effect before becoming fully airborne. In fact, the wing tips became perfectly flexible, rising some four feet before the aircraft was finally airborne and it became a mystery as to how the control rods worked under such conditions.

Various types of engines were fitted to the Windsor bomber in a series of experiments to achieve the best motive power output. The Type 447 was powered by Rolls-Royce Merlin 65 engines, with chin-type radiators, later to be replaced on the Type 457 and Type 461, the second and third prototypes, by Merlin 85s with off-centre annular type radiators, but with improved cowlings. The Type 457 first flew on 15 February 1944 and the Type 461 made its maiden flight on 11 July 1944. Although experimental work was continued by Vickers right up to the end of the Second World War only three aircraft were built. The troubled Windsor had been superseded by the popular and highly successful Lancaster.

The Post-war Era
As aircraft manufacturers contemplated their future following the end of the Second World War; Pierson encouraged Vickers-Armstrongs to move quickly into the civil aviation arena. He immediately began to work on a twin-engined civil airliner based on the design of the Wellington. On 22 June 1945 the prototype of the Vickers VC1 Viking first took to the air at Wisley Aerodrome. The Viking marked a major change for Vickers-Armstrongs that helped the company to develop in the difficult post-war years. The Viking was also an important aircraft for Britain's fledgling airline industry, providing it with a

short and medium-haul airliner that served it well until the turboprop Viscount came into service in 1950.

The first variant was the Viking VC1A, which was able to carry 21 passengers in an unpressurized cabin. The VC1B variant increased passenger capacity to 24 seats and in 1951 British European Airways (BEA), refitted its fleet of Vikings increasing capacity to 36 seats. The VC1B Viking was 65 feet 2 inches long, had a wingspan of 89 feet 3 inches and was 19 feet 6 inches high. It was fitted with two 1,690hp Bristol Hercules 634 14-cylinder two-row radial engines that gave it a maximum speed of 263mph, a cruising speed of 210mph and a range of 1,700 miles. Interestingly, in 1948 an experimental version of the Viking was equipped with Rolls-Royce Nene turbojet engines and became the world's first all-jet passenger aircraft.

On 1 September 1946 BEA started its first regular service using the Viking on the route between Northolt and Copenhagen. The company went on to operate a fleet of Vikings for a further eight years. Of the 163 Vikings manufactured between 1945 and 1949 some 56 were lost in accidents. A number of Vikings can still be seen at aeroplane museums around the world, including G-AGRU at the Brooklands Museum in Surrey, which is located between Weybridge and Byfleet and is just a few minutes from Junction 10 of the London orbital M25 motorway. The museum is at the former motor racing circuit of the same name, which was built in 1907. Brooklands Aerodrome was also the home of one of Vickers-Armstrongs factories. One of the two complete Wellingtons that have survived until today can be seen at Brooklands. Wellington Mk IA serial number N2980 was salvaged from Loch Ness in September 1985. It had ditched into the Loch having lost engine power during a training flight in 1940. The crew was able to bale out and survived, except for the rear gunner whose parachute failed to open and was killed. Wellington N2980 has now been restored except for the damaged propellers, which were kept as they were found as a tribute to the rear gunner.

The second Wellington is a Mk X, serial number MF628, which entered service with the RAF on 11 May 1944. It has been on display at the Royal Air Force Museum, Hendon, since it opened in 1972. Wellington MF628 appeared in the 1955 film *The Dam Busters*, which told the story of Operation *Chastise* when in 1943 RAF Lancasters from 617 Squadron destroyed the Möhne, Eder and Sorpe dams in Germany using Dr Barnes Wallis' unique 'bouncing bomb'. This was not the first time that a Wellington had been the centre of attention on the silver screen. The 1942 propaganda film *One of Our Aircraft is Missing*, produced by Michael Powell and Emeric Pressburger, was part of a series of films made by the Ministry of Information aimed at maintaining morale during the Second World War. The film opens by introducing the crew of the Wellington 'B for Bertie', which is returning home from a raid over Stuttgart. One of the aircraft's engines becomes damaged by enemy fire and the crew is forced to bale out over occupied Holland. They then try to make their way back to Britain. The film is also notable as it includes Peter Ustinov's first film role.

More recently the BBC produced a one-hour documentary called *Wellington Bomber* that recounted the story of Wellington LN514, which in 1943 was built in a record 23 hours and 50 minutes, beating a similar record of 48 hours for the construction of a single aircraft set by an American factory in California.

The record attempt was filmed and a special newsreel was produced called *Workers' Weekend.* Wellington LN514 was built at Vickers-Armstrongs' Broughton plant in Flintshire, which during the Second World War was run by the Ministry of Aircraft Production. At its peak the factory employed over 6,000 people, who each worked twelve-hour shifts to produce some twenty-eight Wellingtons per week. Over half of the workforce at Broughton were women and the film sought to show that not only were Britain's manufacturing capabilities unaffected by German bombing raids, but also the invaluable contribution made by women in the production of essential wartime military equipment. It was hoped by the Ministry that *Workers' Weekend* would not only boost morale but also encourage more volunteer workers to come forward.

Reginald Pierson died at his home in Cranleigh, Surrey, at the age of fifty-six following a long illness. During his life his invaluable contribution to British aviation was recognized many times. He became a fellow of the Royal Aeronautical Society in 1926, received its Taylor Gold Medal for his paper on performance prediction in 1928 and served as vice-president in 1945. He was made an MBE in 1919, OBE in 1941 and CBE in 1943 for services to his country.

Reginald Pierson spent forty years with Vickers-Armstrongs and contributed greatly to the success of its aviation division, remaining as chief designer until 1945 when he passed the mantle to George Edwards. Sir Roy Fedden, who designed most of the Bristol Engine Company's most successful aircraft engines, gave the first RK Pierson Memorial Lecture in the staff mess at Vickers-Armstrongs' Weybridge Works on 12 November 1952. The lecture was introduced by George Edwards. Sir Roy was a close friend and business associate of Pierson and paid tribute to his friend's outstanding achievements. He explained how well Pierson was regarded by his colleagues, how they admired his absolute integrity, his open mindedness and his willingness to listen to criticism. In closing he said there are 'Few of the considerable number of people that passed through his hands who would not say that there was an innate decentness in all his dealings with them'.

Chapter 12

Alliott Verdon-Roe and the Road to Lancaster

lliott Verdon-Roe is remembered for a number of most significant
aviation landmarks. In 1908 he took off from Brooklands Aerodrome and
become the first Englishman to make a powered flight. The following
year at Walthamstow Marshes he became the first Englishman to fly an entirely
British designed and built aircraft. Roe also pioneered the design for the tractor
type biplane and built the first English seaplane.

He will also be remembered as the co-founder of AV Roe & Company
Limited, which he established with his younger brother Humphrey in 1910 and
that went on to produce the iconic Second World War four-engined bomber the
Avro Lancaster, the backbone of RAF Bomber Command and the hero of
countless bombing raids over Germany, not least of all the famous Dambuster
raid of 1943. But the Lancaster entered service fourteen years after Roe had sold
the company to Armstrong-Siddeley in 1928 and he had formed the noted flying
boat manufacturer Saunders-Roe. The Avro mark changed hands for a second
time in 1934 when Armstrong-Siddeley was sold to Hawker Aviation and
Hawker Siddeley was established.

Alliott Verdon-Roe was born on 26 April 1877 in Patricroft, Eccles, the son of
a doctor. At the age of fourteen he went to British Columbia, Canada, to pursue
a career as a surveyor, but the end of the silver rush meant that there were few
opportunities to be had and so after having held a small number of odd jobs he
returned to England. Once back home he took up an apprenticeship with the
Lancashire & Yorkshire Railway. Roe had attempted to join the Royal Navy but
was turned down. However, he did make it to sea on board the British & South
African Royal Mail Company's ship SS *Jebba*, serving as the fifth engineer on the
West African run. It was while at sea that his imagination was first captured by
flight. He watched as the sea birds swooped down onto the ship and soon he
started to put what he had observed into experiments with various aeroplane
models. By 1906 he patented the world's first single cockpit control column that
replaced the previous two lever system. The following year, in April 1907, he won
the *Daily Mail*'s £75 prize for an aircraft model capable of making a sustained
flight at a competition held at Alexandra Palace in London. He used his

winnings to convert the design of the model aircraft into his first aeroplane. Roe planned to make an attempt on the £2,500 prize offered by the Brooklands Automobile Racing Club for the first person to fly a single circuit of its race track before the end of 1907. Unfortunately, despite numerous endeavours no one was able to claim that prize, including Roe who only managed to fly for the first time on 8 June 1908. The Roe I biplane was the first engined aeroplane to be entirely designed, constructed and flown in England. It was originally equipped with a 9hp JAP motorcycle engine, but due to a severe lack of lift Roe borrowed a French Antoinette engine and made a number of successful short flights. The aircraft had a wingspan of 36 feet, was 19 feet long and was powered by an 8-cylinder, 24hp, water-cooled Antoinette engine. Roe managed to make a few short hops in the aircraft on 8 June 1908, but the aircraft was damaged beyond repair shortly afterwards. The following year Roe produced the Roe I Triplane, which uniquely featured a triplane wing and a triplane tail. It was originally equipped with a 6hp JAP motorcycle engine, but this was quickly uprated to a 24hp Antoinette motor. The aircraft first flew, or at least first hopped off the ground, at the Walthamstow Marshes on 5 June 1909. By 13 July Roe had succeeded in making a flight of at least 100 feet and had flown 900 feet before the end of the month. There is some debate as to exactly which was the first flight, as opposed to a simple hop, but it was the flight of the Roe I Triplane that is regarded as the first all-British powered flight.

On 1 January 1910, Roe and his younger brother Humphrey established AV Roe & Company Limited. Roe would provide the design capabilities, whilst his brother assisted with the finance and production facilities at Brownsfield Mill, Great Ancoats Street, Manchester. Howard Pixton, the pilot who subsequently won the Schneider Trophy in Monaco in 1914, joined the company in June 1910 and eventually became Avro's test pilot. He agreed to work without pay in exchange for flying lessons and subsequently the Royal Aero Club awarded him Certificate No. 50 on 24 January 1911. It was with Pixton that Roe established the Avro School of Flying at Manchester, which later moved to a small grass aerodrome at Shoreham-by-Sea in West Sussex.

The Avro 504 was a two-seater that fulfilled a number of different roles as a trainer, reconnaissance spotter, fighter and bomber. It made its maiden flight in July 1913 and accounted for most of the company's output during the First World War. In all, more than 10,000 units were delivered and the 504 remained in service with the RAF until 1934. A flying example of an Avro 504K can be seen today at the Shuttleworth Collection based at Old Warden Aerodrome, near Biggleswade in Bedfordshire, and a second machine can be seen at London's Science Museum. The Avro 504 trainer was 28 feet 6 inches in length, had a wing span of 36 feet and was fitted with a 160hp Armstrong Siddeley Lynx IV rotary engine, which gave it a maximum speed of 80mph and a ceiling of 14,600 feet. The 504 went into service with the Royal Flying Corps and the Royal Naval Air Service before the start of the First World War and was taken across the

Channel when the conflagration started. The first British aircraft that was shot down during the war was an Avro 504 on 22 August 1914. The pilot was Second Lieutenant Vincent Waterfall and his navigator was Lieutenant Charles George Gordon Bayly of RFC 5 Squadron. The Royal Naval Air Service attacked the Zeppelin factory at Friedrichshafen on 21 November 1914 with four Avro 504s that were armed with four 20lb bombs each. However, the aircraft was quickly superseded on the front line and became the RFC's primary trainer. It remained in service until 1934 when it was replaced by the Avro Type 621, a two-seat radial-engined biplane.

The Sale of AV Roe & Company

Most British aircraft manufacturers found business difficult immediately after the First World War due to the sudden and severe drop in the number of government orders for new aeroplanes and AV Roe was no exception. In August 1920 Crossley Motors acquired 68.5 per cent of the company's shares in order to help expand its motor vehicle production facilities. The company outgrew its Brownsfield Mills facilities and in 1924 moved to New Hall Farm at Woodford in Cheshire. In 1928 Crossley Motors decided to sell its shareholding to Armstrong-Siddeley Holdings Ltd and Roe decided to do the same. Roe used the money to buy the company SE Saunders, based at Cowes on the Isle of Wight and formed Saunders-Roe, which later developed a highly successful range of flying boats. It was at this time that Roy Chadwick returned to Avro's Woodford plant as chief designer from the company's experimental facilities at Hamble, near Southampton. He joined the original company in 1911 aged eighteen and worked as Roe's assistant and draughtsman. He is particularly noted for having designed the Avro Lancaster, the Lincoln, the initial designs of the Vulcan and Britain's first pressurized airliner, the Avro Tudor. In 1935 Hawker Aviation acquired JD Siddeley, the car and engine maker Armstrong-Siddeley and the aircraft manufacturer Armstrong Whitworth. As a result Avro became a subsidiary of the new Hawker Siddeley. Following the British government's pressure for consolidation in the British aircraft industry Hawker Siddeley bought Folland Aircraft, de Havilland Aircraft Company and Blackburn Aircraft to become Hawker Siddeley Group and the Avro mark died out for a time following an internal reorganization. In 1994 British Aerospace brought the Avro name back when it was adopted for its regional jet design, named the Avro RJ.

The Road to Lancaster

In 1936 the Air Ministry issued specification P13/36 for a new twin-engined medium-range bomber that could carry a payload of 8,000lb of bombs or two 18-inch torpedoes. By 1937 the Ministry had accepted designs from Avro and Handley Page and as a result commissioned prototypes for what would become the Manchester and the Halifax.

The Avro Manchester made its maiden flight on 25 July 1939. The Mk I featured a central tail as well as twin fins and the first twenty aircraft entered service in November 1940 with 207 Squadron. The next 200 aircraft to be delivered were the Mk IA, which had the central tail removed. The aircraft was significantly underpowered and as a result was not thought to be a success by the RAF, which retired the aircraft from front-line service just two years later in 1942. The aircraft had been ordered directly from the initial designs and was hastened into production by the then imminent threat of war. Had more thorough testing been undertaken the shortcomings of the two Rolls-Royce Vulture 24-cylinder X-block engines would have been identified and perhaps overcome. The engines, originally developed in 1935, generated 1,760hp each and adopted an X shape that was made up of two V-cylinder blocks, the second inverted and mounted below the other that created the X. However, the engines were notoriously unreliable and their power rating was revised downwards to 1,500hp. The Manchester had a crew of seven, was 69 feet 4 inches in length, had a wingspan of 90 feet 1 inch and stood 19 feet 6 inches high. The two Rolls-Royce Vulture I engines gave the aircraft a maximum speed of 265mph, a range of 1,630 miles and an operational ceiling of 19,200 feet. The armament consisted of eight .303-inch Browning machine-guns and a 10,350lb offensive bomb payload.

The Manchester first saw active service on the night of 24/25 February 1941 when a number of the aircraft took part in a bombing raid with 207 Squadron on the port of Brest in north-west France. The aircraft's last sortie was over Bremen, Germany, on 25 June 1942. The Manchesters took part in 1,269 operations and dropped over 1,800 tons of bombs. In order to try and overcome the poor engine performance Roy Chadwick developed the Manchester Mk III, which was equipped with four Rolls-Royce Merlin XX engines and had an increased wingspan. This aircraft became known as the first prototype Lancaster, which made its maiden flight on 9 January 1941.

The Lancaster was distinctive from the Manchester in that it did not have the third tail fin common in early Manchester production aircraft, using instead the wider tailplane and larger elliptical twin fins that became common in later versions. The design included an all-metal fuselage, retractable main landing gear and a fixed tail wheel. Originally the aircraft was equipped with four Rolls-Royce Merlin engines, but with demand for fighter engine production increasing in the early part of the war there was a shortage of supply and so the Lancaster Mk II was fitted with four 1,650hp Bristol Hercules VI or XVI engines as a temporary measure of which 300 were manufactured. However, a number of Mk IIs were lost when they ran out of fuel before they could return home and so the Packard Merlin engines were fitted to the Lancaster Mk III. Production for the Lancaster took place mainly at Avro's factory at Chadderton near Oldham in Lancashire, with test flights taking place at Woodford Aerodrome nearby.

The Lancaster Mk III had a crew of seven; made up of the pilot, flight engineer, navigator, bomb aimer, wireless operator as well as the mid-upper and rear gunners. The aircraft was 69 feet 6 inches long, had a wingspan of 102 feet and stood 20 feet 6 inches tall. It was fitted with four 1,640hp Rolls-Royce Merlin XXVIII or XXXVIII V-12 engines, which gave it a maximum speed of 287mph at 15,000 feet, a range of 1,730 miles with a 12,000lb bomb payload and an operational ceiling of 19,000 feet. The Lancaster had a formidable array of defensive and offensive armament. The aircraft was fitted with eight .303-inch Browning machine-guns. In later designs twin .50-inch turrets were fitted to the tail and dorsal positions. A 33 feet bomb bay allowed for a 4,000lb bomb payload, but with bulged bay doors added the payload was increased to 8,000lb, then to 12,000lb. Later versions of the Lancaster were adapted to carry the 21 feet, 12,000lb Tallboy or the 25 feet 6 inches, 22,000lb Grand Slam bombs that were used to attack particularly difficult and well protected targets.

The Avro Lancaster first came into service with RAF 44 Squadron in early 1942. In all, the aircraft took part in 156,192 missions and dropped 608,612 tons of bombs before the end of the Second World War. Of the 7,374 produced a total of 3,431 aircraft were lost in action and a further 246 were destroyed as a result of operational accidents. Only 35 aircraft managed to complete 100 operations; the most successful managed 139, but that aircraft was scrapped in 1947. RAF Lancasters attacked the *Tirpitz* with Tallboy 12,000lb bombs, first crippling her then eventually sinking her. Two of the aircraft that took part in the attack had to make emergency landings near Yagodnik airfield in north-west Russia. The Soviets were able to repair the aircraft and used them briefly for reconnaissance and transport purposes, but a lack of spares meant that they were soon withdrawn from service. However, the most memorable Lancaster mission was Operation *Chastise*, the Dambuster raid, where nineteen Lancasters from 617 Squadron, led by Wing Commander Guy Penrose Gibson, attacked the Möhne, Eder, Sorpe and Ennepe Dams in Germany's Ruhr industrial region. The attacks were only possible because of the ground-breaking work of the scientist, aviation engineer and inventor Dr Barnes Wallis.

Barnes Neville Wallis was born on 26 September 1887 in Ripley, Derbyshire, and was educated at the prestigious Christ's Hospital school in Horsham. He trained as a marine engineer and in 1922, at the age of thirty-five, he took a degree in engineering through the University of London External Programme. The geodetic design for aircraft construction was first developed while he was working for the Airship Guarantee Company in Hull, which was owned by Vickers-Armstrongs and which built the *R100* airship in 1930. Wallis moved into aircraft design and development with Vickers-Armstrongs and worked closely with RK Pierson on the designs of the Vickers Wellesley and Wellington bombers, both of which used the new geodetic design in their fuselage and wing construction.

In April 1942 Wallis wrote a paper called *Spherical Bomb – Surface Torpedo*, which outlined how a bomb could avoid anti-torpedo defences by skipping across the surface of water and then sinking directly next to a ship or large dam. It was calculated that the volume of water surrounding such objects would concentrate the force of an explosion. Wallis found that with the addition of back spin that was created by spinning the bomb in the aircraft shortly before it was dropped, the bomb was less likely to explode directly under the aircraft and the range could be increased as it skipped across the water. These seemingly outlandish proposals were eventually accepted by a very sceptical RAF following successful tests that were conducted at Reculver in Kent. As a result preparations were put in place for Operation *Chastise* in May 1943. The Ruhr dams were successfully breached in the now infamous Dambuster raid using the Upkeep bouncing bomb. Further developments led to the Highball bouncing bomb that was intended to be used to sink the *Tirpitz* in Trondheim. But the Highball did not see action. On 12 November 1944 the *Tirpitz* was capsized by Lancasters from 9 and 617 Squadrons in Operation *Catechism* using Wallis' Tallboy bombs.

Operation *Chastise*

On the night of 16/17 May 1943 nineteen specially modified Lancaster Mk IIIs from 617 Squadron, led by Wing Commander Guy Gibson, took off from RAF Scampton armed with Upkeep bouncing bombs and attacked the Möhne, Eder, Sorpe and Ennepe Dams in Germany's Ruhr and Eder valleys. There has been some suggestion that Flight Sergeant Bill Townsend, who took off in the third formation, may have attacked the Bever Dam in error, mistaking it for the Ennepe Dam. Much of the internal armour was taken out of the Lancasters and the bomb bay doors removed to compensate for the size and weight of the bomb.

For the attack 617 Squadron was divided into three formations. The first formation was made up of nine aircraft and was assigned to the Möhne Dam and was to move onto the Eder if any bombs were remaining after the attack. The second formation was made up of five aircraft and was assigned the Sorpe Dam. The third formation consisted of five aircraft and was a mobile reserve force that took off two hours after the first two formations, with orders to attack the main targets if required, otherwise to concentrate on secondary targets, the Schwelm, Ennepe and Diemel Dams. A further two aircraft were assigned to the mission but were unable to take part due to illness amongst the crews. Eight of the Dambusters did not make it back. Two were shot down over Holland outbound, another was shot down over Germany outbound, a further two came down outbound after hitting power cables, two were shot down over Germany just after making their attack and one was shot down over Holland on its way back.

The first Lancasters to take off were from the second formation and departed at 9.28 p.m. on 16 May 1943. They flew a longer northern route to the dams. The first formation took off next, leaving in groups of three in ten-minute intervals

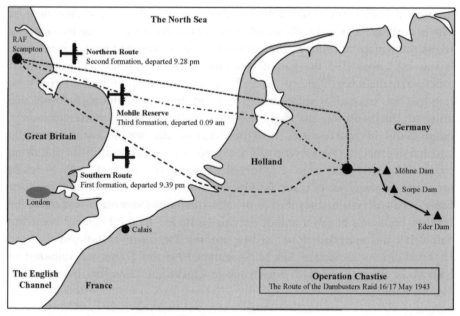

The route of the Dambuster raid, 16/17 May 1943.

from 9.39 p.m. and flew a shorter southern route. The third formation began to take off at 0.09 a.m. on 17 May. To avoid radar detection the aircraft flew at around 100 feet, which explains why two collided with power cables and were lost before reaching their targets.

The first formation made their attack on the Möhne Dam, with Gibson making the first run. Flight Lieutenant John V Hopgood came in second but was hit by flak and was then caught in the blast from his own bomb. Hopgood's Lancaster limped over the dam and Gibson flew in to draw fire away, but it was to no avail and Hopgood crashed shortly after. Two of the three crew members survived. Flight Lieutenant HB Martin made a successful attack next and was followed by Squadron Leader Henry Young and then Flight Lieutenant David Maltby. The attacks finally breached the dam and the whole attack was relayed back to Britain via an airborne GEC 1142 transmitter receiver. Gibson, accompanied by Squadron Leader Henry Melvin Young, Flight Lieutenant Dave Shannon, Squadron Leader Henry Maudslay and Flying Officer Les Knight, moved on to attack the Eder.

There was a thick layer of fog over the Eder Valley, which added to the difficult terrain, meaning that Shannon had to make six runs before he let Maudslay make an attempt, but his bomb clipped the top of the dam damaging his Lancaster in the explosion. Shannon's next run was successful and with Knight then also making a successful attack the dam was breached.

The Sorpe Dam was of earthen construction rather than concrete and was the most difficult to breach. Three Dambusters reached the target, Flight

Lieutenant Joe McCarthy from the second formation, along with Flight Sergeant Ken Brown and Flight Sergeant Cyril Anderson from the third formation. With this attack the Upkeep bomb was static and not given back spin before being dropped and the aircraft approached along the dam and not at right angles. McCarthy arrived at 0.15 a.m. and made ten attempts at his run before dropping the bomb, but despite a direct hit there was little damage. Brown did not manage to breach the dam and in the dense fog Anderson was unable to attempt a run. The remaining aircraft were then diverted to secondary targets. Pilot Officer Warner Ottley was shot down before reaching the Lister Dam and Flight Sergeant Bill Townsend dropped his bomb on the Ennepe Dam but did not cause any damage.

The surviving Lancasters started to return back at their base at RAF Scampton from 3.11 a.m. and Gibson arrived at 4.15 a.m. The last home was Townsend, who touched down at 6.15 a.m. Of the 133 aircrew that set out just a few hours previously, fifth-three had been killed in action, thirteen were Canadian and two Australian. Three members of aircrew survived their crashes; two were from Hopgood's aircraft and one from Ottley's. A total of thirty-four of the survivors received decorations at Buckingham Palace on 22 June 1943. Gibson was awarded the Victoria Cross, whilst there were also five Distinguished Service Orders, ten Distinguished Flying Crosses and four bars, two Conspicuous Gallantry Medals and eleven Distinguished Flying Medals and one bar. A memorial to those that took part in Operation *Chastise* has been erected at Woodhall Spa, south-east of Lincoln in Lincolnshire. Squadron 617 was based nearby at RAF Scampton, just north of Lincoln. It was later moved to RAF Coningsby, then to RAF Woodhall Spa and is now based at RAF Lossiemouth in Scotland.

A memorial to the German dead was erected in Neheim, four miles from the Möhne Dam. German estimates suggest that the operation killed 1,294 people. Of these were 749 French, Belgian, Dutch and Ukrainian prisoners of war and labourers.

Wallis' remarkable contribution to the Second World War went on to include the development of strategic bombs that were used by the RAF to attack either highly defended or what were assumed to be impenetrable targets. The Tallboy, which contained 12,000lb of explosives, was used to attack the German V-1 flying-bomb and V-2 rocket facilities, whilst the Grand Slam deep-penetration earthquake bomb, with 22,000lb of explosives, was used successfully, in particular on 27 March 1945 when it penetrated the Valentin submarine pen.

Wallis was made a Fellow of the Royal Society in 1945 and was knighted by Queen Elizabeth II in 1968. The Royal Commission awarded him £10,000 for his work during the war, which he donated to his old school, Christ's Hospital, in 1951 to establish the RAF Foundationers' Trust, which would pay for the children of airmen killed or injured in action to study at the school.

Wallis married Molly Bloxam on 23 April 1925 and they lived in Effingham in Surrey from 1930 until his death in 1979. They had four children together and his daughter Mary Eyre Wallis married Harry Stopes-Roe, the son of the women's rights and family planning campaigner Marie Stopes and Humphrey Verdon-Roe, co-founder of AV Roe & Company Limited and Alliott Verdon-Roe's brother.

A statue of Wallis by American sculptor Tom White was erected in 2008 at Herne Bay in Kent near Reculver where the bouncing bomb was tested. Numerous public houses and streets have been named after Barnes Wallis and a Red Wheel heritage plaque was erected on 31 May 2009 near his place of birth in Ripley, Derbyshire, by the Transport Trust.

Examples of bouncing bombs can be found at the Aeronautical Museum, Brenzett, on Romney Marsh, at Brooklands Museum in Weybridge, at Dover Castle in Kent, at the Imperial War Museum at Duxford in Cambridgeshire and at the Spitfire & Hurricane Memorial Museum at RAF Manston in Kent. Highballs can be found at Haverfordwest Aerodrome and at the Herne Bay Museum and Gallery, near the Reculver test site. The Newark Air Museum has an example of an Upkeep bouncing bomb.

From Lancaster to York

The Avro York was developed from the Lancaster and made its maiden flight on 5 July 1942. In all, 50 civilian and 208 military versions were delivered. In the post-war era nine squadrons of RAF Transport Command were equipped with Yorks and half of the British contribution to the Berlin airlift was made by the aircraft, flying in excess of 58,000 sorties. The Avro York transport aircraft was 78 feet 6 inches in length, had a wingspan of 102 feet and stood 17 feet 10 inches tall. It was fitted with four 1,280hp Rolls-Royce Merlin XX in-line engines that gave it a maximum speed of 298mph at 21,000 feet. The aircraft served with British Overseas Airways Corporation (BOAC), which operated Yorks between Cairo and Durban in place of the Shorts flying boats that had previously plied that route. British South American Airways operated the Yorks to the Caribbean and South America, until the company was merged with BOAC in September 1949, when the Yorks were moved to freight carriage and then eventually withdrawn from service in November 1957. Air Chief Marshal Sir Trafford Leigh-Mallory was killed when his Avro York crashed in the French Alps on 14 November 1944 killing all ten people on-board. He was flying to Ceylon to take up command of Allied air operations in the Pacific when the aircraft came down thirty miles south of Grenoble. The wreckage was found seven months later in June 1945. The RAF Museum at Cosford and at the Imperial War Museum, Duxford both have static examples of the Avro York.

The first versions of the Avro Lincoln were originally named the Lancaster IV and V, but were renamed the Lincoln I and II shortly afterwards. The Lincoln, which became operational in August 1945, was delivered too late to see active service during the Second World War. It was also the last piston-engined bomber to be used by the RAF. The Lincoln B1 was 78 feet 3 inches in length, had a wingspan of 120 feet and stood 17 feet 3 inches tall. The aircraft was fitted with four Rolls-Royce Merlin 85 engines that gave it a maximum speed of 319mph at 18,500 feet.

The Avro Lincoln was designed by Roy Chadwick and the prototype made its maiden flight from Manchester Ringway Airport on 9 June 1944. In all, 604 machines were manufactured and many saw action with the RAF during the Mau Mau uprising in Kenya from 1952 and with the RAAF during the Malayan Emergency when they were used to help tackle the Malayan National Liberation Army, the military wing of the Malayan Communist Party. An RAF Lincoln was shot down twenty miles north-east of Lüneburg in the former East Germany by a Soviet MiG-15 on 12 March 1953. The aircraft was attempting to reach Berlin as part of a training flight and all seven of the crew members were killed. With the development of jet bombers the Lincolns were slowly removed from service from the late 1950s and by 1963 were retired completely.

The Avro Type 696 Shackleton was also designed by Roy Chadwick and was based on the designs of the Lincoln and the Tudor airliner. It was also the last Avro aircraft to have Lancaster lineage. The Shackleton long-range maritime patrol aircraft MR3 had a crew of between 10 and 13. It was 87 feet 4 inches long, with a wingspan of 119 feet10 inches and stood 23 feet 4 inches tall. The aircraft was fitted with four 1,960hp Rolls-Royce Griffon 57 liquid-cooled V-12 engines that were fitted with 13 feet contra-rotating propellers. The aircraft could reach a top speed of 302mph, had a range of 4,215 miles, and an operational ceiling of 20,000 feet. In all, some 185 Shackletons were manufactured between 1951 and 1958. Coastal Command was the first to take delivery of the new Shackleton, which saw active service during the Suez Crisis and in Aden during the Radfan Emergency in Yemen. The Shackleton never quite came into its own and was perpetually on the brink of being replaced, which finally came about with the introduction of the Hawker Siddeley Nimrod in 1969. The Shackleton did continue in search and rescue operations until 1972, and with the withdrawal of the Fairey Gannet and the continued need for airborne early warning coverage in the North Sea and northern Atlantic the Shackleton won something of a reprieve. In fact, delays to the Nimrod's development meant that the Shackleton was not completely replaced until 1990, after the RAF had taken delivery of its six Boeing E3 Sentry airborne warning and control system (AWACS) aircraft in 1986.

The last great Avro aircraft was the Vulcan, a delta wing subsonic jet bomber that served with the RAF for over thirty years between 1953 until 1984 and fulfilled a central role as part of Britain's nuclear deterrent in the Cold War. However, design work started as early as 1947 by Avro's chief designer Roy Chadwick, who utilized development work completed by Professor Alexander Lippisch during the Second World War. The Air Ministry issued Specification

B35/46 in 1946 for a bomber that could achieve a top speed of 575mph, operate at 50,000 feet, have a range of more than 3,000 miles and that could carry a bomb payload of 10,000lb. Vickers-Armstrongs and Handley Page put forward designs to the Air Ministry as well as Avro. All three were approved and the RAF's V-force took shape with the Vickers Valiant, the Handley Page Victor and the Avro Vulcan.

Sadly, on 23 August 1947 Roy Chadwick was killed in an air crash when the prototype of the Avro Tudor 2 that he was travelling in came down. His work on the Vulcan was continued by Stuart Davies, who took over as Avro's chief designer. In 1948 an experimental prototype, the single-seater Avro 707, was built but it crashed on 30 September 1949. Subsequently, four other versions of the 707 were constructed. Eventually, the Avro Type 698 prototype VX770 made its maiden flight on 30 August 1952 with Avro's chief test pilot, retired Wing Commander Roly Falk, at the controls. The aircraft's outstanding manoeuvrability was later demonstrated at the Farnborough Airshow in 1955. The Vulcan B2 strategic bomber was 99 feet 11 inches in length, had a wingspan of 111 feet and stood 27 feet 2 inches high. It was powered by four 20,000lbf Bristol Siddeley Olympus 301 turbojets that gave it a maximum speed of 645mph at high altitude, a range of 4,600 miles and an operational ceiling of 65,000 feet.

The first Vulcan that was delivered to the RAF was XA897 in September 1956. Air Chief Marshal Sir Harry Broadhurst, Air Officer Commander-in-Chief Bomber Command, took the Vulcan, with a full crew, on a round-the-world tour, with Broadhurst occupying the co-pilot seat. On 1 October 1956 the aircraft returned to the UK and attempted to land in bad weather at London's Heathrow Airport. The Vulcan struck the ground 2,000 feet short of the runway and bounced back into the air. The pilot, Squadron Leader DR Howard and Broadhurst both ejected and survived. The remaining four crew members were killed. After his retirement in 1961 Broadhurst became managing director of Avro, then managing director of Hawker Siddeley in 1965 and finally a director of Hawker Siddeley Group Limited in 1968 before taking full retirement in 1976.

In 1982 the RAF used Vulcan bombers to attack Argentine positions on the Falkland Islands through a number of very long-range missions that were codenamed Operation *Black Buck*. In all, seven operations were planned and five were put into effect. The aircraft flew 3,889 miles from Ascension Island in the South Atlantic to the Falkland Islands. The first attack took place on 1 May when a single Vulcan bombed Port Stanley's main airfield. A further four missions targeted the airfield and Argentinian radar installations. Handley Page Victor aircraft assisted the operation with in-flight refuelling, with each sortie consuming some 1.1 million gallons of jet fuel.

Saunders-Roe Limited

Following the sale of AV Roe & Company Ltd to Armstrong-Siddeley in 1928 Roe acquired a controlling interest in marine manufacturer SE Saunders based at Cowes on the Isle of Wight. With Roe's aviation abilities it became inevitable that Saunders-Roe Limited would move into the development and manufacture of flying boats. Few of the models produced by the company extended into particularly long production runs; the most prolific was the London flying boat that first flew in March 1934 and of which only thirty-one were produced. Whitehall Securities Corporation Limited, which owned a large part of Spartan Aircraft Ltd, acquired a significant shareholding in Saunders-Roe in 1931, and as a result Spartan was merged into the company.

Following a major company reorganization in 1938 the shipyard and boat-building assets were transferred to a new company Saunders Shipyard Ltd, with all of the shares owned by Saunders-Roe Ltd. The plywood business was transferred to a new company Saro Laminated Wood Products Ltd. Later during the Second World War Saunders-Roe manufactured Supermarine Walrus and Otter seaplanes, whilst its Anglesey plant provided service and repair facilities for RAF Catalinas. By the early 1950s the popularity and functionality of flying boats had diminished and although Saunders-Roe developed a new prototype for the Princess flying boat the aircraft did not go into production and no new seaplanes were developed. However, the company continued to make modifications to Short flying boats at its Cowes facilities until 1955.

In an effort to diversify, the company bought the helicopter manufacturer Cierva Autogyro Company in 1951. By the end of the decade Saunders-Roe was experimenting with the construction of hovercraft and in 1959 had built the first SR-N1 that was designed by Sir Christopher Cockerell, the inventor of the hovercraft, and which was built under a contract with the National Research Development Corporation. The SR-N1 could carry four people and travel at a speed of 28mph. On 25 July 1959 the SR-N1 successfully crossed the English Channel between Dover and Calais.

In the same year Saunders-Roe's helicopter and hovercraft business interests were sold to Westland Aircraft. Five years later in 1964, as part of the government's drive for consolidation within the UK aircraft industry, Westland merged with Vickers-Armstrongs to create the British Hovercraft Corporation. A further change of hands meant that the business became Westland Aerospace in 1985. Ten years later Westland was bought by GKN, which subsequently sold Westland to create AgustaWestland, but it kept hold of the Cowes production facilities and continued aircraft component design and production there.

Memories and Memorials
Today there are only two flying Lancasters left. Lancaster BI PA474 *City of Lincoln* is operated by the Royal Air Force's Battle of Britain Memorial Flight and can be seen in numerous air displays around the UK each year. The second is BX FM213, which underwent a ten-year restoration programme and is operated by the Canadian Warplane Heritage Museum. There are fifteen complete or partially complete Lancasters in various museums around the

world. The Lincolnshire Aviation Heritage Centre based at East Kirby Airfield, near Spilsby in Lincolnshire, is able to offer taxiing rides in BVII NX611 *Just Jane* and boasts that it is the only place in the UK where the public can ride in a Lancaster bomber.

Roe was knighted by King George V in 1929 in recognition of his outstanding contribution to British aviation. Later, he was controversially a supporter of Oswald Mosley's fascist Black Shirts. Roe had two sons but unfortunately tragedy struck and both were killed in separate incidents whilst on active service with the RAF during the Second World War. Squadron Leader Eric Alliott Verdon-Roe was killed in 1941 at the age of twenty-six and Squadron Leader Lighton Verdon-Roe DFC was killed in 1943 at the age of twenty-two.

Roe remained chairman of Saunders-Roe until his death in 1958 at the age of eighty. He is buried in the graveyard of St Andrew's Church in Hamble near Southampton, Hampshire, with his parents, Edwin Hodgson Roe and Annie Sophia Verdon. Inside the church is a special memorial plaque that states:

In memory of Sir Edwin Alliott Verdon-Roe OBE, first Englishman to fly, 26 April 1877 – 4 January 1958, and of his sons Squadron Leader Eric Alliott Verdon-Roe RAF, died in action 24 July 1941 and Squadron Leader Lighton Verdon-Roe RAF VR DFC, died in action 13 May 1943, who have no known grave.

Chapter 13

Frederick Handley Page and the Opening of the Imperial Airways

O n 17 June 1909, at the age of twenty-three, Frederick Handley Page established Britain's first publicly listed aviation manufacturing company, Handley Page Limited, one of Britain's most important military and civil aircraft companies. Handley Page was responsible for the Second World War bombers the Hampden and the Halifax, the post-war Victor V bomber and was involved in the creation of Imperial Airways, which became part of today's British Airways. Handley Page Limited refused to be drawn into the British government's attempts led by the then Secretary of State for Defence, Duncan Sandys, to consolidate the aircraft industry in the late 1950s. As a result Handley Page was not part of the formation of either the British Aircraft Corporation or the Hawker Siddeley Group in 1960 and remained independent. The government had warned that contracts would only be awarded to a smaller number of merged companies and it was inevitable that Handley Page would begin to be left out. A steady decline in orders meant that the company went into voluntary liquidation in 1970 and closed down sixty-one years after its formation.

Family Matters
Frederick Handley Page was born on 15 November 1885 in Cheltenham in Gloucestershire and was the son of a Non-Conformist Minister and furniture maker. He married Una Thynne in 1918 at the age of thirty-one and together they had three daughters. In 1938 he was elected President of the Society of British Aircraft Constructors and was President of the Royal Aeronautical Society between 1945 and 1947. He served as Vice Chairman of the Air Registration Board, as President of the Institute of Transport and was Chairman of the Board of Governors of the College of Aeronautics at Cranfield. His outstanding contribution to British aviation, in particular his war efforts, led him to be knighted by King George VI in 1942. Handley Page died at the age of seventy-six on 21 April 1962 in London. He was buried at Langney Cemetery in Eastbourne, East Sussex.

The Second World War fighter ace Wing Commander Alan Geoffrey Page DSO, OBE, DFC and Bar, was Handley Page's nephew and is noted as the founding member of the famous Guinea Pig Club. During 1940 Page was posted to 56 Squadron of the RAF as a Hurricane pilot. He was shot down during the Battle of Britain on 12 August 1940, while attacking a formation of Dornier Do 17 bombers. During the attack the fuel tank in front of Page was hit and it sprayed burning aircraft fuel into the cockpit. He received horrific burns to most of his front side, in particular his hands and face. Despite his appalling injuries he managed to bale out and was later picked up from the English Channel. He received treatment at the Burns Unit at the Queen Victoria Hospital in East Grinstead, West Sussex, from the noted plastic surgeon Sir Archibald McIndoe. It was during his recuperation in hospital that Page established the Guinea Pig Club, with other badly burnt servicemen. Sir Archibald was elected the club's life president, while Page was the first to take the role of chairman. Despite his injuries, and fifteen operations, Page was determined to return to active service. Astonishingly, by 1942 he had regained full operational status with the RAF. On 29 June 1943 Page, along with Wing Commander James MacLachlan, who had lost an arm two years earlier, brought down six enemy aircraft in just ten minutes, while flying south of Paris. Sadly, MacLachlan was killed in action the following month.

Handley Page Limited
The first aircraft to be built by the company was the Type A single-seater monoplane in 1910. The aircraft was 20 feet 6 inches long, had a wingspan of 32 feet 6 inches and was powered by a 20hp Advance air-cooled V-4 engine that gave the aircraft a maximum speed of 35mph. The Type A took to the air for the first time on 26 May 1910, when it made a number of short hops and then unceremoniously crashed. Despite the accident this achievement marked the beginning of the company's long and invaluable contribution to British aviation. By 1912 Handley Page had established its first aircraft factory at Cricklewood, with access to the facilities of Cricklewood Aerodrome nearby. It was from here that Handley Page Transport inaugurated its London to Paris service in 1920.

During the First World War the Germans had built a fleet of Zeppelin airships, which undertook a series of bombing raids on England between January 1915 and June 1917. During the first raid two Zeppelin airships bombed Great Yarmouth and King's Lynn in East Anglia. London was attacked for the first time on 31 May 1915 when twenty-eight people were killed. By June 1916 more than 500 people in England had been killed by German bombs. British pilots had developed highly effective techniques for bringing down the Zeppelins, with a total of seventy-seven of the airships destroyed or severely damaged during the war. Handley Page was asked by the Admiralty to develop a heavy bomber that could not only bomb the Zeppelins' sheds in Germany, but also the German capital Berlin in reprisal for the attack on London. The result was the development of the Handley Page O/100 twin-engined biplane bomber in 1915, followed by the more powerful O/400 twin-engined bomber in 1918 and the four-engined V/1500 long-range bomber that was capable of reaching Berlin, but entered service only as the war was drawing to a close.

The Handley Page O/100 made its maiden flight on 7 December 1915. The aircraft was a twin-engined biplane heavy bomber with a glazed cockpit and in all some forty-six machines were built. The O/100 had a crew of three, was 62 feet 10 inches in length, had a wingspan of 100 feet and stood 22 feet tall. It was fitted with two 250hp Rolls-Royce Eagle II V-12 engines that gave it a maximum speed of 76mph, a range of 450 miles and an operational ceiling of 8,500 feet. The aircraft was armed with four .303 Lewis machine-guns and could carry a 2,000lb bomb payload. The O/100 undertook its first bombing mission on 16 March 1917 when a single aircraft attacked the railway junction at Moulins-lès-Metz, forty miles east of Verdun. The O/100 was considered to be somewhat underpowered and so the cockpit glazing and armour were removed for the design of the O/400, which was deployed in April 1918. The O/400 heavy bomber had a crew of three, was 62 feet 10 inches long, had wingspan of 100 feet and stood 22 feet high. It was fitted with two 360hp Rolls-Royce Eagle VIII inline piston engines, which gave the aircraft a maximum speed of 97mph, a range of 450 miles, an endurance of 8 hours and an operational ceiling of 8,500 feet. The O/400 was armed with four .303-inch Lewis machine-guns and could carry a 2,000lb bomb payload. Despite its relatively late entry into the war 550 were built in Britain and a further 107 assembled from parts manufactured under licence by the Standard Aircraft Corporation in the United States of America. After the war the O/400 remained in service with the RAF until 1919, when it was replaced by the Vickers Vimy. However, a number of the machines were converted for civilian use and nine of the aircraft were used by Handley Page Transport, the company's innovative airline service.

The Handley Page V/1500 was designed by the company's chief designer, George Rudolph Volkert, as a four-engined long-range bomber that could take off from East Anglia in eastern England and attack Berlin as well as the industrial areas surrounding the Saar and the Ruhr rivers. The V/1500 was based on the design of the O/400 and made its maiden flight on 22 May 1918. The aircraft was 62 feet long, had a wingspan of 126 feet and stood 23 feet high. It was equipped with four 375hp Rolls-Royce Eagle VIII V-12 water-cooled engines, which gave it a maximum speed of 97mph, an endurance of 6 hours and an operational ceiling of 10,000 feet. The V/1500 was armed with twin .303-inch Lewis machine-guns in the nose and dorsal positions, with another in the tail. The aircraft could carry a 7,500lb bomb payload. An order for 225 aircraft was issued, but due to the end of the war only 35 were built. The V/1500 was the first four-engined aircraft used by the RAF and the first to be equipped with armament in the tail.

On 13 December 1918 Major AC Stuart MacLaren, Captain Robert Halley and Brigadier General Norman McEwan made the first through flight from

England to India in a Handley Page V/1500. HMA *Old Carthusian* took off from Martlesham and flew via Rome, Malta, Cairo and Baghdad. They reached Karachi on 15 January 1919 and landed with just two engines. Another V/1500 attempted to make the first transatlantic crossing but was beaten to the record by Alcock and Brown in a Vickers Vimy in June 1919. The aircraft later set off for New York but crashed on 5 July in Parrsboro on the northern shore of the Minas Basin in Nova Scotia. Following repairs the V/1500 made it to New York on 9 October 1919 and with it the first airmail to be carried from Canada to the United States of America.

Opening the Imperial Airways
The inevitable sharp drop in government orders for military aircraft that followed the end of the First World War led many manufacturers to rapidly explore new markets. Handley Page was convinced by the opportunities that lay in the civil aviation market, not just with cargo transportation, but also with the commercial airliner and regular passenger services. In 1919 the government lifted restrictions on civil flying in Britain and Handley Page decided to establish its own fledgling airline, Handley Page Transport Limited, which was equipped with converted wartime surplus Type O/400 bombers. On 25 August 1919 Aircraft Travel & Transport Limited (AT&T) started the world's first sustained commercial international air service that flew between London and Paris in a converted de Havilland DH4A day bomber. The aircraft carried only two passengers who had to travel in a small cabin modified from the original gunner's cockpit. Later AT&T introduced DH16 aircraft that were able to carry four passengers. The new airliner G-EAJC took off from Hounslow Heath Aerodrome at 9.10 a.m. with one passenger and a cargo of newspapers, leather and Devonshire cream. It arrived 2 hours and 20 minutes later at Le Bourget, Bonneuil-en-France, seven miles north-east of Paris. In its first ten weeks of operation AT&T made 147 flights on the London to Paris route. Handley Page Transport followed hot on the heels of AT&T, inaugurating its London to Paris service eight days later on 2 September 1919. The O/400 aircraft were considerably more spacious and able to carry between seven and twelve passengers, which provided significantly more income opportunities for the company. At that time a single air fare to Paris would cost £25, with £40 for a return fare.

In July 1922 five companies were operating services between London and Paris, and in that month they collectively made 434 flights and carried 1,271 passengers. During July 1923 Handley Page Transport alone made 118 flights on the route with 1,200 passengers. The level of demand was growing, particularly holiday traffic, and showed no signs of diminishing. In the first four days of August 1923 Handley Page Transport carried 250 passengers between London and Paris. Other operators were also in a similar position. Daimler Airway had to suspend its London to Manchester route in the summer of 1923 in order to cope with the demand for seats on its flights to Amsterdam and Berlin, whilst the Instone Air Line struggled with the number of passengers on its routes to Cologne and Brussels.

In January 1923 the British government, under the Conservative Prime Minister Andrew Bonar Law, was anxious to investigate the prevailing subsidies for cross-Channel civil aviation and to seek advice on the ideal way for the country to continue to subsidise air transport. Sir Samuel Hoare, the Secretary of State for Air, appointed Sir Herbert Hambling, the deputy chairman of Barclays Bank, as chairman of the Civil Aviation Subsidies Committee, also known as the Hambling Committee. After some deliberation the Committee published their recommendations in February 1923 and called for the government to establish a single national civil airline company to provide a European air transport service. On 1 April 1924 Imperial Airways was formed with the merger of the air transport business carried by Handley Page Transport, Instone Air Line, Daimler Airway and British Marine Air Navigation Company. Handley Page Transport Limited became a dormant company and was not reconstituted until 1947 during Handley Page's takeover of Miles Aircraft when it became Handley Page (Reading) Ltd.

Handley Page Transport had been operating routes from London to Paris and Zurich, Daimler Airway was operating services between London and Manchester as well as between Amsterdam and Berlin, whilst British Marine Air Navigation Company was operating services between Southampton and Cherbourg as well as between Southampton and the Channel Islands. Instone Air Line, which was the first airline to transport a racehorse, stopped its London to Paris route in 1922, but introduced a London to Cologne route in May 1922, which became part of the combined Imperial Airways. The company had a share capital of £1 million, which included 500,000 £1 shares that were issued to British subjects only to ensure that the new airline remained completely a British company. To help establish the company the government provided a £1 million subsidy that was to be paid over 10 years and started with a payment of £137,000 per annum during the first four years. Many of the senior executives of the four merged companies served on the board of Imperial Airways, including Sir Eric Geddes as chairman, along with Frank Searle of Daimler Hire Limited as managing director, Sir Samuel Instone from the Instone Air Line, Lieutenant Colonel John Barrett-Lennard of Handley Page Transport Limited, Robert Scott-Paine of the British Marine Air Navigation Company, and Sir John G Beharrell, the managing director of the Dunlop Rubber Company. The government appointed two nominee directors, Sir Herbert Hambling, chairman of the Civil Aviation Subsidies Committee, and Major John W Hills, formerly the government's Financial Secretary to the Treasury. The company secretary was Sydney H Dismore and the registered offices were located at 43 Frederick's Place, Old Jewry, London, EC2.

The government paid the four companies £148,750 for their business operations that had been taken over as going concerns. Handley Page Transport received £51,500, which included £17,166 in cash and 34,334 shares; Instone Air Line received £46,000, which included £15,333 in cash and 30,667 shares; Daimler Hire Limited received £30,000, with £10,000 in cash and 20,000 shares and the British Marine Air Navigation Company received £21,250, with £7,083 in cash and 14,167 shares in the capital of the new company. The profits were divided up such that after 10 per cent had been paid as a return on the capital, one third of the remaining profits would be paid to the government to repay the subsidy, another third to be retained as a reserve and the remaining third to be paid in additional dividends.

Imperial Airways flew its first service between Croydon Aerodrome in London and Le Bourget near Paris on 26 April 1924. The first departure was later than had been scheduled due to a pilots' strike. However, soon the company had built a reputation for promptness, reliability and above all safety. The success of Imperial Airways served as a catalyst for the growth and development of the civil airline industry in Great Britain, with many new smaller airlines being formed. On 30 September 1935 the Whitehall Securities Corporation, owned by the Honourable Clive Pearson, established Allied British Airways by merging the public company Hillmans Airways with its privately owned companies Spartan Air Lines, British Continental Airways and United Airways. Within a month the new company had become simply British Airways and on 11 December 1935 became a publicaly listed company. The acquisition of Highland Airways and Northern and Scottish Airways followed shortly afterwards. Major J Ronald McCrindle was appointed the managing director and Alan Campbell-Orde, who had been with AT&T, was appointed the operations manager.

From 1935 the two companies, Imperial Airways and British Airways, remained in stiff competition with each other for three years. In 1938 the government established the Cadman Committee of Inquiry to investigate the best way to develop British civil aviation and its report recommended the merger of the main airline operators. This led in 1939 to the merger of Imperial Airways and British Airways to form the state-owned British Overseas Airways Corporation (BOAC). Legislation to nationalize the two companies was introduced to Parliament by Sir Kingsley Wood, the Air Minister, on 12 June 1939. The Act received Royal Assent on 4 August and BOAC formally came into being on 1 April 1940, with the BBC's founder Sir John Reith as chairman. In 1971 BOAC was merged with another state-owned airline British European Airways (BEA), along with Cardiff-based Cambrian Airways and Newcastle-upon-Tyne based Northeast Airlines, to form the British Airways Board. Three years later all four companies were dissolved and merged into one State-owned business and the British Airways brand formally reappeared once again. In February 1987 British Airways was privatized by the Conservative government under Prime Minister Margaret Thatcher.

In August 1969, on the fiftieth anniversary of AT&T's first London to Paris scheduled service, BEA was operating Hawker Siddeley Trident airliners on the route, with a cruising speed of around 600mph and a flying time of just 50 minutes. The single fare was £12 and 8 shillings, around half of the 1919 price, with a return fare of £15 and 9 shillings. According to analysis published in *Flight International* in August 1969 some sixty-five minutes were allocated for the journey from the West London Air Terminal to the aircraft's departure at the airport and a further forty minutes allocated at Paris from boarding the coach to the terminal at the Gare des Invalides. Despite the 1969 aircraft having a cruising speed three times that of the 1939 four-engined Frobisher, the total journey time was the same as in 1969. Interestingly, despite the advances in road transport, the transfer times between central London and the UK airport and from central Paris to the French airport were the same in 1919 as they were fifty years later in 1969.

From Halifax to Hastings

By 1929 the Cricklewood Aerodrome, which had been established in 1912, had become encircled by housing developments and was closed. Handley Page continued to manufacture aircraft at its Cricklewood plant until 1964, but a new plant and airfield were developed nearby at Radlett. During the 1920s a high proportion of the company's income came from the patented Handley Page Slot, which involved a small channel being placed on the leading edge of an aircraft's wing to enhance airflow and performance. With the German rearmament programme and the increasing threat of war the British government requested designs for long-range heavy bombers. This set in train the development of two important bombers that served with the RAF. First the twin-engined Handley Page HP52 Hampden, which took part in the first British bombing raid on Berlin and the first 1,000 bomber raid on Cologne. The other was the four-engined Handley Page HP57 Halifax, of which over 6,000 were produced, making it the second most prolific bomber of the war, second only to the Lancaster.

The Handley Page Hampden was a twin-engined medium-range bomber that was designed by Gustav Lachmann. Lachmann was born in Dresden in 1896 and served as a lieutenant with the German Army during the First World War. He joined Handley Page in 1929 as director of scientific research. He was interned on the Isle of Man at the start of the Second World War, but following an intervention by Handley Page, he was released and able to continue his work. He stayed with the company until his retirement.

The Handley Page Hampden first flew in June 1937 and was produced to the same Air Ministry specification that led to the introduction of the Wellington. In all, 1,430 Hampdens were delivered. The Hereford was a version built with Napier Dagger engines of which 100 were built and from 1942 around 140 Hampdens were converted into TB Mk I torpedo bombers. The medium bomber variant had a crew of four and was 53 feet 7 inches in length. It had a wingspan of 69 feet 2 inches and stood 14 feet 11 inches high. The machine was equipped with two 1,000hp Bristol Pegasus XVIII 9-cylinder radial engines, which gave it a maximum speed of 265mph at 15,500 feet, a range of 1,885 miles and an operational ceiling of 22,700 feet. The armament consisted of up to six .303-inch machine-guns and a bomb payload of 4,000lb. The Hampden went into production in 1936 and was first introduced to RAF 49 Squadron in September 1938. The Hampden also served with the Royal Canadian Air Force and the Royal Australian Air Force during the Second World War.

Guy Gibson, the commander of the Dambuster raid, spent the first two years of the war flying Hampdens, which he outlined in detail in his book *Enemy Coast Ahead*. By September 1940 two Victoria Crosses were won within a month of each other by aircrew while flying in Hampdens. On 12 August 1940 Flight Lieutenant Rod Learoyd of 49 Squadron bombed the Dortmund-Ems Canal in Germany. Four other Hampdens had attempted the mission earlier the same night. Two had been shot down and the remaining two were severely damaged by enemy fire. Learoyd flew in at 150 feet through intense enemy anti-aircraft fire. His Hampden sustained considerable damage but he still succeeded in hitting the target. The following month, on 15 September 1940, Sergeant John Hannah, a wireless operator and air gunner of 83 Squadron, was severely burnt while he valiantly fought intense flames on-board a Hampden bomber. His actions succeeded in enabling the aircraft and its crew to return back to England. Tragically, due to his injuries Hannah developed tuberculosis the following year and was discharged from the RAF with a disability pension in December 1942. Back in Civvy Street he was unable to hold down a full-time job and worked briefly as a part-time taxi driver, but soon had to give up. He died in June 1947 after spending four months in the Markfield Sanatorium in Leicester.

The Hampden's light armament meant that it was soon withdrawn from daytime operations and was switched to night sorties, including bombing raids and minelaying duties. The aircraft ceased operations with Bomber Command in 1942 and was then deployed as a long-range torpedo bomber with Coastal Command. The aircraft was retired from the RAF in 1945.

The Halifax was Handley Page's most significant contribution to the Second World War. The Halifax was a four-engined long-range aircraft with heavy bomber, transport and maritime patrol variants produced. The Halifax was introduced in November 1940 and served with the RAF until 1952, as well as seeing wartime service with the Royal Canadian Air Force, the Royal Australian Air Force, the Free French Air Force and the Free Polish Air Force. After the Second World War the Halifax was also deployed by the Royal Egyptian Air Force, the *Armée de l'Air* and the Royal Pakistan Air Force that operated the aircraft as late as 1961.

In all, a total of 6,176 machines were built between 1938 and 1945. During the Second World War the Halifax flew 75,532 sorties and dropped 227,610 tons of bombs. The Halifax Mk III was the most produced voriant, with 2,060 aircraft delivered. The Mk III had a crew of seven and was 71 feet 7 inches long and had a wingspan of 98 feet 8 inches. It was equipped with four 1,615hp Bristol Hercules VI or XVI 14-cylinder two-row radial engines, which gave it a maximum speed of 282mph at 13,500 feet, a range of 1,985 miles and an operational ceiling of 24,000 feet. The armour consisted of nine .303 machine-guns, with four in the tail turret, four in a dorsal turret and one in the nose. The aircraft could carry a 14,500lb bomb payload. Other variants included the C Mk VIII unarmed transport aircraft, which could carry 8,000lb of cargo in the bomb bay area and had room for 11 passengers. The Mk A IX transport aircraft variant had space for 16 paratroopers. Handley Page also developed a civilian airliner variant of the Halifax called the Halton.

The Halifax was first introduced in November 1940 to RAF 35 Squadron based at RAF Linton-on-Ouse. The first combat sortie was flown on the night of 10/11 March 1941 to attack the French port of Le Havre. The Halifax also served extensively with Coastal Command and undertook anti-submarine and reconnaissance operations. During a raid on the German battleship *Tirpitz* on the night of 27/28 April 1942 a Halifax B Mk II, number W1048, S for Sugar, of 35 Squadron, was shot down whilst on its first operational flight. The pilot had managed to drop the aircraft's four 1,000lb mines before he successfully crash-landed on Lake Hoklingen in the municipality of Levanger in the Nord-Trøndelag county of Norway. With the help of the Norwegian resistance the crew were able to make it to safety in Sweden, except for the Flight Engineer who had broken his ankle and was taken prisoner. Shortly after the crash the aircraft went through the ice and sank. In 1973 the wreck of W1048 was recovered from the lake and now forms part of the Bomber Command display at the RAF Museum in Hendon. A restored Halifax is located at the Yorkshire Air Museum, at the former RAF Elvington airbase. A second restored machine was pulled from the bottom of Lake Mjøsa in Norway in 1995, fifty years after it had been shot down, and is now located at the RCAF Memorial Museum at Trenton, Ontario. After the war a number of surplus Halifax aircraft were sold to British airlines and used for freight transport. Forty-one were used during the Berlin airlift in 1948, carrying out 4,653 freight drops and 3,509 flights carrying diesel.

The Post-war Era

In 1947 Handley Page reconstituted Handley Page Transport Limited when it bought the assets of Miles Aircraft, that had previously gone bankrupt. The acquisition included the company's site at Woodley and most importantly the Miles M52, the world's first supersonic aircraft that was designed by Don Brown and developed in secret from 1942. The M52 project was cancelled by the Air Ministry in 1945. Handley Page Transport became Handley Page (Reading) Ltd, which then owned and operated the former Miles Aircraft assets. Miles Aircraft had been established in the 1930s by Charles Powis and Jack Phillips, with

Frederick Miles, initially as Philips and Powis Aircraft. The company formally became Miles Aircraft Limited in 1943. The company went into receivership in 1947 following the drying up of military contracts after the Second World War and was then bought by Handley Page. Frederick Miles established FG Miles Limited in 1948 and continued to manufacture aircraft, along with his many other manufacturing interests, with aeroplane production facilities at Redhill aerodrome and Shoreham aerodrome.

The Handley Page HP67 Hastings was an all-metal long-range monoplane transport and troop carrying aircraft, which replaced the Avro York. In 1946 it was the largest transport plane ever designed for the RAF and could carry thirty paratroopers, thirty-two stretchers and twenty-eight sitting casualties or fifty troops. A civilian version of the Hastings, the Handley Page HP81 Hermes, was developed simultaneously, but was put on hold briefly when the prototype crashed on its maiden flight on 2 December 1945. The Hastings prototype flew for the first time when it took off from RAF Wittering on 7 May 1946. Initial stability issues were resolved with a number of hurried modifications and subsequently the aircraft entered service in October 1948. A total of 151 machines were delivered, primarily to the RAF and the Royal New Zealand Air Force. The RAF had retired all of its Hastings aircraft by 1977. The civil variant, the Handley Page Hermes airliner, was built in response to the Air Ministry's specification for a pressurized civil airliner that was capable of carrying thirty-four first class passengers and fifty tourist class passengers. The Hermes was finally introduced on 6 August 1950 and initially served with BOAC before later being introduced to a number of charter airlines. The Hermes Mk IV variant first flew on 5 September 1948. It had a crew of seven and could carry up to eighty-two passengers, depending upon the cabin configuration. The aircraft was 96 feet 10 inches long, had a wingspan of 113 feet and stood 30 feet high. It was powered by four 2,100hp Bristol Hercules 763 radial engines, which gave it a maximum speed of 350mph, a cruising speed of 270mph at 20,000 feet, a range of 2,000 miles and an operational ceiling of 24,500 feet. The Mk IV flew the West Africa service to Accra for BOAC, via Tripoli, Kano and Lagos. Later in 1950 the aircraft was extended to BOAC's Kenyan and South African services. However, by 1952 the Canadair Argonaut had replaced the Hermes on these routes and the aircraft was retired by the airline, only bringing them back out briefly when the de Havilland Comet was grounded in July 1954 after a number of then unexplained disasters. The smaller airlines bought BOAC's surplus Hermes aircraft, which were operated successfully by such companies as the New Zealand airline Airwork, British Aviation Services Limited and Skyways, which was later taken-over by Dan Air.

The last civil Hermes to fly was operated by Air Links Limited, and was retired from service on 13 December 1964. The aircraft was scrapped nine days later. Two Hermes Mk V aircraft were built and were retained by the Ministry of

Supply for experimental aircraft development work. The first crashed at Chilbolton airfield near Andover on 10 April 1951. The second was used by the Aeroplane & Armament Experimental Establishment at Boscombe Down and the Royal Aircraft Establishment at Farnborough until September 1953. The following month it was given military markings and was then used for experimental work, which included testing airborne radar sets by the Royal Radar Establishment at Defford near Worcester. It was the last Hermes to fly and was retired in 1969.

V is for Victor

The Handley Page Victor was the third of the strategic V bombers that made up Britain's nuclear deterrent during the Cold War, which also included the Avro Vulcan and the Vickers Valiant. The Victor was designed by Reginald Stafford, who was Handley Page's chief designer at that time and became technical director in 1953. The aircraft first flew on Christmas Eve 24 December 1952, but was destroyed following a crash during a low-level run. The second prototype first flew on 11 September 1954. The Victor eventually entered service with RAF 10 Squadron in 1958.

The Victor B2 had a crew of five. It was 114 feet 11 inches long, had a wingspan of 120 feet and stood 30 feet 1 inch high. It was fitted with four 20,600lbf Rolls-Royce Conway 201 turbofans, which gave it a maximum speed of 640mph at 40,000 feet, a range of 4,600 miles and an operational ceiling of 47,000 feet. It was armed with one HS Blue Steel ASM with a Red Snow warhead. In all, a total of 86 aircraft were built between 1952 and 1963.

On 1 June 1956, Handley Page's test pilot Johnny Allam, flying a Victor B1, number XA917, accidentally broke the sound barrier when he let the nose drop. The aircraft's speedometer read Mach 1.1 and observers on the ground from Watford in Hertfordshire, to Banbury in Oxfordshire, claimed to have heard a sonic boom.

By the time that the Handley Page Victor entered service the Valiant and Vulcan had already been deployed with the RAF. The first RAF squadron to take delivery of the Victor B1 was the 232 Operational Conversion Unit stationed at RAF Gaydon in Warwickshire, which received its aircraft at the end of 1957. The first operational bomber squadron was 10 Squadron based at RAF Cottesmore, which took delivery of its Victors in April 1958. Four aircraft equipped with Yellow Astor reconnaissance radar were deployed with the Radar Reconnaissance Flight at RAF Wyton. By 1960 three more Victor squadrons had been established, which were Nos 15, 55 and 57.

At this time the British government was putting considerable pressure on UK aircraft manufacturers to merge into two large corporations. Sir Frederick Handley Page was not in favour of this proposal. He resisted the government pressure and kept his company independent. This meant that Handley Page

Limited received fewer and fewer government contracts. In 1968 fatigue cracks were discovered on the Victor's airframe. A contract to make modifications to the aircraft was delayed by the Ministry of Defence until after Handley Page had gone into voluntary liquidation on 31 March 1970. The work was awarded to Hawker Siddeley, which had bowed to government pressure and merged with a number of its competitors to form the Hawker Siddeley Group in 1960. Reconnaissance variants of the Victor remained in service with the RAF until 1974. One of their last missions was the monitoring of French nuclear tests in the South Pacific.

The Vickers Valiant fleet of airborne tankers used by the RAF for in-flight refuelling were found to have metal fatigue and were withdrawn in 1964. A number of Victor aircraft were modified to replace the Valiants and the Victor K2 became the RAF's main in-flight refuelling aircraft. When the Royal Navy introduced the submarine-launched Polaris missiles in 1969 the V bombers became redundant. The last Victor to fly was retired from service on 15 October 1993.

A K2 tanker can be seen at the British Aviation Heritage Centre at Bruntingthorpe in Lutterworth near Leicester. Another K2 is at the Royal Air Force Museum, Cosford, in Shropshire, in its Cold War building. The Imperial War Museum at Duxford in Cambridgeshire has a Victor B1A, Victor XH673 is at the gate of RAF Marham in Norfolk, the Victor's last home, and XL231 *Lusty Lindy* can be found at the Yorkshire Air Museum in York.

Into the Jetstream

The Handley Page Dart Herald fast short-range turboprop regional airliner was intended as a replacement for the Douglas DC-3. It was evolved from the design of the Miles Marathon airliner that Handley Page inherited when it acquired Miles Aircraft. The Herald first flew on 25 August 1955 and a total of fifty aircraft were built between 1959 and 1968.

Despite attracting a great deal of interest Handley Page failed to secure many orders for the aircraft, mostly because the main competitors at that time, the Fokker F-27 and the Hawker Siddeley HS748, were considerably cheaper. The initial design was developed into the Series 200, which had been lengthened to allow for an increase in seating capacity from 47 to 56 seats. The Herald Series 200 was 75 feet 6 inches long, had a wingspan of 94 feet 10 inches and stood 24 feet high. It was powered by two 1,910hp Rolls-Royce Dart 527 turboprop engines, with a cruising speed of 275mph, a range of 1,635 miles and an operational ceiling of 29,700 feet. The first of this type was delivered to Jersey Airlines in January 1962, but by this time the sales were drying up and only 36 machines were built in a six-year period.

A Series 400 followed in 1964 for the Royal Malaysian Air Force and a larger sixty-seat Series 700 that was fitted with Rolls-Royce Dart 532 engines was designed. The final Herald was a Series 200 and was the fiftieth machine to be built. It was delivered in August 1968 to Arkia, formerly Israel Inland Airlines. Examples of the Handley Page Herald can be seen at the Museum of Berkshire Aviation in Woodley, the Duxford Aviation Society based at Duxford Aerodrome, the City of Norwich Aviation Museum at Norwich Airport, the Yorkshire Air Museum in Elvington and the Highland Aviation Museum at Inverness.

The cancellation of the Herald left Handley Page with the opportunity of developing the HP137 Jetstream pressurized regional airliner. The Jetstream was significantly more successful than the Herald with a total of 458 aircraft delivered; most, however, after Handley Page had gone into liquidation. The Jetstream first flew on 18 August 1967 and was introduced two years later in 1969. The Jetstream 200 had a crew of two and was able to carry up to 19 passengers. It was 47 feet 2 inches long, had a wingspan of 52 feet and was 17 feet 5 inches high. It was fitted with two Turbomeca Astazou XVI C2 turboprop engines, which gave it a maximum speed of 282mph, a cruising speed of 269mph, a range of 1,380 miles and an operational ceiling of 25,000 feet. The new smaller design of the Jetstream attracted a great deal of interest in the United States of America and some 20 aircraft were ordered off the drawing board. The first production Jetstream 1 flew on 6 December 1968 and 36 aircraft were delivered over the following 12 months, with the Jetstream 200 being introduced in 1969. Production delays and engine problems had caused the development costs of the Jetstream to spiral from £3 million to £13 million. Only three Jetstream 2 aircraft were delivered before Handley Page ceased trading in 1970.

Scottish Aviation established Jetstream Aircraft to continue to manufacture the aircraft after it bought the design following the collapse of Handley Page Limited. In 1977 the British government nationalized the aircraft and shipbuilding industries in the UK and Scottish Aviation became part of the state-owned corporation British Aerospace. The following year the company began development of the Jetstream 3, which was equipped with new 1,020shp Garrett turboprop engines and was available with an 18-seat option. This variant became the Jetstream 31 and first flew on 28 March 1980. In 1988 the Jetstream Super 31, also known as the Jetstream 32, was introduced and remained in production until 1993 when 386 of the 31 and 32 types had been built. In the same year British Aerospace used the Jetstream name formally as the brand for its regional airliners. The British Aerospace Jetstream 41, a stretched version of the 31, which could carry up to 30 passengers, flew for the first time on 25 September 1991. A total of 100 aircraft were built between 1992 and 1997. In July 2008 a team from BAE Systems, Cranfield Aerospace and the National Flight Laboratory Centre at Cranfield University, succeeded in flying a converted unmanned Jetstream 31, G-BWWW, on a series of flights that exceeded a total of 800 miles without any human intervention whatsoever. Ironically, Handley Page's most successful post-war aircraft, the Jetstream, only achieved the level of sales that the company deserved after it had gone into voluntary liquidation.

Chapter 14

Charles Fairey and the Journey from Swordfish to Spearfish

After a brief two-year spell with Short Brothers, Charles Fairey established the Fairey Aviation Company in 1915 and so began his forty-year career at the helm of one of Britain's most innovative aircraft manufacturers that led his outstanding contribution to military aviation to be recognized and rewarded in the UK and the US.

Charles Richard Fairey was born on 5 May 1887 in Hendon, Middlesex, and studied electrical engineering and chemistry at Finsbury Technical College. Fairey had a lifelong passion for model making and was a member of the Kite and Model Aeroplane Association. On 4 June 1910, at the age of twenty-three, he won the first prize in a model flying competition at Crystal Palace, where his innovative monoplane design flew more than 150 yards.

Fairey Aviation Company
With the outbreak of the First World War Fairey had attempted to enlist, but was turned down on medical grounds. Undeterred, in 1915 he made up his mind to leave Short Brothers and branch out on his own and set about establishing the Fairey Aviation Company. He set up an office in Piccadilly, London, and decided to locate his first factory in North Hyde Road at Hayes in Middlesex. In 1930 Fairey Aviation built a new factory at Hayes and also established the Great West Aerodrome at Harmondsworth as a home for its test flights. The aerodrome was built on 150 acres of land that had been bought from the church. It was located next to the small hamlet of Heathrow, which was demolished in 1945 to make way for the development of London's main airport. In 1935 the company opened additional manufacturing facilities at Heaton Chapel near Stockport, Manchester, and from 1937 test flights for that plant were made from Ringway Airport. The Stockport factory manufactured the Hendon and Battle bombers, the Fulmar fighter and the Barracuda dive-bomber, as well as the Bristol Beaufighter and the Handley Page Halifax bomber.

From the start Fairey Aviation was responsible for a range of carrier-borne torpedo bombers, beginning with the Campania, which was produced in 1917 for the Royal Navy's first aircraft carrier, HMS *Campania*, a converted ocean liner with a flight deck that extended 200 feet. The Campania was the first ever aircraft to be specifically designed to operate from an aircraft carrier and flew for the first time on 16 February 1917. It was 43 feet in length, had a wingspan of 61 feet 7 inches and stood 15 feet 1 inch tall. It was powered by one 345hp Rolls-Royce Eagle VIII 12-cylinder engine that gave it a maximum speed of 80mph, an operational ceiling of 5,500 feet and a duration of three hours. The aircraft went on to serve on the seaplane carriers *Nairana* and *Pegasus*.

Most notably during the inter-war years was the Fairey Swordfish, a carrier-borne biplane, which first flew in 1934 and although obsolete by the start of the Second World War it played an invaluable part in numerous critical sea battles, including the sinking of the *Bismarck* on 27 May 1941.

The Attack on Taranto Harbour

In early 1941 a group of Japanese naval officers on diplomatic duty in Berlin was escorted by the German *Abwehr* on a liaison visit to Italy. In Rome the Japanese were introduced to the Italian naval authorities and asked if they could investigate the secrets of the Royal Navy's Fleet Air Arm attack of November 1940 on the Italian battleships in Taranto Harbour. A double agent working for the British MI6 secret service acquired the intelligence from a conversation with his *Abwehr* control officer whilst visiting Lisbon. Unbeknown to the West the Japanese Navy was planning an attack on the US naval base at Pearl Harbor in Hawaii. Admiral Isoroku Yamamoto, commander of the Imperial Navy's Combined Fleet, had advised his Navy Minister on 7 January 1941 that a decisive strike crippling the US fleet would bring about the subsequent defeat of the British and Allied forces south of the Philippine Islands. The Japanese knew that if they were to succeed the secrets of Taranto had to be unlocked.

On 10 November 1940 Glenn Martin Maryland reconnaissance bombers of 431 Flight, flying from RAF Malta, photographed the roads and harbour of the Italian naval base at Taranto and revealed the presence of six battleships and miscellaneous naval vessels. The decision was immediately taken by the British Admiralty to attack.

The following day HMS *Illustrious*, under the command of Rear Admiral Lumley Lyster, escorted by four cruisers from the 3rd Cruiser Squadron and four destroyers from the 2nd Destroyer Flotilla, launched aircraft from forty miles south-west of the island of Cephalonia and 170 miles south-east of Taranto. The first strike of twelve Fairey Swordfish torpedo bombers took off at 8.57 p.m. under the command of Lieutenant Commander Williamson of 815 Squadron. Six of the aircraft were armed with torpedoes, four with bombs and two with flares and bombs. The aircraft, with open cockpits and unescorted, flew at a height of 8,000 feet. Taranto Harbour was guarded by balloon barrages,

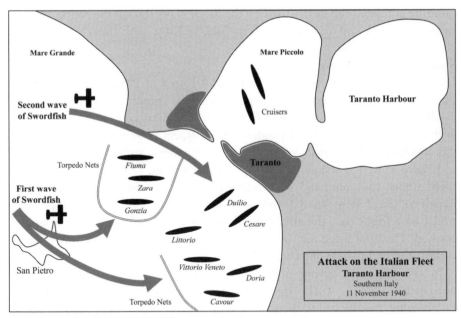

Attack on Italian fleet at Taranto Harbour, 11 November 1940.

guard ships, shore batteries and anti-aircraft sound detectors, whilst the Italian warships were protected by torpedo nets. At 11.00 p.m. flares were dropped over the eastern side of the outer harbour, the Mare Grande. The torpedo bombers dived down to 4,000 feet, then to a height of 30 feet over the harbour to make their torpedo runs. Meanwhile, the Swordfish aircraft armed with bombs attacked and destroyed the cruisers in the inner harbour, the Mare Piccolo, as well as the port installations. A second strike of nine Swordfish aircraft under the command of Lieutenant Commander JW Hale RN of 819 Squadron comprised five aircraft armed with torpedoes, two armed with bombs and two with flares and bombs. Once again, the same method of attack was used as the Italian naval forces put up a heavy curtain of anti-aircraft fire. As the low-level attack proceeded, anti-aircraft shells from the Italian batteries crashed into ships and harbour facilities as the gunners trained their weapons on the low-flying torpedo bombers. Later photographic reconnaissance of the harbour showed the battleship *Littorio* disabled with three torpedo hits and probably out of action for at least a year. The battleship *Caio Duilio* beached having received one torpedo hit and the *Conte di Cavour* sunk in shallow water after being struck by one torpedo. The heavy cruiser *Trento* had been hit by a heavy bomb, whilst the destroyers, the seaplane base and the harbour fuel tanks had sustained heavy damage. Overnight the strategic balance in heavy capital ships in the Eastern Mediterranean had changed in favour of the Royal Navy. Allied convoys could now sail from Gibraltar to Alexandria without interference. The Japanese officers carefully evaluated the tactics used by the Royal Navy during the course of their successful attack and took their findings back to Tokyo with them.

Swordfish to Albacore

Completed as a private adventure by Charles Fairey in 1933 the Fairey TSR-1 was designed as a three-seater torpedo bomber, spotter and reconnaissance machine to Air Ministry specification S09/30. The pilot's cockpit was sited high in the fuselage, with a fin and rudder of high aspect ratio, and the landing gear was attached to the fuselage via spats. The wings were two-bay of differing span and chord as well as staggered. On 21 March 1933 the TSR-1 made its maiden flight under the command of Flight Lieutenant CS Staniland from Fairey Aviation's Great West Road Aerodrome near London. On 11 September 1933, whilst on a flight test, the aircraft could not be extracted from a flat spin and crashed. The pilot baled out, but was blown back by the slipstream into the rear cockpit and had to bale out a second time.

In the following spring of 1934 the second prototype was completed, designated TSR-2, works number K4190 and airframe number F2038. Engineering modifications incuded a four-degree sweep back on the upper wings, as well as an additional bay in the fuselage that eradicated the tendency to spin. On 17 April 1934 Flight Lieutenant Staniland flew the TSR-2 for the first time. The new prototype was designed by Marcel Lobelle, Fairey Aviation's chief designer. It was equipped with a Bristol Pegasus III M engine rated at 690hp, as well as a new rudder of lower aspect ratio and revised upper wing tips. Long anti-spin stakes were installed to the rear fuselage and a broad chord Townsend Cooling Ring encased the engine. The flight tests involved trials with the wooden Watts two-bladed propeller as well as the Fairey-Reed two-bladed metal propeller. On 10 November 1934 flight tests on the River Hamble took place with the TSR-2 equipped with floats for catapult launches from HMS *Repulse*. Successful trials were later completed at the Aircraft and Armament Experimental Establishment at RAF Martlesham Heath, Suffolk, and the TSR-2 was ordered into production for the Fleet Air Arm as the Fairey Swordfish Mk I with a contract for eighty-six aircraft in April 1935.

The Swordfish had a crew of three. It was 35 feet 8 inches long, had a wingspan of 42 feet 6 inches and stood 12 feet 4 inches tall. The 820hp Bristol Pegasus XXX radial engine gave the aircraft a maximum speed of 138mph at 4,750 feet, a range of 546 miles, an endurance of over five hours and an operational ceiling of 19,250 feet. The extensive armoury included one fixed forward-firing .303-inch Vickers machine-gun, a second .303-inch machine-gun in the rear cockpit and one 18-inch torpedo. The first production aircraft were delivered to 815 Squadron in July 1936, and were fitted with three bladed Fairey-Reed metal propellers. The Swordfish remained in production until 18 August 1944, by which time a total of 2,391 had been manufactured.

On the eve of the Second World War 126 Swordfish torpedo bombers, out of a total of 232, were on duty in Royal Navy aircraft carriers. On the China Station HMS *Eagle* had eighteen aircraft, in the Mediterranean Sea HMS *Glorious* had thirty-six, in Scapa Flow HMS *Ark Royal* had a further thirty-six aircraft, the carrier HMS *Courageous* was stationed at Portsmouth with a complement of twenty-four Swordfish and HMS *Hermes* was at sea with one squadron of twelve Swordfish torpedo bombers.

When war was declared in September 1939 Britain's aircraft carriers were quickly deployed on anti-submarine operations but without very much success. With the German invasion of Norway in April 1940 and the decision to send a British Expeditionary Force to assist in the defence of that country the Royal Navy's aircraft carriers assumed an offensive role. On 11 April 1940 HMS *Furious* was on patrol with 816 Squadron commanded by Lieutenant CN Gardiner and 818 Squadron under the command of Lieutenant J Fenton, with orders to immediately attack the German heavy cruiser Admiral *Hipper* and four destroyers in Trondheim Harbour. Unfortunately, the Admiral *Hipper* had departed on 10 April 1940 and the Swordfish torpedo force returned without making a strike. It was later discovered that the Trondheim Harbour waters were too shallow for successful torpedo runs.

The following day nine Swordfish attacked shipping in Narvik Harbour, each armed with four 250lb and four 20lb bombs. They flew in appalling weather conditions with snow, sleet and wind speeds of 35 to 45mph. The cloud ceiling had closed-in from an altitude of 1,000 feet down to 200 feet. Observations during the course of the attack revealed that Narvik Harbour contained five German Maas Class destroyers, eleven merchant ships, with one destroyer alongside the iron ore jetty, three moored alongside the pier and one destroyer at anchor in the roads. The aerial attack on Narvik Harbour achieved two direct hits on shipping with one ship seriously damaged. During 13 April 1940 a combined air-sea operation was conducted, when ten Swordfish and the battleship HMS *Warspite*, accompanied by nine British destroyers entered Narvik Fjord. Eight German destroyers were sunk, with U-boat *U-64* destroyed by HMS *Warspite*'s own Swordfish, for the loss of two aircraft. HMS *Furious* launched photographic reconnaissance and anti-submarine patrols along the Vaag Fjord on 15 April. Nine Swordfish bombers attacked German Junkers Ju 52 3MZ transport planes parked on a frozen lake. Two German planes were destroyed, whilst the remainder were machine-gunned in low-level attacks. During the operation one Swordfish was forced to land but fortunately the crew were rescued by HMS *Zulu*.

Three days later HMS *Furious* was attacked by a Heinkel He 111, with two near bomb misses. The port side near miss damaged the port steam engine turbine and shook the blades on the turbine shaft out of alignment, which reduced the carrier's speed to 23mph. By 25 April 1940 HMS *Furious* was withdrawn from Norwegian operations. The ship's Swordfish had flown 23,870 miles, launched 18 torpedoes and dropped 15½ tons of bombs, for the loss of half of the complement of Swordfish. Enemy anti-aircraft fire had damaged 17 reconnaissance aircraft, but 295 photographs had been taken for three men killed, seven wounded and two missing, presumed dead. Hastily, the aircraft carriers HMS *Ark Royal* and HMS *Glorious* were withdrawn from the Mediterranean. During the evacuation of the British Forces from Norway the two carriers were flying thirty-six Swordfish torpedo bombers, four squadrons of Blackburn Skuas and three squadrons of Gloster Gladiator biplane fighters. Operating 100 miles off the Norwegian coast the two aircraft carriers provided vital air cover over Namsos and Åndalsnes, whilst the Swordfish attacked Trondheim and the Værnes airfield. On 2 June 1940 the aircraft carriers covered the final evacuation as *Luftwaffe* bombing attacks on Royal Navy warships increased in intensity. The Allied defence of Norway was a failure owing to the inability of the RAF to provide adequate air cover and conduct bombing missions against enemy forces. The Royal Navy's Fleet Air Arm urgently required a modern fighter to provide adequate aerial defence of the fleet whilst on overseas operations. The Swordfish was outmoded and urgently required a replacement, though it did continue as a radar reconnaissance and anti-submarine aircraft. The new torpedo bomber to equip the Fleet's aircraft carriers was to be the Fairey Albacore.

The Sinking of the *Bismarck*

The German battleship *Bismarck* was laid down on 1 July 1936 and was commissioned on 24 August 1940. The *Bismarck*, along with the heavy cruiser *Prinz Eugen*, were assigned by Admiral Günther Lütjens to the German operation codenamed *Rheinübung*, where these two formidable ships were to break out into the Atlantic and destroy British and Allied shipping. During the Battle of the Denmark Strait the *Bismarck* and *Prinz Eugen* fought their way out into the Atlantic and HMS *Hood* paid the ultimate price on 24 May 1941. The British battlecruiser was sunk almost immediately when one shell from the *Bismarck* penetrated *Hood*'s deck and hit the ammunition magazine, which caused the ship to explode and sink almost instantly. Of the complement of 1,325 on-board the *Hood* there were only three survivors. With the two German warships loose in the Atlantic the race was on for the Royal Navy to locate and sink them both. The Swordfish of the Fleet Air Arm's 800, 808, 810, 818, 820 and 825 Squadron's earned their battle honours well and truly in the days that followed. Shortly after the *Hood* was sunk all nine Swordfish from 825 Squadron under the command of Lieutenant Commander Eugene Esmonde took off from HMS *Victorious* and made the first attack on the *Bismarck*.

The Squadron was followed by three Fulmar aircraft from 800Z Flight, with orders to watch the attack and to keep in contact with the quarry. Two days later, on 26 May 1941, the five Fleet Air Arm Swordfish Squadrons aboard HMS *Ark Royal* joined the chase from their base in Gibraltar. Lieutenant Commander

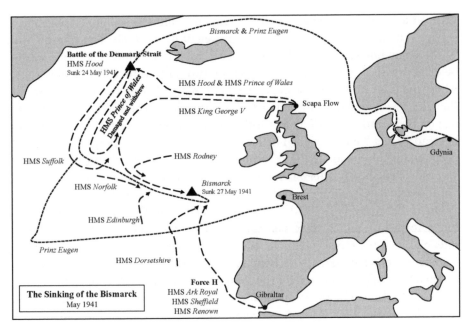

The sinking of the *Bismarck*, 27 May 1941.

James Sholto Douglas DSO commanded 807 squadron, Lieutenant Commander Rupert Claude Tillard commanded 808 Squadron, Lieutenant Commander Mervyn Johnstone commanded 810 Squadron, Lieutenant Commander Trevenen Penrose Coode commanded 818 Squadron and Lieutenant Commander James Andrew Stewart-Moore was in command of 820 Squadron.

Later that day two waves of Swordfish attacked the *Bismarck* and *Prinz Eugen*, the first wave was led by 818 Squadron and the second wave was led by 810 Squadron. During the attacks a torpedo struck the *Bismarck*'s rudder and succeeded in crippling the ship, which forced it to slow down and crucially allowed the Royal Navy sufficient time to catch up and launch its final attack. On 27 May 1941 a barrage of shells from HMS *King George V*, HMS *Rodney* and HMS *Dorsetshire* finally sank the *Bismarck*. The *Prinz Eugen* crept away and made it back to Brest in North West France.

Albacore to Barracuda

On 8 September 1936 specification M7/36 had been issued for a torpedo bomber, spotter and reconnaissance aircraft that was armed with an 18-inch Mk XII A torpedo. The crew of two or three were to be accommodated in a heated and sound proof cockpit, insulated with padding for fire prevention and with dual controls including full navigation and observation equipment, as well as a sling for stowage by a ship's lifting crane. The leading edge wings and tailplane were to be metal covered. It was to be equipped with one or two British engines with variable pitch propellers, with a maximum stalling speed of 58 knots and a service ceiling of 20,000 feet at an all-up weight of 10,000lb. The take-off run was to be no longer than 200 feet against a 20mph head wind. The plane was to be armed with a gun turret amidships for two guns with 1,000 rounds each, whilst the pilot would have a single fixed gun with 400 rounds. A good view for the pilot was essential for torpedo attacks. With a length of 37 feet on wheels, 44 feet on floats and a span of 50 feet with wings folded to 18 feet, the machine was to stand 14 feet 9 inches high. The Fairey Aviation Company prepared a detailed proposal for submission to the government, but disappointingly the requirement was cancelled shortly afterwards. However, despite this Fairey was determined not to waste its extensive research and development work on the design.

On 11 February 1937 the Air Ministry issued a further specification S41/36 for a torpedo, spotter, dive-bomber and reconnaissance machine that was intended to be a replacement for the Fairey Swordfish. The Fairey Aviation Company's chief designer, the Belgian aeronautical engineer Marcel Lobelle, adapted the designs prepared for the 1936 specification and developed the Fairey Albacore biplane. The prototype made its maiden flight on 12 December 1938 from the Great West Road Aerodrome with Flight Lieutenant Christopher Stainbank Staniland at the controls. Following the successful maiden flight an initial order was made and the Mk I entered service in March 1940. In all, a total of 798 aircraft were produced.

The Albacore Mk I was 39 feet 11 inches in length, had a wingspan of 49 feet 11 inches and stood 12 feet 6 inches tall. The production machines had a 1,130hp Bristol Taurus XII motor that gave them a maximum speed of 161 mph, a range of 930 miles and a ceiling of 20,700 feet. The aircraft had a metal monocoque fuselage and the crew was accommodated in an enclosed heated greenhouse cockpit.

Handling trials for an Albacore mounted on floats were undertaken by the Marine Aircraft Experimental Establishment at Helensburgh on 28 March 1940. The machine was powered by a Bristol Taurus I Ma engine and tests were conducted at the Fairey Aviation works at Hamble on the River Solent. The machine took off at a speed of 70mph in 26 seconds or 29 seconds with a heavy load. Air handling was considered acceptable and the aircraft was passed for catapult flights.

At that time Italian high-speed battleships and cruisers operated in the Mediterranean Sea. Savoia-Marchetti SM79 torpedo bombers flew from Sardinia and Sicily to successfully attack Royal Navy convoys en route for Alexandria, Egypt. On 27 March 1941 the Italian fleet, under the command of Admiral Angelo Iachino, was steaming westwards for Brindisi, southern Italy, and was continuously attacked by Blenheim bombers flying from Greece. The pursuing British Mediterranean Fleet commanded by Admiral Cunningham consisted of the slow and ageing British battleships HMS *Warspite*, HMS *Valiant* and HMS *Barham*, accompanied by the aircraft carrier HMS *Formidable* and escorting destroyers. The carrier was flying Fairey Fulmar fighters from 806 Squadron, Fairey Albacores and Fairey Swordfish bombers. At 11.27 a.m. six Albacore aircraft of 826 Squadron, under the command of Lieutenant Commander WGH Saunt, made unsuccessful attacks on the Italian battleship *Vittorio Veneto* and the heavy cruiser *Bolzano*. At approximately 3.10 a.m. three Albacore and two Swordfish, under the command of Lieutenant Commander Dalyell-Stead, again attacked the *Vittorio Veneto* from the port and starboard sides from a range of 1,000 yards. The battleship was struck on the port upper screw and her speed was considerably reduced, as near bomb misses were registered by the attacking Bristol Blenheim bombers. Meanwhile, at 7.30 a.m. six Albacore and two Swordfish were despatched from HMS *Formidable* to attack the 8,000-ton cruiser *Pola*. By 7.46 a.m. *Pola* was hit, had lost speed and dropped back from her sister ships. The Italian heavy cruisers *Zara* and *Fiume* with two destroyer escorts, the *Alfieri* and *Carducci*, were despatched by Admiral Iachino to support the stricken *Pola*. That night Admiral Cunningham's battleship force caught up with the Italian squadron and in a night action off Cape Matapan the heavy Italian cruisers and destroyer escorts were sunk with the use of heavy calibre gunfire using radar-controlled gun-laying techniques. The effect was to further reduce the ability of the Italian Navy to interfere with Allied convoys sailing to Alexandria.

The Fairey Albacore bombers of the Fleet Air Arm 826 and 821 Squadrons attacked eight enemy ships in the Mediterranean Sea during the latter half of 1941. Other Albacore aircraft assisted RAF Wellington bombers by illuminating enemy targets and port installations for bombing attacks. Normally intelligence reports filed by forward Army patrols would indicate enemy motor transport, gun emplacements and installations for attack. Late during daylight hours RAF reconnaissance flights would photograph the targets for that night's operation. When darkness descended the black painted Albacore bombers, armed with 32 flares and 250lb bombs, would take off and when over the target at an altitude of 3,000 feet, 15 minutes before the Wellington bombers arrived, would drop flares to illuminate the target.

Far away in the Pacific Ocean, during the early hours of Sunday 7 December 1941, the Japanese Combined Fleet's tactical carrier strike force, known as the *Kido Butai*, sailed at speed under the command of Vice Admiral Nagumo to approximately 200 miles north of Hawaii. The six aircraft carriers HIJMS *Soryu*, *Shokaku*, *Zuikaku*, *Hiryu*, *Kaga* and *Akagi*, with over 350 aircraft, were escorted by seventeen warships. All had left their home port of Kure one by one late in November 1940 and during their voyage Imperial Navy Headquarters, Tokyo, had transmitted orders and intelligence information in the new Admiral's Code. Though these transmissions had been picked up as far away as the East Indies and by an American liner voyaging from Hawaii to San Francisco, the key to the new code had remained unbroken and deciphering the messages was impossible.

At approximately 7.49 a.m. the Japanese dive-bombers climbed to 12,000 feet, the horizontal bombers descended to 3,500 feet, with the torpedo bombers skimming the wave tops, adopting a similar attack strategy as employed by the Swordfish at Taranto harbour the year before. A second wave attacked at 8.45 a.m. The operation crippled the US Pacific Fleet at Pearl Harbor. At Singapore the Royal Navy had failed to send the necessary fleet to defend the city-island and the Malayan archipelago. As a result the warships in southeast Asia had been hunted down and sunk due to inadequate RAF aerial defence and an inability to concentrate naval strength in force.

The Bite of the Barracuda
The successor to the Albacore was the Fairey Barracuda. It was designed as a torpedo and dive-bomber to specification S24/37 and made its maiden flight on 7 December 1940. However, a three-year delay caused by design problems meant that the first thirty Barracuda Mk I aircraft to be produced were not introduced until May 1942. The aircraft had occasionally failed to pull out of a dive, problems had arisen retracting the undercarriage and the high wings required a block and tackle to manually fold, whereas foreign designs had hydraulically operated folding wings. The machine looked ungainly and was considered difficult to fly. It was said that the Barracuda was designed by committee and contained 'bits of the Forth Bridge'. Nevertheless, the Barracuda first saw action off Salerno flying with 810 Squadron from HMS *Illustrious*. Comparison with the Grumman Avenger torpedo bomber of the United States Navy did little to boost the Barracuda's reputation. The Avenger had superior performance and load-carrying capacity with internal stowage for offensive weapons, whilst the wings folded hydraulically and were operated from inside the cockpit. Even the Douglas Devastator had this facility when introduced to US Naval Air Squadrons during 1938 and 1939.

The Barracuda Mk II had a crew of three, was 39 feet 9 inches long, had a wingspan of 49 feet 2 inches and stood 15 feet 1 inch high. The 1,640hp Rolls-Royce Merlin 32 V-12 liquid-cooled engine gave the aircraft a maximum speed of 228mph, an operational ceiling of 16,600 feet and a maximum range of 1,150 miles. The Barracuda Mk II was armed with two .303-inch Vickers K machine-guns mounted in the rear cockpit and a 1,620lb aerial torpedo, four 450lb depth charges or six 250lb bombs beneath the wings.

The Barracuda Mk III was similar to the Mk I and Mk II, except that a radar ASV Mk X was installed and a crew of two was required, whereas a crew of three had previously been carried with rear defensive armament. The Mk V was introduced during the summer of 1946. The production of the Fleet Air Arm's variant of the Barracuda commenced in 1945 at the company's Stockport factory and the aircraft were fitted with rocket-assisted take-off equipment or accelerator gear. An air-sea rescue version was also built. Increased performance was obtained by replacing the Rolls-Royce Merlin 32 with the 2,020hp Rolls-

Royce Griffon 37 engine and the bomb payload was increased to 2,000lb. The structure was strengthened to take increased loads and the increased G factor from the effects of dive-bombing attacks. Larger fuel tanks were installed and a taller rudder was designed to provide adequate directional stability due to the Rolls-Royce Griffon installation.

On 6 September 1943 the German battleship *Tirpitz* accompanied by the battle cruiser *Scharnhorst* bombarded the strategic island of Spitzbergen. This island was located on the route that the British convoys would take sailing to the Soviet ports of Murmansk and Archangel. The German capital ships then sailed to the Kaafjord to take up a strategic anchorage that gave easy access to attack British shipping rounding the north of Norway, as well as the waters of the North Atlantic Ocean. Protected by anti-torpedo nets, anti-submarine booms and with the waters of the fjord constantly patrolled by small craft, the *Tirpitz* represented a serious threat. During September 1943 an attack was made on the *Tirpitz* by midget submarines and though seriously damaged the battleship was not put out of commission. By March 1944 the damage was repaired.

On 3 April 1944 twelve Barracudas from 827 Squadron and nine from 830 Squadron, escorted by forty fighter planes, attacked the German battleship *Tirpitz* as part of Operation *Tungsten*. Flying from 120 miles west of Altenfjord the aerial strike force crossed the Norwegian coast at 5.10 a.m. and turned onto a southerly course. The German battleship was caught by the first air strike as preparations were being made to depart seawards and as no German fighter defences were encountered two direct hits were achieved with 1,600lb bombs and a further five with 500lb bombs. The second airstrike commenced at 6.35 a.m. with nineteen Barracudas from 820 Squadron and the *Tirpitz* sustained a further five direct hits. In the two air attacks 122 German crewmen had been killed, 316 had been wounded and the *Tirpitz* damaged such that it required a further period at anchor to effect repairs. The British lost three Barracudas and one Grumman Hellcat, with a total of eight airmen killed.

As the heavy German battleship had not been completely put out of action it represented a continuing threat to British shipping and the Admiralty planned further attacks. Operation *Planet* was cancelled on 26 April due to bad weather, as was Operation *Brown* on 15 May. Operation *Mascot* on 17 July launched an attack at 2.20 a.m. with 44 Barracudas from 827, 830, 820 and 826 Squadrons and fared little better. They encountered heavy anti-aircraft fire and the target was deliberately obscured by dense smoke. Operation *Goodwood* followed in which thirty-three Barracudas were unable to reach the target due to bad weather and the operation was cancelled. A further force of thirty-three Barracudas escorted by Grumman Hellcats, Chance-Vought Corsairs and Fairey fighter planes attacked the *Tirpitz* on 24 August and only registered two hits. One 1,600lb bomb crashed through eight armoured decks and failed to explode. The German naval bomb disposal team reported that the missile was only half filled with explosive. Five days later another attack took place with twenty-six

Barracudas escorted by Fleet Air Arm fighters, but they did not achieve one direct hit, only near misses. The Admiralty concluded that to sink such a big armoured ship, a big weapon was required and the destruction of the *Tirpitz* was assigned to the Royal Air Force.

Spearfish and the Post-war Era

The original design of the Spearfish was produced as a result of specification O5/43 and was conceived when the Barracuda had been introduced in 1943. The plan envisaged a Rolls-Royce Exe motor with either the Sabre or Bristol Centaurus engine as an alternative. At one point a twin-engined version was considered as well as a combination motor utilizing a coupled piston and jet engine. Finally, a decision was taken to install the Bristol Centaurus 57 in the production aircraft and manufacturing commenced at Fairey Aviation's Hayes factory in 1946.

The Fairey Spearfish, the successor to the Barracuda, first flew on 5 July 1945, it was the largest and heaviest aeroplane ever built for aircraft carrier operations by the Royal Navy and the first British Fleet Air Arm aircraft with a power-operated gun turret controlled by the observer. Radar apparatus operated by the observer was installed for sea and air search. A spacious fuselage allowed all equipment to be stowed internally and an ejector gear could be fitted to the interior of the bomb bay to allow the missile to fall clear of the rotating propeller during dive bombing sequences. The aeroplane had multiple uses, including torpedo bombing, precision dive-bombing, reconnaissance, radar surveillance, minelaying and rocket strafing operations for which the pilot was given a broad unobstructed forward view.

The Spearfish had a crew of two and was 45 feet 4 inches in length, had a wingspan of 60 feet and stood 16 feet 6 inches tall. It was fitted with a 2,585hp Bristol Centaurus 57 two-row air-cooled radial engine that gave it a maximum speed of 301mph at 16,000 feet and a range of 900 miles at 196mph. Defensive armament comprised two .50-inch fixed forward-firing machine-guns operated by the pilot and two further machine-guns mounted in a Nash & Thomson power operated aft turret. The aircraft could also carry either one 18-inch torpedo or a bomb payload of 2,000lb. Only five Spearfish were built before victory over Japan brought an end to the Second World War. At the time plans for the Fairey Gannet were already progressing and so despite the Spearfish's successful design the British government withdrew funding and the manufacturing programme was subsequently cancelled.

The post-war era forced Fairey Aviation to diversify into a number of new areas, including rocketry and boat building to supplement its aircraft division. Immediately after the war Fairey Aviation focussed its efforts on the FB-1 Gyrodyne, the Primer trainer and the anti-submarine early warning aircraft the Fairey Gannet. The Gannet AS4 was 43 feet long, had a wingspan of 54 feet 4 inches and stood 13 feet 8 inches high. It was powered by a 3,035hp

Armstrong-Siddeley Double Mamba 101 coupled turboprop engine, with two contra-rotating four bladed propellers that gave it a top speed of 299mph at sea level and an operational ceiling of 25,000 feet. The Gannet made its maiden flight on 19 September 1949 and was ordered into production shortly afterwards. The first operational aircraft went into service with 826 Squadron in January 1955.

The Fairey Delta

Sir Charles Fairey and the Fairey Aviation Company were without doubt innovative and forward thinking, as was illustrated by the Delta 1 and Delta 2 aircraft. The Delta 1 was the first British-designed delta wing aeroplane, built as a research aircraft to develop understanding of the delta wing design and the most effective ways of controlling an aircraft travelling at transonic speeds. A 3,600lbf Rolls-Royce Derwent 8 turbojet engine was fitted that gave the Delta 1 a maximum speed of 628mph. The aircraft made its maiden flight on 10 March 1951, but poor handling and stability led the Ministry of Supply to cancel its contract for two further prototypes. Sadly, the only Delta 1 that was manufactured ended its days as a target at the Shoeburyness weapons range.

The Delta 2 was an experimental supersonic delta wing monoplane designed by Dundee-born Robert Lickley and which first flew on 6 October 1954. The Delta 2 was 51 feet 7 inches in length, had a wingspan of 26 feet 10 inches, stood 11 feet tall and was powered by a 10,250lbf Rolls-Royce Avon turbojet engine. The Delta 2 earned its place in the record books when on 10 March 1956 it became the first aircraft to reach 1,000mph and broke the world airspeed record. It achieved a top speed of 1,132mph, an increase of 300mph on the previous record.

Fairey's Rotodyne, a compound gyroplane vertical take-off airliner, made its maiden flight on 6 November 1957, but it was to become a victim of the changing times in the aviation industry. The British government felt that there was a need for consolidation and that Britain's helicopter needs would be best served if Fairey Aviation was to merge with Westland Aircraft. Westland had just acquired the Saunders-Roe group and the Bristol Aeroplane Company's helicopter division and a merger was completed in 1960.

The remainder of the many Fairey engineering, survey and marine subsidiaries continued trading as the Fairey Group, but in 1977 the company collapsed. The British government nationalized the business, acquiring all of the share capital for just over £200 million. Fairey was managed by the National Enterprise Board until 1980 when it was sold to the stoneware manufacturer Doulton & Company Limited. In 1986 Doulton sold the Fairey engineering division to Williams Holdings and a management buy-out occurred in 1988 that subsequently acquired Burnfield in 1997, Servomex plc in 1999 and Spectris AG in July 2000. In May 2001 the company changed its name from the Fairey Group to Spectris plc.

Legacies and Memorials

Fairey's significant contribution to military aviation saw the company produce a wide range of innovative aircraft that clearly demonstrates its capability as an aircraft designer and manufacturer. Its legacy goes well beyond even that of the Swordfish, Albacore and Barracuda. During the inter-war years the company produced the Flycatcher fighter that replaced the Gloster Nightjar in 1923. The Fairey Fox light bomber first flew in January 1925 and was a good 30mph faster than any contemporary RAF fighter. The Fairey Hendon night bomber was produced in 1930 and was the first low-wing monoplane bomber to be built in Britain and the first to enter service with the RAF. The Fairey Battle light bomber entered service in May 1937 and ten squadrons of the Advanced Air Striking Force were deployed with the aircraft to France on 2 September 1939. Due to poor armaments the Battle was relegated to second-line duties early in the war, but the aircraft did take part in numerous night attacks on invasion barges in German-occupied ports along the Channel. The Firefly was a two-seater naval fighter that made its maiden flight on 22 December 1941 and entered service in October 1943. The Firefly provided invaluable fighter cover during the numerous attacks on the *Tirpitz* in the summer of 1944, as well as attacks on Japanese oil refineries in Sumatra in January 1945. The Fairey Fulmar first flew on 4 January 1940 and had entered service in the Mediterranean by mid-1942. The Fulmar played an important role in the defence of the Malta convoys.

Many examples of the Fairey Aviation Company's extraordinary and diverse output can be seen around the UK and overseas. The Imperial War Museum at Duxford in Cambridgeshire has a Swordfish and a Gannet AEW3 is on display at the Gatwick Aviation Museum at Charlwood in West Sussex. The Fleet Air Arm Museum near Yeovil in Somerset has the original Delta 2, which was rebuilt by the British Aircraft Corporation and designated as BAC 221. It also has a Firefly, a Fulmar, the only remaining example of the Albacore and a Gannet AEW3. A second Delta 2 can be seen at the Royal Air Force Museum at the Defence College of Aeronautical Engineering at Albrighton in Shropshire. The Royal Navy Historic Flight based at the Royal Naval Air Station in Yeovilton is a registered charity staffed by civilians that provides aircraft for air displays. Its collection includes three Swordfish, a Mk I, Mk II and Mk III, as well as a Firefly AS5.

Sir Charles Fairey died on 30 September 1956 at the age of sixty-nine. During his lifetime his outstanding contribution to British aviation was acknowledged by his peers and recognized by his country. He was made a Member of the Order of the British Empire in 1920, served as President of the Royal Aeronautical Society in 1930 and 1932, was awarded the Sir Charles Wakefield Gold Medal by the Society in 1936 for his work on aircraft flaps and he was knighted by King George VI in June 1942. He also served as Director General of the British Air Commission in Washington during the Second World War and in 1948, in recognition of his work with aircraft research he was awarded the Presidential Medal of Freedom with silver palm by the government of the United States of America.

Chapter 15

Robert Blackburn and the Brough Buccaneers

On 24 May 1910 Robert Blackburn made a short, ill-fated flight from the sands at Marske-by-the-Sea, near Redcar on the north-east coast of England. The flight lasted for just over a minute and finished with a crash that virtually destroyed his aeroplane. The Blackburn First Monoplane was a high-wing design, which was 23 feet in length, had a wingspan of 24 feet and was 9 feet 6 inches high. It was fitted with a 35hp Green C4 engine, which used a chain to drive an 8 feet 6 inches propeller on the wing's leading edge. Blackburn's father, George Blackburn, was the General Manager at Thomas Green & Son, which manufactured a range of equipment from lawnmowers to locomotives at its Smithfield Foundry engineering works. He was able to secure space for a while at the foundry to allow Blackburn to start building his monoplane. Blackburn was assisted by Harry Goodyear, who later joined AV Roë, and the aircraft was eventually completed at a nearby clothing factory. The first flight was made after a long period of trials along the beach between Marske and Saltburn from April 1909.

Undeterred by the crash of his first aircraft, Blackburn set about the development of his second. The design was influenced by the Antoinette monoplane designed by Léon Levavasseur and was manufactured by the French Antoinette company. Blériot was with Antoinette when in 1906 they were asked to construct an aircraft for Captain Ferdinand Ferber. Blériot feared that this would create too much competition for his own business and attempted to persuade them not to get into aircraft manufacturing, but his advice was ignored and he left the company. Blackburn's second monoplane was 32 feet long, had a wingspan of 30 feet and was fitted with a 40hp Isaacson 7-cylinder radial engine. On 8 March 1911 Bentfield Charles Hucks, the noted aviator, took the monoplane out for its first flight from the beach at Filey in North Yorkshire. Hucks flew around 30 feet and reached a speed of 50mph before he crashed into the sands when he attempted his first turn. Later that year Hucks competed in the *Daily Mail* newspaper's £10,000 Round Britain air race, which in 1911 was won by Lieutenant de Vaisseau Conneau in a Blériot XI monoplane.

The Mercury monoplane two-seater trainer was designed for the Blackburn Flying School at Filey and became the first successful aircraft made by Blackburn, with a total of nine being built. The Mercury was seen by the public for the first time at the Olympia Aero Show. On 17 May 1911 it flew a return trip from Filey to Scarborough in Yorkshire in just 19 minutes, reaching a top speed of 50mph and an altitude of over 1,200 feet. The next day, however, the aircraft crashed. Two Mercury II aircraft were built with 50hp Gnôme engines and a further six Mercury III machines were manufactured. The development of his first two monoplanes and in particular the success of the Mercury gave Blackburn the confidence in June 1914 to establish the Blackburn Aeroplane and Motor Car Company.

Robert Blackburn was born on 26 March 1885 in Leeds. He attended the Leeds Modern School before graduating with an engineering degree from Leeds University in 1906. He held a passion for aviation and soon after leaving university he travelled to France to spend time mixing with and observing the leading aviation pioneers across the Channel. This experience led him to design and construct his own aircraft. Blackburn was married twice and had three children. He died in Devon at the age of seventy in September 1955. Blackburn's brother Norman became a director of the Blackburn Aeroplane and Motor Car Company in 1920 and was appointed joint managing director in 1949. He remained on the board until 1958. Norman William George Blackburn was born on 25 May 1895 in Leeds. He became Flight Sub Lieutenant Blackburn on 5 June 1915 after qualifying at the Grahame White Flying School at Hendon Aerodrome. He served with the Royal Naval Air Service during the First World War and even flew Blackburn Kangaroo bombers. By the end of the war he was appointed Acting Major at RAF Tern Hill and commanded 132 Squadron. He later returned to Leeds to re-join the company with Robert Blackburn. During the inter-war years he ran the RAF Reserve training school at Brough and taught, amongst many others, The Hon. Mrs Victor Bruce to fly. A mere eight weeks after completing her training Mrs Bruce flew around the world in a Blackburn Bluebird. Norman Blackburn died at Bridlington in Yorkshire, in January 1966.

The Blackburn Aeroplane and Motor Car Company

One of the first aircraft that was built by the newly formed Blackburn Aeroplane and Motor Car Company was the Blackburn Type L racing seaplane. It was the first biplane designed by Robert Blackburn and was intended for the 1914 *Daily Mail* £5,000 Circuit of Britain seaplane race. Only one version of this aircraft was built, but the outbreak of the First World War meant that the race was cancelled. The Type L was a two-seater that was 32 feet 6 inches long, had a wingspan of 49 feet 6 inches and stood 12 feet 6 inches tall. It was fitted with a 130hp Salmson Canton-Unné 9-cylinder water-cooled radial engine that was produced under licence by the Dudbridge Iron Works Ltd, Stroud, in

Gloucestershire. The engine gave the aircraft a maximum speed of 81mph, a range of 445 miles and an operational ceiling of 11,000 feet. The Type L was built at the company's Olympia Works in Leeds, which was a former skating rink. The aircraft was based at Scalby Mills near Scarborough during the First World War and performed off-shore reconnaissance duties. The Type L crashed in 1915 near the cliffs at Speeton, just south of Filey, Yorkshire.

In 1916 the company built a new factory at Brough in Yorkshire, which became the main production facility and allowed the business to flourish, particularly during the First World War. The plant was located a few miles west of Hull and near the shore of the Humber Estuary, which enabled the company to develop seaplanes more easily. The main aircraft built by Blackburn during the First World War was the Blackburn Kangaroo, a twin-engined land-based biplane that had initially been designed as the Blackburn GP (General Purpose) floatplane. This design was not accepted by the Air Ministry and so Blackburn re-engineered it into the Kangaroo and the first machine was delivered to Martlesham Heath for evaluation in January 1918. However, the results were disappointing and consequently the initial order was reduced and only twenty-four were produced. The first of the Kangaroos entered service on 1 May that year and ten were issued to No. 246 Squadron at Seaton Carew on the Durham coast.

The Blackburn Kangaroo was one of the last heavy bombers built in Britain during the First World War. It was 46 feet long, had a wingspan of 74 feet 10 inches and stood 16 feet 10 inches tall. It was fitted with two 255hp Rolls-Royce Falcon II liquid-cooled V-12 engines that gave it a maximum speed of 100mph at 6,500 feet and an operational ceiling of 10,500 feet. It was armed with two .303-inch Lewis machine-guns and had a 1,000lb bomb payload. The Kangaroo did see active service during the First World War with the Royal Naval Air Service, where it performed anti-submarine duties over the North Sea. After the war three of the remaining machines were sold by the RAF to the Grahame White Aviation Company at Hendon Aerodrome and eight were sold back to Blackburn. On 30 September 1919 the North Sea Aerial Navigation Company, also based at Brough Aerodrome, used three Kangaroo aircraft to begin regular passenger services between Roundhay Park in Leeds and Hounslow Heath in London, around two miles east of today's Heathrow Airport. The following year the company became the North Sea Aerial & General Transport Company and began regular services to Amsterdam. The Kangaroo was also used by this company from 1924 to provide refresher training for the RAF and in 1929 the last machine was finally retired.

The Inter-war Years
The Blackburn Aeroplane and Motor Car Company continued to develop strong military aircraft designs during the inter-war years, which included the Blackburn Dart, a single-seater carrier-based torpedo bomber biplane that was

introduced in 1923 and served with the Royal Navy's Fleet Air Arm until 1933. Initially the design was intended as a replacement for the Sopwith Cuckoo and was developed by Blackburn as a private venture. Blackburn's chief designer, Major Frank Arnold Bumpus, was responsible for the aircraft's design, which was named the T1 Swift and included staggered wings that could fold back to enable easier storage on-board an aircraft carrier. The prototype made its maiden flight in September 1920 and following some changes to the design led to three machines being ordered by the Admiralty for further evaluation, which became named the Blackburn Dart.

The Blackburn Dart was 35 feet 4 inches long, had a wingspan of 45 feet 6 inches and stood 12 feet 11 inches tall. It was fitted with a 450hp Napier Lion IIB 12-cylinder engine, which gave the Dart a maximum speed of 107mph, a range of 285 miles and an operational ceiling of 12,700 feet. The machine was armed with one 1,650 lb torpedo. A version of the Dart, which retained the Swift name, was sold to naval air forces abroad. The Japanese Navy bought two of the machines, the Spanish bought three and a further two were sold to the United States Navy for evaluation. The Dart served with the Fleet Air Arm aboard HMS *Eagle* and HMS *Courageous* in the Mediterranean, on-board HMS *Furious* around the British Isles and a single aircraft was stationed with the RAF's 36 Squadron Coastal Defence Torpedo Flight. On 6 May 1926 Canadian born Air Commodore GH Boyce performed the first night deck-landing after safely bringing his Blackburn Dart down onto the floodlit deck of HMS *Furious*.

A version of the Dart, the Blackburn Velos, was developed for the Greek Navy. It was a two-seater twin-float seaplane that flew for the first time in 1925 and the first four machines were built at Brough Aerodrome. The Velos became the first Greek licence-built aircraft that was constructed in a factory developed by Blackburn at Phaleron, near Athens, which later became the Greek National Aircraft Factory. The Velos was retired from service by the Greek Navy in 1936.

The Blackburn Bluebird was a twin-seater biplane trainer and tourer that had a side-by-side seating arrangement and folding wings. It was intended as a competitor in the 1924 Lympne light aircraft trials but was not completed in time. The Bluebird won the Grosvenor Cup air race in 1926 and, with the interest in the machine that followed, the aircraft went into production and a total of twenty were built. The Bluebird design was developed further in 1929 and eventually became the all-metal Blackburn Bluebird IV. The aircraft was 23 feet 2 inches long, had a wingspan of 30 feet and was 9 feet high. It was fitted with a 100hp de Havilland Gipsy I 4-cylinder inline engine, which gave the aircraft a maximum speed of 120mph and a range of 320 miles. The first Bluebird IV flew from England to South Africa in 1929. It took off from Croydon Aerodrome on 7 March and arrived in Durban on 15 April. A total of 58 aircraft were built, with 55 machines constructed by Saunders-Roe, with the wings manufactured by Boulton & Paul Aircraft Limited.

Blackburn's attempt at developing a long-range maritime patrol flying boat was less successful. In 1927 the Air Ministry had issued Specification R5/27 and in response Blackburn proposed the Sydney, which flew for the first time on 18 July 1930. The aircraft was 65 feet 7 inches long, had a wingspan of 100 feet and stood 20 feet 4 inches tall. It was fitted with three 525hp Rolls-Royce F XII MS engines that gave it a maximum speed of 123mph, an endurance of 7 hours 30 minutes and an operational ceiling of 16,500 feet. The design was not accepted by the Ministry and no further machines were built. A cargo version, known as the Nile, which had been in development at the same time, was also cancelled.

On 20 May 1929 the Blackburn Aeroplane and Motor Car Company established the Blackburn Aircraft Corporation in Detroit, Michigan, in the United States of America. The new company's objective was to acquire the North and South American design and patent rights of the British company. This included some rights in Canada, but excluded Brazil. The new company would purchase all tools and patterns from the British company at cost price. This venture was owned by the Detroit Aircraft Corporation, which held 90 per cent of the capital and Blackburn, which owned the remaining 10 per cent. The Detroit Aircraft Corporation was established on 10 July 1922 as the Aircraft Development Corporation. The corporation owned the Ryan Aircraft Corp., Aircraft Development Corp., Aviation Tool Co., Grosse Airport, Inc., Marine Aircraft Corp., Park's Air College and Affiliated Companies, Detroit Aircraft Export Co., Gliders, Inc., Eastman Aircraft Corp. and almost all of the Lockheed Aircraft Company. On 27 October 1931 the Detroit Aircraft Corporation was driven into receivership by the Great Depression.

Blackburn expanded into the manufacture of aero engines with the acquisition of Cirrus Hermes in 1934 and immediately introduced the Blackburn Cirrus range. Cirrus Aero Engines Limited was established in 1927 and became Cirrus Hermes four years later in 1931, when it was bought by the Cirrus Hermes Engineering Company. The Blackburn Cirrus division traded independently from the main company and remained in operation until the late 1950s.

The Blackburn Ripon was a more successful aircraft for the company. It operated with the Fleet Air Arm as a torpedo bomber, as well as with the Finnish Air Force, where it saw active service as a reconnaissance aircraft during both the Winter and Continuation Wars between Finland and the Soviet Union. The Ripon was developed from the Dart and first flew on 17 April 1926. The aircraft entered service in 1929 and production continued until 1933. In all, Blackburn built ninety-one examples of the Ripon, which was later superseded by the Blackburn Baffin. The Fleet Air Arm 811 Naval Air Squadron was the last to operate Ripons and decommissioned its aircraft as the new Baffins arrived in January 1935. The Finnish Air Force retired its last Ripons in 1944. The Blackburn Baffin was designed by Major Frank Bumpus; it first flew on 30 September 1932 and entered service two years later in 1934. The Baffin was a twin-seater biplane torpedo bomber that was 38 feet 3¾ inches long, had a wingspan of 44 feet 6 inches and stood 12 feet 10 inches high. The design differed from the Ripon by being fitted with a 565hp Bristol Pegasus IM3 9-cylinder radial engine, replacing the Napier engine. The Baffin had a maximum speed of 136mph at 6,500 feet, a range of 540 miles, an endurance of 4 hours 30 minutes and an operational ceiling of 15,000 feet. It was armed with a fixed forward-firing .303-inch Vickers machine-gun, a .303-inch Lewis machine-gun in the rear cockpit and carried either one 18-inch torpedo or a 2,000lb bomb payload. The Baffin was in service for two years before it too was superseded, in this case by the Blackburn Shark and the Fairey Swordfish. The Royal New Zealand Air Force bought twenty-nine Baffins for its Territorial Air Force reserve squadrons based in Auckland, Wellington and Christchurch. With the outbreak of the Second World War twenty-four of these aircraft were still in service as trainers and in March 1940 were deployed with the NZ General Reconnaissance Squadron. They were later retired in 1941, before the attack on Pearl Harbor.

In all, Blackburn manufactured 269 of the Shark carrier-borne torpedo bomber reconnaissance aircraft, which saw service with the Fleet Air Arm and the Royal Canadian Air Force from 1934 until 1945. However, the pace of aircraft development in the late 1930s meant that the Shark also quickly became obsolete and was replaced by the Fairey Swordfish in 1937. The Swordfish itself was also lagging behind and by the time the Second World War was declared in 1939 it too was obsolete. However, that did not stop it achieving a great deal of success during the war, not only against the Italian fleet at Taranto Harbour, but also when it delivered the decisive torpedoes against the *Bismarck* in May 1941.

The Shark Mk III had a crew of two, was 35 feet 2 inches long, had a wingspan of 46 feet and stood 12 feet 1 inch tall. It was equipped with a 760hp Armstrong-Siddeley Tiger VI 14-cylinder radial engine that gave it a maximum speed of 152mph, a range of 625 miles and an operational ceiling of 16,400 feet. It was armed with a forward-firing .303-inch Vickers machine-gun and either a .303-inch Vickers K machine-gun or a Lewis machine-gun. It could carry either one Mk VIII or Mk X 18-inch torpedo or a 1,576lb bomb payload. The prototype Blackburn B6 first flew on 24 August 1933 when it took off from Brough Aerodrome. In August 1934 the aircraft successfully completed deck-landing trials and the Fleet Air Arm placed its first order. The Shark entered service with the Fleet Air Arm 820 Naval Air Squadron in May 1935, where it replaced the Fairey Seal carrier-borne spotter-reconnaissance aircraft. The Royal Canadian Air Force kept a number of Blackburn Sharks in service as late as 1944.

The Gathering Storm

By 1939 the company had simplified its name to Blackburn Aircraft Limited. During this time in the run-up to the outbreak of the Second World War Blackburn had developed the Skua that combined the roles of a dive-bomber and a fighter. It was an all-metal duralumin, low wing, two-seater, carrier-borne aircraft that was designed by Blackburn's GE Petty. The Skua was the Fleet Air

Arm's first monoplane and had an enclosed cockpit, unlike the Swordfish biplane torpedo bomber. The Skua first flew on 9 February 1937 and was introduced into service with the Fleet Air Arm in November 1938. A total of 192 Skuas were delivered. The aircraft was 35 feet 7 inches long, had a wingspan of 46 feet 2 inches and stood 12 feet 6 inches high. It was fitted with an 890hp Bristol Perseus XII 9-cylinder radial engine that gave it a maximum speed of 225mph at 6,500 feet, which compared unfavourably with the 290mph that could be achieved by the Messerschmitt Bf 109. The Skua had a range of 758 miles and could operate at a ceiling of 19,100 feet. The machine was armed with five .303-inch forward-firing Browning machine-guns and could carry up to a 740lb bomb payload.

The Skua is believed to be the first British aircraft to have brought down an enemy aeroplane in the Second World War, when three Skuas of 803 Naval Air Squadron from HMS *Ark Royal* attacked a Dornier Do 18 on 26 September 1939 over the North Sea. On 10 April 1940 Lieutenant Commander William Lucy led sixteen Skuas from 800 and 803 Naval Air Squadrons based at RNAS Hatston in the Orkney Islands in an attack that sank the German cruiser *Königsberg* in Bergen Harbour. On 15 June 1940 a further fifteen Skuas attempted to sink the German battleship *Scharnhorst* at Trondheim in Norway. Eight of the aircraft were shot down.

The Skua was withdrawn from front-line active duties in 1941 due to the heavy losses the aircraft experienced, especially at the hands of the faster and more manoeuvrable German fighters. It was replaced by the Fairey Fulmar, which could achieve a further 50mph. The Skua was relegated to advanced trainer duties and was finally retired in March 1945.

The Blackburn Roc was designed by Boulton & Paul Aircraft Limited and was derived from the Skua. The primary difference consisted of a powered dorsal turret, which housed four .303-inch Browning machine-guns. The aircraft could also carry eight 30lb bombs. The Roc first flew on 23 December 1938 and was introduced into service in April 1939. In all, some 136 were built. The aircraft served primarily in 1940 at Scapa Flow in Scotland to protect the fleet; they also flew from HMS *Glorious* and HMS *Ark Royal* during the Norwegian Campaign. They also performed air support duties during the evacuation of Allied troops from Dunkirk between 27 May and 4 June 1940 as part of Operation *Dynamo* and with further evacuations from northern French ports during Operation *Aerial* between 15 and 25 June 1940.

Blackburn's chief seaplane designer in 1940 was Major JD Rennie, who developed an experimental flying boat that used a large float under the main fuselage and two smaller floats under the wings for stability. When in flight the main float would retract into the fuselage to create a more streamlined machine. The wing floats folded outwards to form wing tips. The Blackburn B20 was unsuccessfully put forward in response to the Air Ministry's Specification R1/36. The Ministry selected the Saunders-Roe Lerwick to go into production, but was sufficiently interested in the B20 concept to commission a prototype to be built. The B20 first flew on 26 March 1940, but twelve days later on 7 April, while on a test flight, the aircraft crashed. The crew were able to bale out but three were killed and the remaining two were picked up by HMS *Transylvania*. Development work on the B20 was then stopped.

The Blackburn Firebrand single-engined fighter designed by GE Petty first flew on 27 February 1942. The Fleet Air Arm was already equipped with the Supermarine Seafire variant of the Spitfire as a carrier-borne fighter and so the Firebrand was envisaged as a torpedo bomber. The Firebrand TF Mk II was redesigned to allow for a torpedo to be carried and this variant first flew on 31 March 1943. However, only twelve machines were built. The Mk III flew for the first time on 21 December 1943, but technical problems meant that it was deemed unsuitable for aircraft carrier duties. The Mk IV incorporated new design features and a newer Centaurus IX engine. This version first flew on 17 May 1945 and was the first to go into mass production. The Mk IV entered service in September 1945 with 813 Squadron. The Mk V was 38 feet 11 inches long, had a wingspan of 51 feet 3 inches and stood 14 feet 11 inches tall. It was fitted with a 2,500hp Bristol Centaurus IX 18-cylinder radial engine, which gave the aircraft a maximum speed of 350mph, and a range of 746 miles. It was armed with four 20mm Hispano Mk II cannon, and could carry either one 18-inch 1,850lb torpedo or two 1,000lb bombs. A total of 225 Firebrands were built.

By the time the Firebrand had gone into significant production it was too late for the aircraft to see active service during the Second World War. However, the Firebrand did remain in service with the Royal Navy's Fleet Air Arm until 1953 and spawned a new variant, the Blackburn Firecrest.

The Post-war Era

The Blackburn Firecrest was a single-engined naval fighter that first flew on 1 April 1947. Three prototypes had been ordered by the Air Ministry, but by the time that the first of these had made its maiden flight the Ministry had decided that the Westland Wyvern would be selected to meet its requirement for a strike fighter. The second prototype never flew, but the third did fly in early 1948. The results of the test flights were disappointing. The pilot reported that the Firecrest was more sluggish and less manoeuvrable than the Firebrand. The pilot sat behind the wing's trailing edge and with the aircraft's long nose the visibility was rather inadequate, particularly for carrier operations. The two flying prototypes were sold back to Blackburn in 1950 and were subsequently scrapped.

At around the same time Blackburn produced the B54 and B88 carrier-borne anti-submarine monoplane aircraft. The design was intended for deployment with the Fleet Air Arm and was created in response to the Air Ministry's specification GR17/45. Again Blackburn would lose out to Fairey, whose design for the Gannet was eventually accepted. The primary difference between the two

Blackburn designs was that the B54 had a conventional piston engine, while the B88 was powered by a gas turbine motor driving a contra rotating propeller. The aircraft was a two-seater, with the pilot and observer sitting one behind the other. It made its maiden flight on 20 September 1949. The Admiralty added radar apparatus and an operator to its requirements in 1950, which led to a redesign and the development of the B54 version that first flew on 3 May 1950, with a Rolls-Royce Griffon 56 piston engine powering a contra rotating propeller. The B88 flew for the first time two months later on 19 July 1950 and was fitted with an Armstrong-Siddeley Double Mamba engine. The Fairey Gannet also had a Double Mamba engine and had completed landing trials by the time the B88 made its maiden flight. As a result the Ministry lost interest in the Blackburn designs. The B88 was 42 feet 8 inches long, had a wingspan of 44 feet 2 inches and stood 16 feet 9 inches tall. The 2,950hp Armstrong-Siddeley Double Mamba ASMD 1 turboprop engine gave it a top speed of 320mph. In all, only three aircraft were built and the project was cancelled in 1950.

Blackburn Aircraft Limited, like many other aircraft manufacturers, struggled to find new contracts in the years that immediately followed the Second World War. The company took on a wide range of work, including making bread tins for Jackson's Bakeries in Hull. In 1949 Blackburn amalgamated with General Aircraft Limited and became Blackburn and General Limited. General Aircraft Limited was founded on 27 February 1931 by the Swiss engineer Helmut J Stieger to manufacture aircraft with the monospar wing design that Stieger had invented and produced through his other business the Mono-spar Company Limited based at Croydon Aerodrome. In October 1934 the investment group British Pacific Trust financed the merger of General Aircraft and Mono-spar, along with the assets of National Flying Services Limited that owned London Air Park and the premises built in 1917 by Whitehead Aircraft Limited. During the late 1930s General Aircraft was busy constructing aircraft as a sub-contractor for other manufacturers, including Hawker. It was also part of the wartime Civilian Repair Organization and designed a number of gliders. After the war the company diversified in an effort to maintain its business and manufactured pre-fabricated houses and automobile bodies. At this time General Aircraft had developed the GAL 60 Universal freighter aircraft, but did not have the production capacity to manufacture the machine in quantity. General Aircraft approached Blackburn, which was anxiously looking for new contracts to keep its plant running at Brough in Yorkshire. This approach led to the two companies merging on 1 January 1949. The GAL 60 was moved to Brough and soon became the Blackburn Beverley.

The Blackburn Beverley was a four-engine, heavy transport, high-wing cantilever monoplane that served with Royal Air Force Transport Command for more than ten years from April 1956. The aircraft had a crew of six and could carry up to 94 fully equipped troops or a payload of 45,000 lb. The Beverley was 99 feet 5 inches long, had a wingspan of 162 feet and stood 38 feet 9 inches tall.

It was fitted with four 2,850hp Bristol Centaurus 273 18-cylinder radial engines that gave the aircraft a maximum speed of 238mph at 5,700 feet and a cruise speed of 273mph at 8,000 feet. It had a range of 1,300 miles and an operational ceiling of 16,000 feet. The internal cargo space was around 6,000 cubic feet, which made it the largest aircraft in the RAF when it was introduced. The Beverley was noted for its short take-off and landing lengths that were achieved by the use of the Bristol Centaurus engines with reverse pitch propellers. The aircraft could take off with a standard payload within 790 yards and could land within 310 yards. The Beverley was intended as a bulk freighter capable of landing on difficult uneven runways.

The prototype first flew on 20 June 1950 and the RAF placed its initial order for twenty aircraft in 1952. In all, forty-nine aircraft were manufactured and the last one rolled off the production line in 1958. The first aircraft in operational service were delivered to 47 Squadron based at RAF Abingdon on 12 March 1956. RAF 84 Squadron based at RAF Khormaksar in Aden flew Beverleys between 1958 and August 1967, when Hawker Siddeley Andovers were introduced.

The Blackburn Buccaneer

The last major aircraft to be developed and manufactured by Blackburn was its most successful. It came at the end of its history as an independent aircraft manufacturer. The Blackburn Buccaneer was a low-level nuclear and conventional strike aircraft that served with the RAF and the Fleet Air Arm from 17 July 1962 until it was retired in 1994. The Buccaneer first flew on 30 April 1958, just two years before the company was absorbed into the Hawker Siddeley Group. The aircraft was introduced two years later and although it was initially called the Blackburn Buccaneer, a reorganization within Hawker Siddeley meant that the Blackburn name was dropped in 1962 and the aircraft became the Hawker Siddeley Buccaneer. The aircraft saw action during the Gulf War in 1991, when 12 machines flew a total of 218 missions. The Buccaneer was retired in March 1994 when RAF 208 Squadron was disbanded.

In August 1952 the Ministry of Supply issued specification M148T, which sought a new two-seater aircraft that was able to reach a maximum speed of Mach 0.85 at 200 feet, had a range of 460 miles and was capable of deploying a nuclear weapon. Blackburn's designer Barry P Laight produced the B103 design for the Buccaneer, which was eventually chosen by the Ministry. The Buccaneer S2 was a mid-wing twin-engine monoplane that had a crew of two, the pilot and the observer. The aircraft was 63 feet 5 inches long, had a wingspan of 44 feet and stood 16 feet 3 inches high. It was equipped with two 11,255lbf Rolls-Royce Spey 101 turbofans, which gave it a maximum speed of 667mph at 200 feet, a range of 2,300 miles and an operational ceiling of 40,000 feet. The Buccaneer had four underwing pylon stations and one rotating bomb bay that could carry 12,000lb of incendiaries and four Matra rocket pods with eighteen SNEB 68 mm rockets in each, two AIM 9 Sidewinder missiles, two AS–30L missiles, two AS–37 Martel missiles or two Sea Eagle missiles. The Buccaneer was approved for nuclear operations and could carry either Red Beard or WE177 drop-bombs that were stowed in the rotating internal bomb bay.

The Fleet Air Arm was the first to take delivery of the new Buccaneers, receiving its machines in 1962. They served with Naval Air Squadrons 800, 801, 803 and 809, with Squadron 700B/Z of the Intensive Flying Units Trial, 736 Training Squadron as well as on-board HMS *Victorious*, HMS *Eagle*, HMS *Ark Royal* and HMS *Hermes*. Buccaneers from RNAS Lossiemouth bombed the wrecked tanker *Torrey Canyon* on 28 March 1967 in an effort to destroy the ship's crude oil before it could invoke a major environmental disaster. When HMS *Ark Royal* was decommissioned in 1978 the Buccaneer was also retired from the Fleet Air Arm.

In 1969 12 Squadron based at RAF Honington was the first RAF unit to receive Buccaneers, which were later supplemented by the Fleet Air Arm's decommissioned aircraft in the late 1970s. In all, six squadrons operated the aircraft, with five assigned to Supreme Allied Commander Europe in order to support Allied land forces against the Warsaw Pact land forces that were stationed on the Continent and a further squadron allocated to maritime strike duties under the Supreme Allied Commander Atlantic. By 1983 the Tornado was being introduced and was used to take up the land strike duties that had previously been the preserve of the Buccaneer. The Buccaneer was finally stood down in 1994.

With the consolidation of the aircraft industry in 1960 Blackburn Aircraft was taken over by Hawker Siddeley and became a division of the new Hawker Siddeley Group. The companies within the group had been allowed to continue to use their original names with their new aircraft, but by 1963 Hawker Siddeley had decided to use the initials 'HS' as part of all new aircraft designations and the Blackburn name, like many others, was dropped.

Bristol Siddeley Engines Limited was formed in 1959 when Bristol Aero-Engines Limited and Armstrong-Siddeley Motors Limited were merged. In 1961 the de Havilland Engine Company and the Blackburn Cirrus division of Blackburn Aircraft were also merged into the company. Bristol Siddeley Engines was acquired by Rolls-Royce Limited in 1966.

Today Blackburn aircraft can be seen in both static and airworthy condition at numerous aviation museums across the UK and around the world. The Shuttleworth Collection at Old Warden Aerodrome in Bedfordshire has a replica 1912 Blackburn monoplane Type D, the RAF Museum in Hendon has a Buccaneer S1 and the Fleet Air Arm Museum in Yeovilton also has a Buccaneer S1 on display. A blue plaque can be found on the site of the original Blackburn plant in Roundhay Road, in Leeds, which in 2012 was the location of a supermarket.

Chapter 16

Robert Watson-Watt and the
Prowlers of the Night Sky

With the air war over Britain during the Second World War bringing regular daytime attacks, the need for early warning so as to scramble Britain's air defences was critical. In the early part of the war Britain had developed a chain of radar stations along the English coast to listen for enemy aircraft as they approached far out to sea. Whilst daytime raids took place Britain's scrambled air defences could see their quarry and were able to quickly engage the enemy. However, when German tactics changed and regular night-time raids became the norm, early warning of their arrival was not enough and in the dark the country was blind. In 1940 airborne radar sets were installed to numerous aircraft that became the prowlers of the night sky and once again Britain was able to take the fight to the enemy.

It was James Maxwell, the British physicist, who started a train of thought that would ultimately lead to the development of radar. In 1864 Maxwell laid down a series of mathematical equations related to the behaviour of electromagnetic waves. These equations deal with the laws of radio wave reflection and the principles behind them were demonstrated by the German physicist Heinrich Hertz in 1886. The German engineer Christian Huelsmeyer put forward the concept of using the echoes generated by radio waves to assist with marine navigation. In 1924 the British physicist Sir Edward Victor Appleton measured the height of the earth's ionosphere in the world's first demonstration of range finding with the use of radio waves. But it was Robert Watson-Watt who in 1935 developed the first workable radar system.

Watson-Watt was born in Brechin, Angus, Scotland, on 13 April 1892 and was descended from James Watt, who is credited as the inventor of the steam engine and as the person who introduced the principle of horse power as a measure of motive power. He graduated in 1912 with a degree in engineering from the University of St Andrews, which later became University College, Dundee. Professor William Peddie offered him an assistantship and encouraged him to study wireless telegraphy.

In 1934 the Air Ministry had set up a special committee, chaired by Sir Henry Tizard, to explore ways to improve Britain's air defences, in particular against enemy bombing missions. The following year, on 12 February 1935, Watson-Watt approached the Air Ministry with proposals for his radio detecting and ranging system. Sir Henry was impressed with his ideas and asked for a demonstration, which took place on 26 February 1935 in a farmer's field in the small Northamptonshire village of Stowe Nine Churches, around seven miles south-east of Daventry. During the test Watson-Watt and John Knowles Wilkins proved that radar could work when they detected an old Handley Page bomber as it approached at a distance of eight miles.

On 2 April 1935 Watson-Watt was granted a patent for a radio device for detecting and locating aircraft. The Air Ministry then appointed him head of its Bawdsey Research Station at Bawdsey Manor near Felixstowe in Suffolk. It was work carried out at this establishment that by 1939 led to the creation of a network of aircraft early warning detection stations along the east and south coast of England called Chain Home. Three stations had been built by 1937 and following a series of tests the government ordered a further seventeen stations to be built. Over fifty radar stations were in use by the end of the Second World War.

The Air Ministry had rightly predicted that enemy bombing raids might well switch from daytime to night-time, making it difficult for Britain's defensive fighter forces to intercept and counter the attacks. The Welsh physicist Edward Bowen, a member of Watson-Watt's team at the Radio Research Station, developed a radar system that could be installed and used in a fighter. The problem faced by Bowen was how to overcome the size and weight of the equipment needed to make the system work. The requirement was for a radar system that could detect both ships at sea and aircraft in flight. In September 1937 Bowen demonstrated his new system unofficially when he sought out British ships in the North Sea during poor visibility and managed to detect three vessels. As a result an airborne interception (AI) system was made available in 1940 and an air-to-surface vessel (ASV) system was introduced shortly afterwards.

The Start of the Air War

For the first time since 1918 British bombers crossed the German frontier in September 1939 on offensive operations to attack the warships of the *Kriegsmarine* in the north German ports and the 'phoney war' started when the British Expeditionary Force sailed for France. Shortly afterwards, German forces occupied Norway and the British forces were compelled to withdraw. In April 1940 Holland was similarly attacked and occupied. During the early part of May 1940 German forces smashed through the French defences of the Ardennes, between Namur and Montmédy, to make a wide sweep towards the Channel ports and the estuary of the River Somme. In the north General von

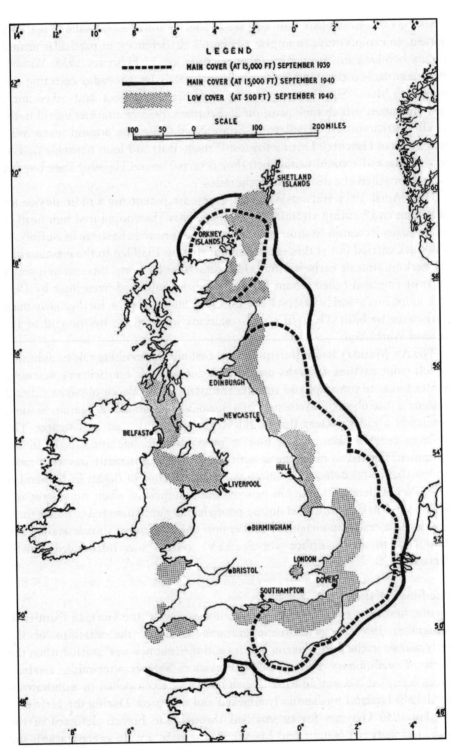

Chain Home radar coverage, 1939–1940.

Bock with Army Group B, supported by *Luftflotte* 3, commanded by *Generaloberst* Sperrle, attacked westward with General Putzier leading the transport planes of *Fliegerkorps z.b.V*. A total of 126 German divisions with 10 Panzer divisions, 2,700 vehicles and 4,050 aircraft rapidly moved into France and Belgium, outflanking the French fortified Maginot Line. With the Panzer divisions and Stuka dive-bombers welded as a single weapon they thrust deep through the Allied armies; with intensive and continued *Luftwaffe* reconnaissance operations over Britain and France, and the forward German units supplied by aerial transports, the French General Staff became operationally paralysed. French resistance soon collapsed and the British forces gradually disintegrated as severely mauled regiments retreated under the constant pressure and speed of the German *Blitzkrieg*. By 25 and 26 May 1940 the Panzer divisions had reached the Atlantic coast. The remnants of the British Expeditionary Force had lost all of their equipment. By 6 June 1940 they had been evacuated from Dunkerque and by 22 June 1940 the French Premier Marshal Pétain had surrendered to the Germans. France had fallen and Britain was on the verge of invasion and conquest.

By early 1940, despite an integrated air defence system, with squadrons of single-engined interceptor aircraft and a chain of aerial control and reporting radar stations, the RAF recognized that it needed a twin-engined escort night fighter. Originally, the Air Ministry had issued specification F37/35 for the design of a twin-engined fighter subsequently named the Westland Whirlwind Mk I, which made its maiden flight on 11 October 1938. The Mk IA long-range fighter-bomber had a wing span of 45 feet, a length of 32 feet 3 inches, stood 10 feet 6 inches tall and was powered by two 765hp Rolls-Royce Peregrine V-12 liquid-cooled engines. Armed with the unprecedented armament of four 20mm Hispano I cannons, the new machine had a rate of climb of 3,000 feet per minute, an operational ceiling of 30,000 feet and a top speed of 360mph. However, the aircraft was bedevilled by engine problems. Rolls-Royce had developed the Peregrine from the Kestrel aircraft engine and a long period ensued before final changes were incorporated to free the motors from frequent breakdowns. Fowler flaps were installed, whilst the landing speed of 80mph was too high and precluded its use at grass field aerodromes. Nevertheless, the Air Ministry ordered 200 and deliveries started in June 1940, but of the original 200 ordered only 112 were built.

At the time of the French military collapse on 22 June 1940 the only other British twin-engined fighter available for service was the Bristol Blenheim IF. This machine had originally been conceived in 1934 for newspaper magnate Lord Rothermere as a high-speed executive twin-engined plane capable of carrying a pilot and six passengers at a speed of 240mph. The Bristol Aeroplane Company, under the direction of the chief designer Captain Frank Barnwell, produced the prototype Bristol Type 142 as a twin-engined monoplane with flaps, a retractable undercarriage and stressed skinned covering. It achieved a top speed of 307mph, much to the surprise of the Bristol engineers and the Air Ministry, who requested the design to be re-engineered for service use. The new Blenheim Mk I emerged as a twin-engined mid-winged monoplane bomber with a redesigned fuselage, a bomb bay beneath the mid wing, a glazed nose that housed a pilot and either a navigator or an observer seated side by side and was armed with a rotating Bristol type gun turret located in the mid upper fuselage. Two hundred of the earlier models were converted to the Mk I NF night fighter configuration when a ventral gun pack containing four rifle-calibre Browning machine-guns was added. Some models were fitted with the AI Mk III airborne radar sets and became the first operational twin-engined radar equipped night fighter planes in the world. Once France had accepted Germany's surrender terms Britain stood alone, waiting for the next phase of the air war to begin.

Adler Tag

Between 25 June and 17 July 1940 the *Luftwaffe* had withdrawn from operations, refitted and rested to be re-organized in strategic locations situated between Hamburg in north Germany and Brest in northern France. Some minor aerial attacks had been made on British ports and the centres of aircraft production, and limited minelaying activities had been undertaken at ports and estuaries around the coast. The *Luftwaffe* was assigned to prepare for the invasion of Britain by destroying the RAF and its ground installations, as well as destroying ports and shipping so as to deny Britain the war supplies that came in from America and the Empire. The forces assigned to these tasks were *Luftflotte* 2, which attacked targets in southern and eastern England, *Luftflotte* 3, which attacked targets in southern and western England and *Luftflotte* 5, which was based in Norway and targeted ports and cities in northern England and Scotland. Some 2,600 German aircraft were assembled to complete the task of eliminating the RAF and to pave the way for the final invasion of Britain. Among the aircraft were 1,480 long-range bombers and dive-bombers, 980 single and twin-engined fighter planes and 140 reconnaissance aircraft. By 17 July 1940 the air armada was organized and on full standby ready to commence offensive operations on 10 August 1940, codenamed *Adler Tag* (Eagle Day). Three days previously the *Luftwaffe* commanders, intelligence chiefs and the fighter leaders had been advised that an organizational link existed between the RAF fighter squadrons and the chain of radar stations around the British coast. *Adler Tag* dawned shrouded in bad weather that curtailed aerial operations, although the Stukas from *Fliegerkorps* VIII had operated successfully and had attacked shipping in the English Channel. Long-range bombers had attacked ports and shipping in the North Sea during the last two weeks of July and had occasionally bombed some airfields. On 13 August 1940 the day broke with fine sunny cloudless skies, the major battle was about to begin!

   Adler Tag witnessed the airfields of the RAF being attacked over the entire South of England by 485 German bombers and 1,000 fighters from *Luftflotte* 2 and 3. Newcastle was bombed by *Luftflotte* 5 and subsequent raids were conducted by both day and night against ports, shipping, airfields and aircraft factories. By day spectacular air battles took place over southern England between the massed German planes and the radar directed Spitfires and Hurricanes. As losses of bomber air crews and machines mounted the *Luftwaffe* realized that a different enemy had been encountered. By 19 August 1940 bad weather had closed in once again and did not clear until 23 August when mass bomber attacks were resumed against RAF airfields, ground installations, aluminium works and centres of aircraft production. Once again the *Luftwaffe* found British radar directed Spitfires and Hurricanes waiting. The RAF fighters were more manoeuvrable than the German Messerschmitt Bf 109Es, which were withdrawn to the London area at the extreme range and limit of their combat time. Thus the lightly armed German bombers became a hunted prey and losses rose. The Messerschmitt dive-bombers were found to be virtually defenceless against modern fighters and were withdrawn. The remaining 220 Stukas of the original 280 were withdrawn to the Pas de Calais region of northern France to await the final assault. By 31 August 1940 the *Luftwaffe* had lost 880 bombers and fighters during air operations in that month alone. The *Luftwaffe* was behind schedule in the destruction of the RAF, which originally was expected to take just four days. Due to the deterioration in the course of the air war and mounting losses a *Luftwaffe* staff conference was arranged to take place in The Hague, Holland, between officers commanding the *Luftflotten* and *Reichsmarschall* Göring, chief of the *Luftwaffe*. A serious difference of opinion existed among the senior officers as to their future strategy. Faulty intelligence had failed to inform the German commanders of the serious loss of qualified RAF pilots, which was a critical problem for the British. The situation rapidly changed when a directive issued by the *Führer* ordered the reprisal bombing of London and other British cities.

Blitz

The second phase of the air war opened on 7 September 1940, when 372 German bombers, with fighter escorts, attacked the East End docks of London and started major fires among the warehouses. These aerial attacks continued by night and day throughout the month with 220 bombers on 9 September and then a further 123 by day and 233 by night on the 15 September. Once again German losses were heavy, with 298 German bombers and fighters shot down between 7 and 15 September. Again serious differences of opinion arose among the German commanders regarding the Messerschmitt Bf 109E and battle tactics over southern England. Finally, *Reichsmarschall* Göring ordered the German fighters to close escort the bombers. This decision wasted all the tactical fighter lessons acquired during the Spanish Civil War, during the Polish campaign and the air war over France. The German fighter pilots were unable to exploit any tactical advantage that presented itself during the air war over England. The

RAF had destroyed 1,178 German aircraft and serviceability problems among the *Luftwaffe* bomber squadrons further reduced the number of operational aircraft for air attacks, which had recommenced on 27 September 1940.

By the end of September 1940 small groups of *Luftwaffe* bombers, heavily escorted by fighter planes, attacked targets in south-east England in place of the flights of mass formations of long-range bombers. Bad weather in early October 1940 caused the *Luftwaffe* to cease operations and to temporarily cancel further daylight attacks. The battle over southern England had been lost to the RAF. With the lull caused by the weather the future strategy and tactics to be used by the *Luftwaffe* against England were changed again. In an attempt to cut the heavy German bomber losses *Reichsmarschall* Göring ordered a further change that dramatically increased the number of night-time attacks on London and other principal cities. Previously, the *Luftwaffe* had conducted limited night-time raids on numerous occasions that utilized the moonlight and in some instances the raids were supported by radio beam navigation. This change in policy required the RAF to urgently find a suitable high-speed night fighter and an efficient airborne radar system that could hunt down the raiders amongst the darkened cloudy skies over England.

Development of the Night Fighter

The RAF recognized that the Bristol Blenheim I NF was no match for a fast Junkers Ju 88, particularly at night. No suitable twin-engined night fighter had been designed before the war other than the Westland Whirlwind day fighter, which was not equipped with radar. The Bristol Aeroplane Company proposed that the most economical solution was to design a new twin-engined fighter that utilized components and sub-assemblies from the Bristol Blenheim and the Beaufort. As no specification existed for such a machine, other than specification F11/37, a fighter plane with a heavy cannon turret, the Air Ministry was privately approached and gave its blessing for the development of the Bristol Type 156, subsequently named the Beaufighter. It was a snub-nosed aircraft that was highly manoeuvrable and possessed great structural strength. However, instability at slow speeds was experienced, with a tendency to swing on take-off and landing. The first to be equipped with the Bristol Beaufighter Mk IF NF in September 1940 was 29 Squadron based at RAF Digby, followed by 25 Squadron at RAF Northolt, North Weald, shortly afterwards. These aircraft were equipped with AI Mk IV airborne radar sets that were characterized by the arrow head type antenna aerials mounted on the nose. They were guided towards the German aircraft by the ground-controlled interception radar stations, until they were able to use their AI radar sets for short-range tracking, sighting and firing.

The *Luftwaffe* raids continued both by day and night during September 1940 but in greatly reduced numbers, with groups of between 35 and 280 aircraft in each attack on London. During 1940 the *Oberkommander der Luftwaffe* realized that the Knickebein radio navigational beams over England were being jammed.

The X-Gerät and Y-Gerät radio systems were brought into use with only two *Kampfgeschwader* equipped for pathfinding night operations to counter this. On 9 October 1940 *Reichsmarschall* Göring switched aerial tactics to massive night attacks on London during the period of the full moon. The number of German bombers ranged from 150 to 487 aircraft for each of these attacks, but they were too scattered and the bombs dropped were not sufficiently heavy enough to demoralize the citizens of London. Nevertheless, in November 1940 Göring announced his strategic bombing plan. The main target was to be London, bombarded by day and night by equal numbers of bombers from *Luftflotte* 2 and 3. Other objectives included bombing the industrial areas of Coventry, Birmingham and Liverpool, mining rivers, estuaries and harbours, the destruction of the Rolls-Royce factory in Glasgow by *Kampfgeschwader* 26 using radio navigational Y-Gerät radio beams, and the bombing of other aircraft factories. Fighter sweeps were also planned across southern England and more importantly special bomber attacks were to be made against the RAF night fighter bases. Following the planning of these attacks a night raid took place on Coventry on the night of 14 November 1940 led by KG 100, the Pathfinder group using the X-Gerät radio navigation bombing system, when 469 German bombers dropped 420 tons of high explosive and incendiary bombs. Five nights later a similar raid took place on Birmingham, with 700 German bombers. During the remainder of November and December similar night attacks took place on London and five other cities, including four ports and one steel centre. On 19 December 1940 London was again severely bombed.

In many of these attacks the *Luftwaffe* achieved very little since the X beams were severely jammed and decoy fires were organized near potential targets to confuse the enemy bomb aimers. Between January and March 1941 *Luftwaffe* bombers penetrated in land to targets during bright moonlight, whilst the main bombing effort was directed against the port of Bristol and four other main ports over which the radio navigational beams could still be used. By May 1941 *Luftwaffe* activity had tailed off as units of *Luftflotte* 2 were withdrawn eastwards.

The Development of Airborne Interception Radar

The AI airborne interception Mk IV radar sets installed at the end of 1940 in the Bristol Beaufighters operated on a wave length of 1½ metres and had greatly contributed to the defeat of the German night bomber operations. Unfortunately, this equipment had certain limitations in that the radar pulses radiated from the arrowhead aerial array located on the nose of the aircraft were reflected from the ground back to the fighter plane. This tended to produce echoes on the cathode-ray tube, which blotted out much of the target data displayed. At times the forward range of the AI Mk IV was equivalent to the altitude of the aircraft above ground level and was limited to some four miles range. Flying over the sea, unless rough weather was encountered, the electromagnetic pulses tended to be reflected away from the emitting aircraft since the sea acted like an optical mirror. The capacity of the high powered valves used in 1939 and 1940 did not enable wavelengths below 1½ metres to be generated. Thus for high definition detection new high-powered valves would have to be devised.

A scientific group under the leadership of Professor Marcus Oliphant of Birmingham University was designated by the Royal Navy in 1939 to develop a centimetric radar apparatus for gun-laying purposes. Central to the designing of this new equipment was the construction of a new type of high-powered valve known as a klystron valve. Two members of the scientific team, Sir John Randall and Dr Harry Boot, who had been working on the Barkhausen Kurz Oscillator, reached the conclusion that neither the Barkhausen Kurz Oscillator nor the klystron would be able to produce the short wavelength radar pulses needed. This caused the research teams to look at combining the principles of the cavity magnetron, hitherto a laboratory curiosity, with the resonating capabilities of the klystron. The klystron had been developed in the United States of America by the Varian brothers and worked on the principle of employing two resonators, which acted as electric oscillators at the frequencies of the klystron valve. This was considered to be the key to centimetric valve development.

Owing to the poor results obtained in using the klystron valve, permission to proceed with the new avenue of research was given by Professor Marcus Oliphant. By 21 February 1940 a Heath Robinson apparatus had been assembled that consisted of transformers borrowed from the Admiralty Establishment at Portsmouth and an old electromagnet found among surplus laboratory equipment, high-tension rectifiers built by Sir John Randall and Dr Harry Boot, a copper cylinder specially machine turned by the mechanical workshop at the laboratory, a vacuum pump and a cavity magnetron with its ends sealed in wax with two half penny coins. The tests found that it could produce a measured wave length of 9.87cm, just within the required 10cm.

In May 1940 development work by Mr ECS McGaw of GEC Ltd, North Wembley in Middlesex, resulted in more effective sealing of the water-cooled apparatus, but this proved too large and heavy for airborne usage. Nevertheless, the original scientific work and its subsequent development were far ahead of German radar developments at that time. On 29 June 1940 an air-cooled cavity magnetron, NT 98, was successfully operated for the first time and generated a wave length of 10cm, using a 6lb magnet, with a pulse output of 10 kilowatts. On 4 July 1940 cavity magnetron NT 98 No. 2 was despatched to Professor Dee and his group of scientists located at the Air Ministry Research Establishment at Worth Matravers for use in the first experimental 10cm airborne radar set aboard a night fighter aircraft. GEC Ltd manufactured many copies of the cavity magnetron NT 98, of which No. 12 was sent to the United States of America with the Tizard Mission in August 1940. This cavity magnetron was considered by the Americans as the most important and the most valuable item ever imported into the USA. Together with plans for the Rolls-Royce Merlin aero engine for future US production, the anti-aircraft proximity fuse and later an example of a British jet engine, the Americans had acquired advanced scientific military knowledge beyond the capability of their own armed forces' research establishments and at a cost of some deep-held misgivings in certain British quarters.

Unhappily, the early magnetrons suffered from wave length jumping, which was cured when alternate segments of the copper block were strapped on so that the cavities oscillated in phase. This development was undertaken by Dr J Sayers of Birmingham University, which resulted in the magnetron becoming a reliable, stable and efficient operational device. The original use of the cavity magnetron was in AI Mk VII airborne radar sets, which became operational in late 1941 on-board the Bristol Beaufighter. Whereas the 1½ metre airborne sets were plagued with ground returns, the new 10cm units produced a narrow pencil beam not affected by the terrain below the aircraft. In May 1942 the AI Mk VII sets were superseded by the Mk VIII with the strapped cavity magnetron CV 64, which generated a pulse of 25 kilowatts on a wave length of 9.1cm that produced a helical scan from a parabolic reflector that gave a maximum range of 6 miles and a minimum of 400 feet. The ground returns had been eliminated, though on the new sets discreet returns from the coast line and built up areas could be obtained by tilting the aerial array downwards. This was to form the basis of the airborne radar sets used for town finding, later codenamed H2S and used successfully by RAF Bomber Command in the aerial offensive over Germany.

The *Luftwaffe* Looked to the East

Unbeknown to the Allies secret preparations were made in May 1941 for the invasion of the Soviet Union by the Axis powers in a campaign codenamed Operation *Barbarossa*. Ground units and flying groups were moved from *Luftflotte* 2 to bases in western Poland. In the meantime 550 *Luftwaffe* bombers attacked London on the night of 10 May 1941 with 708 tons of high explosive and 86,700 incendiary bombs that caused great damage. Three nights later London was bombed again. At the end of May *Generaloberst* Kesselring and the remaining units of *Luftflotte* 2 moved to Eastern Europe and *Fliegerkorps* IV and V were withdrawn from *Luftflotte* 3. The remaining aircraft in France consisted of a mixed force of bombers, reconnaissance planes, minelayers and fighter planes. No firm policy existed for further aerial attacks on England. No preparations for radio warfare had been laid, there were no plans for radio jamming suppression and no planning policies at Staff level had been drafted. From May 1941 onwards the German bomber force was concerned with miscellaneous operations, minelaying, anti-shipping strikes and occasionally night bombing attacks against such targets as Hull and Portsmouth, with a force of bombers which never exceeded 30 aircraft operating as part of *Fliegerkorps* IX, *Luftflotte* 3.

On the night of 28 March 1942 the RAF carried out a particularly heavy raid against Berlin, which prompted the *Führer* to call for reprisal raids against London. The *Oberkommando der Luftwaffe* moved the planes of *Kampfgeschwader* 100, the Pathfinder group, back into France and immediately commenced a retraining programme. On the night of 23 April 1942 German bombers attacked Exeter with forty-five aircraft, a further attack took place on 24 April 1942 with sixty bombers and on 25 April German bombers raided Bath with 150 aircraft and night raids took place on 27 April on Norwich and York. The German bombers flying on these raids had been the minelaying and anti-shipping specialists, together with the aircraft from the Bomber Training Units based in France and Belgium. The *Luftwaffe* bomber losses were mounting owing to the increased efficiency of RAF Fighter Command's night fighting techniques, with the advantage of the Bristol Beaufighter that was successfully operating AI airborne radar in conjunction with the ground-controlled interception stations. A particularly heavy raid rook place over Birmingham at the end of July 1942, but the *Luftwaffe* bombers available for such operations were fast diminishing. Indeed, during 1940 and 1941 *Luftwaffe* bombers had flown largely unmolested by British night fighters, but from the autumn of 1941 and during 1942 the efficiency of British night fighters had placed an increasing drain on the *Luftwaffe*'s bomber strength. As a result fighter bomber tactics were initiated.

In January 1942 *Geschwader* JG 2 and JG 26 were organized flying Messerschmitt Bf 109Es on reprisal raids that machine-gunned ports and towns along the south coast of England. By March 1942 the Bf 109E was equipped to carry a bomb for low-level attacks and eventually was replaced by the Focke Wulf Fw 190 fighter bombers. The aerial attack on Canterbury in October 1942 by a force of thirty fighter bombers was followed by a heavy raid of night bombers. Such tactics continued during the course of the winter of 1942 and into 1943. In the early months of 1943 a further fighter bomber unit was organized, *Schnellkampfgeschwader* 10, which was equipped with Focke Wulf Fw 190 aircraft. But German operations were neutralized by the activities of Allied bombers and fighter sweeps over northern France and Belgium. Meanwhile, Göring changed the strategy once more and organized a special England Attack Command under the command of *Oberst* Peltz, who had successfully completed the dive-bomber leaders' course held at the Foggia Airbase, Italy. The aircraft under his command consisted of a collection of Junkers Ju 88, Ju 188, Dornier Do 217, Heinkel He 177, Messerschmitt Bf 410 and Focke Wulf Fw 190 aircraft. A special Pathfinder Force was organized and trained to use an elaborate target illuminating and marking system based upon RAF methods. The standard of bomber training was inferior to that of the RAF and the opening of the bomber campaign was delayed until 21 January 1944. German bombers found that radar tail devices needed to be installed to give the crews early warning of the presence of RAF night fighters that were tracking an otherwise unwary quarry.

The Mosquito Joins the Battle

In January 1942 a new protagonist had appeared in the skies over England to harass German bomber crews, when the de Havilland Mosquito NF Mk II night fighter joined RAF 157 Squadron. The aircraft was planned as early as 1938 to be an unarmed high-speed bomber built in wood, but the design was initially rejected by the Air Ministry. In early 1940 the de Havilland Aircraft Company had approached the Air Ministry once again and obtained a reluctant acceptance for a reconnaissance version. Between January and June 1940 a prototype aircraft was constructed by twelve engineers at Salisbury Hall, a small estate located near St Albans in Hertfordshire. The secret development of the aircraft came to the attention of the *Luftwaffe* intelligence service, which was sufficiently concerned about the new aircraft's potential that it dropped agents by parachute into a nearby wood to obtain photographic evidence or at least a date for the new machine. Fortuitously, British counter intelligence officers apprehended an agent, who was despatched to London for interrogation. In the meantime the yellow-painted bomber prototype Mosquito made its maiden flight during November 1940. The fighter version flew for the first time on 15 May 1941, with a strengthened wing structure and a revised, repositioned crew entry. The de Havilland Mosquito NF Mk II night fighter was armed with four 20mm Hispano I cannons and four rifle-calibre Browning machine-guns, with the installation of AI Mk IV airborne radar sets identified by the arrowhead-type antennas located on the aircraft nose. In early 1943 the radar was replaced by the much improved AI Mk V. Eventually, Mosquito night fighters Mk XII and Mk XIII were equipped with the new centimetric radar AI Mk VIII or AI Mk X sets. Operating on a wave length of 10cm the new radar sets gave a finer definition for tracking enemy bombers and were extremely accurate, which resulted in further *Luftwaffe* bomber losses. As the German night bombing of England decreased, the de Havilland Mosquito was used in the British bomber offensive over Europe. It mingled with the Avro Lancaster and Handley Page Halifax bombers. The Mosquito was used to attack the German night fighters over German cities, as radio warfare planes that carried a German speaking wireless operator and as a high speed bomber that was much feared and hated in the Germanic skies.

In 1945 at the end of the European war the Mosquito continued in front-line service as a night fighter and long-range reconnaissance machine until January 1951, when the Mosquitoes of 29 Squadron were replaced by the Gloster Meteor NF II jet night fighters. Other Mosquito squadrons exchanged their aircraft for the de Havilland Vampire jet fighters. However, the Mosquito soldiered on and it was discovered during the Falklands War in the South Atlantic that the Chilean Air Force still operated this type of twin piston-engined bomber very successfully on active service as late as 1983.

Clearing of the Skies

On the night of 21 January 1944 an aerial attack took place on London in which 30 tons of bombs were dropped in the centre and a further 270 tons dropped over a wide scattered area of Greater London. The *Luftwaffe* considered this raid a failure. Eight days later a further raid took place on London with some 100 to 140 sorties being made, but this raid was also considered a failure. Raids continued and on 13 February 1944 a total of 175 tons of bombs was dropped. On 18 April half of the German bombers failed to locate their targets. Two attacks were later made on the port of Hull and one on Bristol in which the attacking planes were also unable to identify their targets. Meanwhile, aerial attacks were made on the Portsmouth Solent and the Swanage shipping areas near Poole, but again with little result due to the intervention of the RAF's night fighters, anti-aircraft guns and radio warfare units. Since the *Luftwaffe* Pathfinder Force began to experience widespread jamming of their radio navigation beams, successful attacks could only be made on moonlight nights, otherwise special anti-jamming radio equipment would need to be installed in all bomber aircraft, which hitherto had not been available. The next aerial attack took place on Plymouth on 30 April 1944 by bombers of *Fliegerkorps* IX plus fifteen aircraft from the specialist anti-shipping group armed with 1,400lb high-explosive Fritz X radio controlled glider bombs. Fortunately, none of the objectives were hit and no further attacks took place with such glider bombs.

The bombers were never to return in force; the prowlers of the night sky, armed with their airborne interception radar sets had ensured the raiders' eventual eclipse. On 6 June 1944 Operation *Overlord*, the Allied invasion of Europe, took place and victory came in May 1945. The night prowlers continued to guard the skies of England with Gloster Meteor and de Havilland Vampire jet fighters, enabling RAF Fighter Command to maintain its nocturnal vigil well into the future.

Chapter 17

Frank Whittle and the Power Jets Company

Flight Lieutenant Philip Sayer joined the RAF in 1924 and qualified as a pilot officer the following year. In 1930 he resigned his commission and took up a post as Hawker Aircraft's second test pilot, where he worked alongside Group Captain Paul Bulman, the first person to fly the Hurricane. When Hawker acquired the Gloster Aircraft Company in 1934 Sayer was appointed Gloster's chief test pilot. On 15 May 1941 at 7.45 p.m. Sayer took off from RAF Cranwell near Sleaford in Lincolnshire, in W4041, the prototype Gloster Pioneer E28/39, Britain's first turbojet aircraft. Sayer flew for a total of 17 minutes and reached a maximum speed of around 340mph. Over the following two weeks the aircraft logged a total of 10 hours 28 minutes flying time during seventeen test flights that included a demonstration for the Air Ministry on 21 May 1941. During these flights Sayer achieved a top speed of 370mph at 25,000 feet, faster than any other conventional aircraft at that time. Later the following year on 21 October 1942 Sayer, the first Briton to fly a jet aircraft, disappeared having taken off from RAF Acklington, near Newcastle, on a test flight in a Hawker Typhoon.

Britain's first jet aircraft test flight took place almost two years after the German *Reich* Air Ministry's chief test pilot, Flight Captain Erich Warsitz, took off at 6.00 a.m. on 27 August 1939 from Heinkel's works at Rostock-Marienehe on the Baltic Coast in the Heinkel He 178 turbojet aircraft. Two months earlier, on 20 June 1939, Warsitz was the first person to fly the Heinkel He 176, the world's first liquid-fuelled rocket-powered aircraft.

The Gloster Pioneer E28/39 was the result of the unique efforts of two important aviation pioneers, Gloster's chief designer, George Carter, and Wing Commander Frank Whittle, the man who had invented the turbojet engine, the father of the jet age and modern military and civil aviation. The E28/39 was a single-seater, single-engined aircraft with a low-wing design that had its jet intake in the nose and had the tail fin and elevators mounted above the jet-pipe at the rear. The aircraft was 24 feet 3 inches long, had a wingspan of 29 feet, stood 8 feet 6 inches tall and was fitted with a Power Jets 860lbf W1 turbojet engine.

The Air Ministry placed an order for two prototypes on 3 February 1940. W4041 was the first to be completed and was delivered to RAF Brockworth for initial ground tests on 7 April 1941. This version of the aircraft had a non-flightworthy engine fitted to enable the ground tests to be completed. Once these had been accomplished satisfactorily the flightworthy W1 engine was fitted and the aircraft was transferred to RAF Cranwell ready for the first test flight in May 1941. The second prototype, W4046, was delivered on 1 March 1943 and the following month it flew a demonstration flight at Hatfield for Prime Minister Winston Churchill and senior Air Staff officers. This variant was later fitted with the more powerful 1,500lbf W2B engine and achieved a maximum speed of 466mph. The second prototype crashed on 30 July 1943 when its ailerons jammed. The pilot was Squadron Leader Douglas Davie who at 33,000 feet became the first person to bale out from a jet aircraft. The one remaining prototype was subsequently fitted with the W2/500 engine that generated 1,700lbf and was successfully tested at 42,000 feet. This aircraft continued in use until 1944 and was instrumental in the development of the Gloster Meteor, Britain's first operational jet aircraft. Today W4041 can be seen in the Flight Gallery at the Science Museum in London. Two full-sized replicas were built as memorials to Whittle's outstanding achievements and were placed on roundabouts. The first is located on the perimeter road around Farnborough Airfield and the second is at Lutterworth in Leicestershire, near where Whittle's turbojet engines were originally manufactured.

Air Commodore Sir Frank Whittle OM, KBE, CB, FRS, FRAeS

Frank Whittle died on 9 August 1993 at the age of eighty-nine in Columbia, Maryland in the United States of America where he had settled in 1976 after joining the Faculty of the Naval Academy at Annapolis, a long way and a lifetime away from his humble beginnings in Coventry.

Whittle was born on 1 June 1907 in a small terraced house in Newcombe Road, Earlsdon in Coventry, and was the eldest son of engineer Moses Whittle. He developed his own practical engineering skills while helping his father in his workshop and it was here that he first became interested in aviation. During the First World War he saw aircraft being built at the local Standard Motor Company works, which increased his interest in aviation, particularly when one of the aircraft on a test flight was forced to land near his home. At the age of fifteen, Whittle was determined to become a pilot and applied to join the RAF, but was turned down because he was too short and he had failed his medical. A second attempt also failed. However, a third attempt under an assumed name in September 1923 was more successful and he was able to join the No. 4 Apprentices Wing at the No. 1 School of Technical Training. It was here that his commanding officer saw something of Whittle's potential and in 1926 recommended him for officer training at RAF Cranwell. This change in fortune gave Whittle the opportunity to take flying lessons, initially in an Avro 504 and later in the Bristol Fighter. The final stage of his training required him to write a thesis and Whittle wrote 'Future Developments in Aircraft Design', which explored the potential for flying at high altitude at speeds in excess of 500mph. In this paper he described how the motorjet, a piston engine that forced compressed air into a combustion chamber that then generated thrust through its exhaust, could out-perform conventional engines at altitude. Whittle came second in his class and his paper won him the Andy Fellowes Memorial Prize for Aeronautical Sciences. Having successfully graduated from his course he was commissioned as a pilot officer in July 1928.

Whittle was a keen flyer and took part in numerous aerobatic displays and by 1929 he was posted to the Central Flying School in Wittering. He had continued to develop his ideas on the motorjet and concluded that if a piston engine were used to generate the compressed air then the motor would weigh as much as a conventional engine developing the same amount of thrust. He speculated that if a turbine were used instead of the piston engine to provide the compressed air and if it could derive power from the exhaust to drive a compressor, similar to those used in superchargers, then the remaining exhaust could power an aircraft. With this thought the turbojet idea was born.

Whittle was encouraged by Flying Officer Pat Johnson, a former patent examiner, who in late 1929 suggested, with the support of their commanding officer, that he should send his proposal to the Air Ministry. However, in the Ministry's view the engine proposal was impracticable and the idea was not taken forward. Undeterred Whittle, with Johnson's assistance, applied for a patent for his idea in 1930.

In 1932 Whittle took the Officers' Engineering Course at RAF Henlow in Bedfordshire and passed with the exceptional aggregate score of 98 per cent, completing the course in only eighteen months rather than the usual two years. In February 1934 he was promoted to the rank of flight lieutenant. In the same year his performance at Henlow led to his being allowed to study a two-year Mechanical Sciences Tripos course at Cambridge University's Peterhouse College.

Power Jets Limited
In January 1935 Whittle's patent came up for renewal. He was unable to afford the £5 renewal fee and the Air Ministry refused to pay it for him. As a result the patent lapsed. In May 1935 he was contacted by a former RAF Cranwell colleague, Rolf Dudley-Williams, who introduced Whittle to James Collingwood Tinling, a retired RAF serviceman. They formed an agreement that allowed Dudley-Williams and Tinling to seek finance to develop Whittle's engine further. On 11 September 1935 a meeting was arranged with investment bankers Sir Maurice Bonham-Carter and Lancelot Law Whyte of OT Falk & Partners. Sir Maurice's granddaughter is the actress Helena Bonham-Carter, noted not only for her roles in the recent Harry Potter films, but also for playing the Queen

Mother opposite Colin Firth in the acclaimed 2010 film *The King's Speech*. Following a favourable independent engineering review of the engine proposal a Four Party Agreement was signed on 27 January 1936 between OT Falk, the Air Ministry, Whittle and Williams and Tinling to form Power Jets Limited. Whyte became chairman and Bonham-Carter was appointed as a director to oversee OT Falk's interests. Whittle, Williams and Tinling held 49 per cent of the share capital, with the remaining 51 per cent held by OT Falk in exchange for an initial capital investment of £2,000 and an option for £18,000 that could be called upon within eighteen months of the company's formation. Whittle was still studying at Cambridge and was a full-time RAF officer. As a result he was put on the special duties list by the RAF and allowed to continue to work on his design for no more than six hours per week. He was given the title of Honorary Chief Engineer and Technical Consultant by Power Jets. Production facilities were secured at the specialist steam turbine maker British Thomson Houston (BTH), based at Rugby in Warwickshire and within the year the first prototype was well on the way to being completed.

Sir Henry Tizard, the chairman of the Aeronautical Research Committee, encouraged the Air Ministry to investigate Whittle's design further. A report was produced in March 1937 by Mr AA Griffith, who as early as 1926 had been developing ideas on compressors and turbines at the Royal Aircraft Establishment. Previously, Griffith had been dismissive of Whittle's ideas, but on this occasion was a little more positive, in part because he was working on his own turbine engine design. The Engine Sub-Committee of the Aeronautical Research Committee reviewed the report and chose to fund further development of Griffith's ideas, rather than Whittle's. The Air Ministry's apathy towards Whittle and his engine led OT Falk to reduce the level of funding that the firm was prepared to put into Power Jets to just £5,000. They eventually walked away completely from the company and returned their shares to Whittle, Williams and Tinling on 1 November 1937. The first successful run of the Whittle Unit WU engine took place on 12 April 1937, which enabled the company to secure an investment of £5,000 from the Air Ministry. BTH agreed to invest £2,500 in the business and moved production from Rugby to its Ladywood foundry at Lutterworth in Leicestershire. However, with the involvement of the Air Ministry the project became covered by the Official Secrets Act, which prevented Power Jets from being able to promote the project and secure more private investment.

While Whittle and Power Jets were struggling to raise sufficient funds to keep their business and engine development going, Hans von Ohain in Germany was making great strides forward. Whittle had patented his ideas in 1930, while von Ohain was nineteen years of age. It is claimed that details of Whittle's patent found their way to Berlin in the early 1930s, which helped the Germans considerably in the development of their own turbojet engine. Von Ohain lodged patents for his design five years later in 1935. Whittle is credited with having run the first turbojet engine and von Ohain is credited with being the first to power an all-jet aircraft, the prototype Heinkel He 178 in August 1939. If Whittle had received the support that he deserved from the Air Ministry from the beginning then it is highly likely that his engine would have been the first to make a jet-powered flight. After the Second World War Whittle and von Ohain met for the first time in 1966 and became friends.

In June 1939 Whittle ran the WU engine for twenty minutes for a group of visiting engineers from the Air Ministry, which included David Randall Pye, the Director of Scientific Research. This visit led to a dramatic turnaround in attitudes and the Air Ministry issued a contract for a flyable version of the engine to be built. To help Power Jets achieve this they bought the WU engine and lent it back to the company in order to help finance the development of the new version that became the W1 turbojet. The Air Ministry then issued specification E28/39 for an aircraft capable of testing the W1 in flight and in January 1940 issued a contract to the Gloster Aircraft Company for the development of two Gloster Pioneer E28/39 aircraft, which were also known as the Gloster Whittle and the Gloster Pioneer. Further contracts were placed with Power Jets for a larger and more powerful design, which became the W2, followed by the W1A that was the same size as the W1 but utilized the mechanical layout of the W2. In early 1941 it became clear that the first Gloster airframe would be completed long before the W1 and so Whittle created the W1X experimental engine from a range of spare parts. It was this engine that took the E28/39 through its ground tests in April 1941, which included a number of taxiing runs and several short hops into the air. The W1 finally ran for the first time on 12 April 1941 and was ready for the first test flight on 15 May at RAF Cranwell.

Having secured the future of his engine and sufficient finances for Power Jets in the short term, Whittle was faced with the deterioration in many of the working relationships around him, in particular with BTH, which believed that conventional aero engines would prove themselves over Whittle's jet engine. In early 1940 the Air Ministry awarded shared production contracts to BTH and Rover, excluding Power Jets which was relegated to the position of a research organization. The Air Ministry made matters worse when it ignored the E28/39 design and agreed that the Gloster Aircraft Company could instead develop a twin-engined jet interceptor that became the Gloster Meteor. In 1941 the Air Ministry's director of engine production agreed to modifications to the engine's design that were proposed by Rover, without consulting with Whittle first. As a result of the difficulties experienced during the development of his engine and then having discovered that production was to go ahead without him, Whittle began to drink and smoke heavily, which took a devastating toll on his health.

The Air Ministry made details of Whittle's engine available to other engine manufacturers in Britain and in the United States of America. With this Rolls-Royce, de Havilland and Metropolitan-Vickers began their own work in this area. In the United States of America, General Electric manufactured the engine under licence and Whittle went out to Boston in June 1942 to help the company overcome a number of early teething problems. The Bell Aircraft P-59 Airacomet, America's first jet fighter aircraft, flew for the first time five months before the Gloster Meteor. In Britain Power Jet's new plant at Whetstone, although a vast improvement on what Whittle had been used to until a short time before, was not able to cope with the level of demand that was on the horizon and so production of the W2B was taken over by Rolls-Royce in 1943. With Rolls-Royce having so much influence over Power Jets Whittle was concerned that many of the company's technological achievements could be exploited by other commercial enterprises. Consequently, following a demonstration of the Gloster Pioneer E28/39 for Prime Minister Winston Churchill in April 1943, Whittle suggested to Sir Richard Stafford Cripps, the Minister of Aircraft Production, that Power Jets should be nationalized. His argument was that the private investors had risked a great deal to develop the engine, but the production contracts and the opportunity for their investment to be repaid was being passed to other companies. To help the arrangement go through Whittle offered to give his shares in Power Jets to the Air Ministry. Whittle soon regretted having made the offer, but it was too late. Stafford Cripps set a price of £135,563 10 shillings for the company and all of its assets. On 28 March 1944 the company was taken into state ownership and was immediately renamed Power Jets (Research & Development) Limited. Whittle had already offered his shares to the Air Ministry and as a result received nothing, even though his shares were worth £47,000. Williams and Tinling received almost £47,000 each for their shares. Harold Roxbee Cox was appointed both chairman and managing director by Stafford Cripps and Whittle was retained as chief technical advisor. On 5 April 1944 the Air Ministry paid Whittle an award of £10,000 for his shares, a fifth of their true value. Whittle resigned from Power Jets (Research & Development) Limited in January 1946. Six months later it was merged with the gas turbine division of the Royal Aircraft Establishment to form the National Gas Turbine Establishment and was based at Farnborough. Shortly afterwards sixteen Power Jets engineers took their lead from Whittle and also resigned.

The Gloster Meteor
The first British jet fighter and the first operational jet during the Second World War was designed by George Carter, chief designer of the Gloster Aircraft Company. The Meteor first flew on 5 March 1943 and came into operational service with RAF 616 Squadron on 27 July 1944. In all, 3,545 Meteors were manufactured and were deployed by numerous countries, including the Royal Australian Air Force, the Belgian Air Force and the Israeli Air Force.

George Carter became Gloster's chief designer in 1937 and was appointed technical director in 1948. He remained on the company's board until 1954. His aviation pedigree was quite significant. He served an apprenticeship with the engineering company WH Allen, Sons & Company Ltd between 1906 and 1912.

He was chief draughtsman at the Sopwith Aviation Company between 1916 and 1920, when he joined the newly formed Hawker Engineering Company after Sopwith Aviation's voluntary liquidation. In 1924 he joined Short Brothers at Rochester; in 1928 he moved to de Havilland and finally joined the Gloucestershire Aircraft Company at Brockworth in Gloucestershire in 1931. His most noted designs at Gloster included the Gauntlet and the Gladiator. Following Gloster's acquisition by Hawker in 1934 the company's chief designer, Henry Folland, chose to leave to establish his own business and as a result he was succeeded by Carter. It was during a visit to Gloster by Whittle that Carter's interest in jet aircraft came alight and in 1940 he designed the Gloster Pioneer E28/39 specifically for Whittle's new engine. The Air Ministry believed that the Pioneer was underpowered as a fighter aircraft and that a suitable engine, with at least 2,000lbf, would be needed if the aircraft was to be a success in the short term. The Ministry asked Carter to put forward a proposal for a new aircraft that could meet the challenge and Carter produced a design for a twin-engined aircraft that was designated the F9/40. The aircraft flew for the first time on 5 March 1943 and was later named the Gloster Meteor.

In January 2011, following the death of Carter's son, Wilfred Maxwell Carter, a small collection of aeronautical effects that had belonged to Carter, which included a pocket watch, diaries and letters from Frank Whittle, were discovered at his home, *Haroldstone House* at Crickley Hill in Witcombe, Gloucester, and were put up for auction. Among the lots was a copy of Whittle's book *Jet, The Story of a Pioneer*, which had a handwritten dedication from Whittle to Carter on the title page. The inscription read, 'To George Carter, as a small memento of our joint efforts with very best wishes, from Frank Whittle, 24 Nov 1953'. The book generated a surprising amount of interest and was sold for £680.

The Meteor was an all-metal low-wing single-seater aircraft, with mid-mounted twin turbojets on the wings. In all, eight prototypes of the Gloster Meteor were built. The fifth, DG206, was fitted with two de Havilland Halford H1 engines due to problems with the Whittle W2 and it was this aircraft that was the first to take to the air. The first Meteor to fly with a Whittle engine was DG205/G, which took its maiden flight on 12 June 1943. The Meteor F1 variant took off for the first time on 12 January 1944 from Moreton Valence and the first twenty aircraft were fitted with 1,700lbf Rolls-Royce Welland turbojet engines that were based upon the Whittle W2 design.

The Meteor first saw action during the Second World War on 27 July 1944 with the RAF's first jet combat sortie being fought against the German V-1 flying bomb. The first confirmed victory against the V-1s was on 4 August 1944, with thirteen flying bombs destroyed by the end of the war. On 18 December 1944 616 Squadron's F1 aircraft were replaced by Meteor F3s, which were fitted with two new Rolls-Royce Derwent engines. The Gloster Meteor F3 was 41 feet 3 inches in length, had a wingspan of 43 feet and stood 13 feet tall. It was powered by two 2,000lbf Rolls-Royce Derwent 1 turbojet engines that gave it a maximum speed of 415mph, a range of 988 miles and an operational ceiling of 43,000 feet. The aircraft was armed with four 20mm Hispano cannons. The F4 first flew in April 1945 and was fitted with two Rolls-Royce Derwent 5 turbojet engines.

On 7 November 1945 Group Captain HJ Wilson achieved the first officially confirmed speed record for a jet aircraft, reaching a maximum speed of 606mph in a F4 over Herne Bay in Kent. The aircraft was fitted with two 3,500lbf Rolls-Royce Derwent 5 turbojets. The following year Group Captain Edward Donaldson set a new world airspeed record, achieving 616mph in a Meteor F4 on 7 September 1946. Earlier, Wing Commander Roland Beamont, a former fighter pilot and then test pilot for the RAF, had flown the same aircraft beyond its normal safety limits and it is claimed achieved a top speed of 632mph, but this was not officially recorded. However, Beamont did enter the record books when on 26 August 1952 he made a double crossing of the Atlantic Ocean flying an English Electric Canberra B5 VX185 airliner from Aldergrove, now Belfast International Airport, to Gander in north-east Newfoundland, and then back to Aldergrove in 10 hours 3 minutes.

The F5 variant was a photo-reconnaissance aircraft and the F6 was a swept wing design concept that never went into production. The F7 was a twin-seat trainer aircraft, of which 640 were manufactured. The F8 was as a redesign of the F4 that enabled Gloster to go into production without the need for expensive retooling. The F8 variant entered service in October 1948 and was fitted with a Martin-Baker ejection seat. The F8 was powered by two 3,500lbf Rolls-Royce Derwent 8 turbojet engines that increased the maximum speed to 598mph at 10,000 feet.

The F8 became the dominant jet fighter with RAF Fighter Command as well as with many other air forces around the world. By the early 1950s the Meteor design was becoming out-dated compared with the newer North American F-86 Sabre fighters. The Sabre had a swept-wing design and was fitted with a 5,910lbf General Electric J47-GE 13 turbojet that was developed in the United States of America and gave the aircraft a maximum speed of 675mph. Production of the Meteor ended in 1954 and the aircraft was moved away from front line duties.

Subsequent variants included the FR9 fighter-reconnaissance aircraft, the PR10, which was developed for photo-reconnaissance and the NF11, NF12, NF13 and NF14 variants that were night fighters. The Meteor rapidly became obsolete in the 1950s with the introduction of faster aircraft and the development of surface-to-air missiles. As a result the aircraft was phased out by 1956.

Frank Whittle's Post-war Years

Following the end of the Second World War Whittle became technical advisor for engine design to the RAF Controller of Supplies (Air) in 1946. He also began to receive considerable recognition for his outstanding contribution to aviation. He had been made a Commander of the British Empire in 1944 and was awarded the Order of the Bath in 1947. In 1946 he was made a Commander of the US Legion of Merit, the first decoration specifically created by the United States of America for citizens of other nations. In May 1948 the Royal Commission on Awards to Inventors gave him an ex-gratia award of £100,000 in recognition of his work on the jet engine and in July he was made a Knight of the Order of the British Empire (KBE) by King George VI.

The stress and strain of developing his turbojet engine and the constant battle for resources took its toll on Whittle's health. He suffered his first nervous breakdown in 1940 and suffered a second breakdown in 1944 when Power Jets Limited was nationalized. His poor health remained a difficulty for him for the rest of his life and he eventually retired early from the RAF on 26 August 1948 on medical grounds. By the time his career with the RAF had ended he was an Air Commodore. After a period of recuperation Whittle joined the state-owned airline British Overseas Airways Corporation as a technical advisor, which enabled him to travel a great deal to review and inspect engine developments in North America, Africa, the Middle and Far East. He published his autobiography, *Jet, The Story of a Pioneer* in 1952 and was awarded the Royal Society of Arts' Albert Medal. Between 1953 and 1957 he worked as a mechanical engineering specialist with Shell and developed a new self-powered drill. In 1957 he moved to the Bristol Engine Company, which set up Bristol Siddeley Whittle Tools in 1961 in order to develop the new oil drill. However, following the acquisition of Bristol Siddeley by Rolls-Royce in 1966 and the company's bankruptcy in 1971, the Whittle turbo drill was shelved. In the late 1990s the design was incorporated with a continuous coiled pipe that allowed drilling to take place at any angle and included the ability to tap into pockets of oil sideways, which allowed the oil to flow out quicker. In 1969 Whittle received the Tony Jannus Award for his contributions to commercial aviation. The Tony Jannus Award recognizes outstanding individual achievement in scheduled commercial aviation and has been conferred annually by the Tony Jannus Distinguished Aviation Society since 1964. On 1 January 1914 the aviation pioneer Tony Jannus piloted the first flight of the St Petersburg Tampa Airboat Line, the first scheduled commercial airline flight in the world using heavier-than-air aircraft. In 1977 Whittle emigrated to the United States of America, a year after his forty-six-year marriage to Dorothy was dissolved and he had married American Hazel S Hall. In the US he took up a position as a Research Professor at the United States Naval Academy at Annapolis in Maryland. In 1981 he published a text book *Gas Turbine Aero-thermodynamics: With Special Reference to Aircraft Propulsion*.

Whittle met up with von Ohain at the Wright-Patterson Air Force Base in 1978, where von Ohain was the chief scientist at the Aero Propulsion Laboratory, and the pair gave a number of talks together in the United States of America. In 1986 Whittle was appointed a member of the Commonwealth Order of Merit and became a fellow of the Royal Society and of the Royal Aeronautical Society. In 1991 Whittle and von Ohain were both jointly awarded the Charles Stark

Draper Prize for their independent work on the development of the turbojet engine. The Charles Stark Draper Prize is one of three that make up the Nobel Prizes of Engineering, along with the Russ and Gordon Prizes. The Prizes are awarded annually by the National Academy of Engineering and the winner of each receives an award of $500,000. Charles Stark Draper was an MIT professor, the founder of the Draper Laboratory and is regarded as the father of inertial navigation, a computerized navigational aid that uses motion sensors and rotation sensors to continuously calculate the position, orientation and velocity of a moving object. Inertial navigation is used extensively for shipping, aircraft, missiles and spacecraft.

Memorials

Sir Frank Whittle died of lung cancer on 9 August 1996. Following his cremation in the United States of America his ashes were flown back to Britain where they were interred at the Protestant Chapel at RAF Cranwell. A bronze statue of Sir Frank Whittle is located under the 'Whittle Arches' in his home town of Coventry and is located outside the Coventry Transport Museum in Millennium Place. The statue was unveiled on 1 June 2007 by Whittle's son Ian on what would have been Whittle's 100th birthday. A commemorative plaque was also placed on the wall of the terraced house where he was born in Newcombe Road in Coventry.

A wide range of memorabilia can be found at the Lutterworth Museum, just south of Leicester. Among the museum's collection are original papers, including Whittle's patent and Power Jets' autograph book. A replica Gloster Pioneer is located on a roundabout near the museum. The Royal Academy of Engineering in London awards the Sir Frank Whittle Medal each year to an engineer in recognition of their sustained achievement and their contribution to the overall wellbeing of the nation. The Royal Academy of Engineering also has on display all of Sir Frank Whittle's honours, medals and awards.

The Royal Air Force Chapel is located at the eastern end of Westminster Abbey in the Lady Chapel that was built by King Henry VII. The chapel was dedicated to the memory of those RAF servicemen who lost their lives during the Battle of Britain and contains the graves of Lord Trenchard, who is described as the Father of the Royal Air Force and Lord Dowding, Air Chief Marshal and commander of Fighter Command during the Battle of Britain. On 12 April 2000 a memorial stone was unveiled in the Royal Air Force Chapel in memory of Sir Frank Whittle, with the inscription, 'Frank Whittle. Inventor & Pioneer of the Jet Engine. 1907–1996'.

Chapter 18

Harold Wilson and the Aircraft and Shipbuilding Industries Act 1977

Towards the end of the 1950s it became apparent that the British government was determined to drive through a series of mergers within the UK aviation industry. It enticed aircraft manufacturers with the offer of lucrative new opportunities post-merger, such as for the BAC TSR-2 strike aircraft, as well as sizeable maintenance contracts and the possibility of funding for research into new experimental civil and military aircraft. An attempt by the de Havilland Aircraft Company to have its new DH121 airliner manufactured by Hunting Aircraft and Fairey Aviation under the old name of Airco was not what the Minister of Supply had in mind. Airco's management had pursued its plans right up to the last minute, which included a proposal that Boeing would manufacture the DH121 in place of its 727. In the end the plan failed and the DH121 eventually became the Hawker Siddeley Trident. Despite tremendous opposition from the boardrooms the majority of the British aviation industry merged into just two organizations in 1960, which created the British Aircraft Corporation (BAC) and Hawker Siddeley Group. Handley Page chose to remain independent and stayed outside of the mergers, a decision that was to lead to its eventual collapse in 1970. Aero engine production was consolidated into Bristol Siddeley and Rolls-Royce. In 1966 Bristol Siddeley was sold to Rolls-Royce, which subsequently went bankrupt five years later in 1971. Helicopter production was consolidated into Westland Helicopters in 1960, which acquired Fairey Aviation, Saunders-Roe and the Bristol Aeroplane Company's helicopter division.

During the years that followed their respective mergers both BAC and Hawker Siddeley Group continued the legacy of the old aircraft manufacturers and maintained production of some of Britain's most iconic military and civil aircraft, including the Harrier, Tornado, Trident, Lightning and Concorde, the world's only supersonic airliner. Speculation over a possible take-over of BAC by Hawker Siddeley Group persisted throughout much of its short life, but all was to change again when legislation to nationalize the British aircraft and shipbuilding industries was announced in 1974. The Aircraft and Shipbuilding Industries Act received Royal Assent in March 1977, which took BAC, Hawker Siddeley Group and Scottish Aviation into state ownership and reconstituted them as British Aerospace.

British Aircraft Corporation 1960–1977

In 1960 English Electric Aviation Limited, Vickers-Armstrongs (Aircraft) and Bristol Aeroplane Company were merged to form the British Aircraft Corporation. Bristol, English Electric and Vickers-Armstrongs held 40 per cent, 40 per cent and 20 per cent of the share capital respectively. BAC then acquired 70 per cent of Hunting Aircraft a few months later.

Hunting Aircraft began as the Percival Aircraft Company, which was established by Edgar Percival in Gravesend in 1933. In 1936 the company changed its name to Percival Aircraft Ltd and relocated to Luton. It was acquired by Hunting & Son Ltd in 1944.

Edgar Percival was born on 23 February 1898 in Albury, New South Wales, Australia. Following the outbreak of the First World War he enlisted with the 7th Australian Light Horse in 1915 and the following year was transferred to the Royal Flying Corps, where in 1917 he was posted to 60 Squadron, which was commanded by the Canadian ace Billy Bishop. In 1918 Percival was posted to Egypt and it was while he was stationed there that he designed his first aircraft.

After the war he returned to Australia with two surplus Avro 504s and a surplus de Havilland DH6. In 1923 he won the Melbourne to Geelong Race and launched himself into a string of high-profile flights. In 1929 he came to England and was appointed as a test pilot for the Air Ministry. The following year he designed the Saro Percival Mail Carrier with Saunders-Roe Limited. He then established Percival Aircraft in 1933 in order to manufacture his own designs and established a factory at Gravesend Airport in Kent. During the Second World War Percival served in the Royal Air Force Volunteer Reserve and in September 1944 he sold Percival Aircraft to Hunting & Son Ltd. Percival later moved to the United States of America, where he died in 1984.

Hunting was established in 1874 as a shipbuilder by Charles Hunting who was a veterinary surgeon. The company moved into aviation in the 1930s when it provided manufacturing and maintenance services to other aircraft companies. The aviation division was formalized in 1944 with the acquisition of Percival Aircraft and in 1945 the company established the airline Hunting Air Travel that was based at Luton Airport. In 1954 the company's aviation subsidiary was renamed and became Hunting Percival Aircraft Limited, but the Percival was removed three years later. In 1960 Hunting Aircraft was split from the main company, Hunting plc, and was merged into the British Aircraft Corporation.

The first aircraft to be branded British Aircraft Corporation was the BAC 111, a short-range jet airliner that was originally designed by Hunting Aircraft. The 111 was intended as a replacement for the Vickers Viscount and it made its maiden flight on 20 August 1963. The design was highly successful and it saw service well into the 1990s. The 111 could carry up to 119 passengers and was operated by numerous airlines, including British United Airways, British Airways, Braniff Airways and American Airlines. In all, some 244 machines were built.

BAC acquired the Bristol and English Electric guided missile divisions in 1963 and established the British Aircraft Corporation (Guided Weapons) subsidiary, which developed the Rapier, Sea Skua and Sea Wolf missiles. Later the division worked closely with Hughes Aircraft and was awarded a number of electronics and space systems contracts. In April 1965 the experimental Cold War BAC TSR-2 strike and reconnaissance aircraft project was cancelled and the prototypes were scrapped.

In May 1966 BAC formed a joint venture with the French aircraft manufacturer Breguet to create the Société Européenne de Production de l'Avion d'École de Combat et d'Appui Tactique (SEPECAT), which developed the Jaguar ground attack aircraft. The Jaguar first flew on 8 September 1968 and entered service in 1973. In all, some 543 aircraft were delivered to the RAF and the French *Armée de l'Air*, where their role was expanded to include reconnaissance and tactical nuclear strike activities. The Jaguars were in service in France until 2005 and until 2007 in the UK.

The single-seater Jaguar GR MK IA, was 55 feet 2 inches long, had a wingspan of 28 feet 6 inches and stood 16 feet tall. It was fitted with two Rolls-Royce/Turbomeca Adour Mk 102 turbofans that generated 5,115lbf of dry thrust each or 7,305lbf of thrust each with afterburner. This enabled the aircraft to reach a maximum speed of 990 mph, with a combat radius of 357 miles and an operational ceiling of 50,000 feet. The Jaguar was armed with two 30mm French DEFA cannons, could carry a bomb payload of 10,000lb under the wing and could carry two over-wing mounted AIM-9L Sidewinders. In 1969 a concerted effort was made to sell the Jaguar abroad, but without much success. Negotiations were held with both Japan and Turkey for them to build the aircraft under licence, but failed to reach a positive conclusion with either country. India did deploy a specially designed Jaguar International export variant with its air forces, as did Oman, Nigeria and Ecuador.

When the Saudi Arabian government decided to strengthen and modernize its armed forces BAC demonstrated the English Electric Lightning supersonic jet fighter in Riyadh in 1964, which led two years later to an order for forty Lightnings and forty BAC 167 Strikemaster training and light attack aircraft, as well as a number of Thunderbird surface to air missiles. The order surprised many, not least of all American manufacturers who had thought that the contract would almost certainly go to them. BAC consolidated its position in Saudi Arabia in 1973 when a further contract was agreed that named the company as the main supplier for all of the country's defence system requirements.

The English Electric Lightning was unique as it was the only British-designed and built supersonic fighter that could reach Mach 2.0. The Lightning was one of two aircraft designed by William Petter that demonstrated English Electric's capability to develop aircraft under its own name. The second aircraft was the Canberra high-altitude bomber.

The English Electric story began in 1917 when Glaswegian merchants WB Dick and John Kerr took over the United Electric Car Company, based in Preston, Lancashire, and the following year created The English Electric Company Limited. The company acquired numerous businesses over several decades to establish itself as a dominant tram, railway and aviation manufacturer in the UK. Many of its original trams are still ferrying passengers around the streets of Hong Kong today.

English Electric had started manufacturing aircraft before the First World War, but when the conflict started it was engaged by the Air Ministry to support production and built numerous machines for other companies, which included seaplanes designed by the Seaplane Experimental Station at Felixstowe and several Short Brothers designs.

The English Electric Wren was designed by William Manning and was the first machine built under the company's own name. The Wren was the first ultralight aircraft and was built in 1921. An example of the Wren can be seen at the Shuttleworth Collection at Old Warden Aerodrome in Bedfordshire; it is 24 feet 3 inches long, with a wingspan of 37 feet and stands 4 feet 9 inches tall. It is powered by a 3hp ABC flat-twin engine and can reach a maximum speed of 50mph. During the inter-war years English Electric developed a number of flying boats, which included the Kingston, a twin-engined biplane also designed by Manning and the Ayr, a single-engined biplane, both with hulls designed by Linton Hope. However, with the gathering storm of the Second World War the Air Ministry requested that English Electric establish a shadow factory at Samlesbury Aerodrome in Lancashire in order to manufacture Handley Page Hampden bombers. In 1940 the company extended the runway at Samlesbury and built a second plant in order to build the four-engined Halifax bomber. Then in 1942 English Electric acquired the aero engine manufacturer Napier & Son. By the end of the war the site had three runways and over 2,000 Halifax bombers had been delivered. However, it was during the post-war era that English Electric became a noted aircraft designer and manufacturer in its own right, with the Canberra and Lightning. In 1944 William Petter had left Westland Aircraft and joined English Electric as chief engineer. Under the leadership of George Nelson, who had been English Electric's chairman since 1930, Petter designed the Canberra, a first generation light-bomber that remained in service with the RAF for fifty-five years. The Canberra first flew on 13 May 1949 and entered service with the RAF on 23 May 1951. The aircraft could fly at a higher altitude than any other aircraft during the 1950s and in addition to nuclear strike capabilities was deployed in tactical bombing and reconnaissance roles. The

Canberra B2 variant was 65 feet 6 inches in length, had a wingspan of 63 feet 11 inches and was 15 feet 8 inches high. It was powered by two 6,500lbf Rolls-Royce Avon 101 turbojets that gave it a top speed of 570mph at 40,000 feet, a range of 2,656 miles and an operational ceiling of 48,000 feet. The Canberra saw active service in many parts of the world and was flown by the RAF in Malaya and during the Suez Crisis in the 1950s.

The English Electric Lightning supersonic fighter first flew on 4 August 1954 and began to enter service with the RAF in July 1960. An example of a Lightning can be seen at the Tangmere Military Aviation Museum, near Chichester in West Sussex. The initial design work was undertaken by William Petter, but he left English Electric in 1950 and went to work for Folland Aircraft. The design work was completed by Petter's assistant, Frederick Page, who later became Sir Frederick Page OBE. Page would later work on another major BAC development, the TSR-2.

The first production Lightning was the F Mk 1 variant that made its maiden flight on 29 October 1959. The later F Mk 3 version was 55 feet 3 inches long, had a wingspan of 34 feet 10 inches and stood 19 feet 7 inches tall. It was fitted with two 15,680lbf Rolls-Royce Avon 211R turbojets that gave it a maximum speed of 1,500mph, a range of 800 miles and an operational ceiling of more than 60,000 feet. The aircraft was the last all-British jet fighter to be produced and served with the RAF until it was retired in 1976. In all, 388 aircraft were manufactured, which includes a total of 57 machines exported to foreign air forces.

English Electric established the English Electric Aviation Limited subsidiary in 1958 and it was this company that was merged into the British Aircraft Corporation in 1960. The parent company's missiles division was sold to BAC in 1963.

The twin-engined Tornado was born when BAC, Messerschmitt-Bölkow-Blohm (MBB), Fiat and Fokker joined forces on 26 March 1969 to form Panavia Aircraft GmbH. The new company then developed two new aircraft designs, the single-seater Panavia 100 and the two-seater Panavia 200. In September 1971 the British, Italian and German governments agreed to proceed with the development of the Panavia Tornado. The first of nine Tornado prototypes made its maiden flight in Germany on 14 August 1974. Both RAF and Italian Tornados saw action during the 1991 Gulf War. The last Tornado to be built was delivered to the Royal Saudi Air Force in 1998.

The Tornado GR Mk 1 variant had a crew of two, was 54 feet 10 inches long, had a wingspan of 45 feet 7 inches with swept wings and stood 19 feet 6 inches tall. It was fitted with two Turbo Union RB199-34R Mk 103 afterburning turbofans that gave the aircraft a maximum speed of 1,452mph, a combat radius of 864 miles and a ceiling of 50,000 feet.

Without doubt BAC's most memorable contribution to British aviation was the Aérospatiale BAC Concorde, the world's only supersonic passenger airliner.

The Concorde 001 made its maiden flight on 2 March 1969, when French pilot Major André Edouard Turcat took off from Toulouse Airport for the first time. The aircraft made its first supersonic flight on 1 October 1969. The British prototype, Concorde 002, made its maiden flight on 9 April 1969, when pilot Brian Trubshaw flew the aircraft from Filton near Bristol to RAF Fairford in Gloucestershire.

In all, 20 Concordes were built. The aircraft had a flight crew of three and could carry up to 100 passengers, but with changes to the internal configuration this could have been increased to 128. The production Concorde was 203 feet 9 inches long, had a wingspan of 83 feet 10 inches and stood 37 feet 5 inches tall. It was fitted with four Rolls-Royce/SNECMA Olympus 593 Mk 610 afterburning turbojets, which produced 32,000lbf each, increased to 38,050lbf with 17 per cent afterburning. The Concorde could reach a maximum speed of Mach 2.04, 1,354mph, at 51,300 feet. The aircraft had a range of 4,090 miles and an operational ceiling of 60,000 feet.

Concorde entered service with Air France and British Airways on 21 January 1976 on the London to Bahrain and the Paris to Rio routes. Problems with the sonic booms created by the Concorde limited the routes that it was allowed to fly and put off a number of international airline operators from buying the aircraft. A ban on Concorde flying into New York's JFK Airport was finally lifted on 17 October 1977 and on 22 November scheduled services from London and Paris to New York started for the first time. The New York routes proved very popular and profitable for both airlines. The Concorde story was brought to an abrupt end when Air France flight 4590 crashed on 25 July 2000 in Paris. After a long inquiry and some modification work the Concordes were brought back into service. However, Air France and British Airways jointly announced in April 2003 that the aircraft would be retired. The last Air France flight took place in May 2003 and British Airways made its last Concorde flight in October 2003.

Hawker Siddeley Group 1960–1977

In 1959 de Havilland was acquired by Hawker Siddeley, which with the purchase of Folland Aircraft and Blackburn Aircraft in 1960 became the Hawker Siddeley Group. In 1961 the company was reorganized into three divisions, HS Aviation, HS Industries and AV Roe Canada, with other subsidiaries in South Africa and Australia. Initially, aircraft designs kept the name of their respective company, but by 1963 this idea was dropped and all subsequent aircraft adopted the 'HS' Hawker Siddeley prefix. One of the first aircraft to adopt the new initials was the HS 121 Trident three-engined airliner, which was originally the de Havilland DH121. The Trident was developed in response to a BEA requirement for a short and medium haul airliner, first flying on 9 January 1962 from Hatfield Aerodrome. The aircraft was intended to be able to carry up to 140 passengers, but interference from BEA in the Trident 1's layout led to design changes that may have met the company's requirements but which delayed development and limited the aircraft's saleability. As a result it lost out significantly to the Boeing 727. In all, around 110 Tridents were built, compared to over 1,800 727s.

In 1965 the Trident was the first airliner to make fully automatic approaches and landings. It remained the only aircraft able to do so until the Lockheed TriStar was authorized to do the same almost 10 years later. The aircraft had a flight crew of three and was able to carry 115 passengers. The Trident 2E was 114 feet 9 inches long, had a wingspan of 98 feet and stood 27 feet high. It was fitted with three Rolls-Royce RB163-25 Spey 512-5W engines that each generated 11,960lbf, giving the aircraft a cruising speed of 605mph, a range of 2,464 miles and an operational ceiling of 33,000 feet.

The Hawker Siddeley Group continued to produce a prolific range of aircraft in the years between the merger in 1960 and nationalization in 1977, which included the pioneering delta-winged Vulcan bomber that remained in production until 1965. The company's pioneering work continued with the development of the Hawker Siddeley Harrier, a vertical and short take-off and landing (V/STOL) ground attack aircraft that was evolved from the Kestrel. The first production Harrier flew on 28 December 1967 and entered service with the RAF on 1 April 1969. The Harrier was also deployed with the United States Marine Corps, the Spanish Navy and the Royal Thai Navy. Later variants included the British Aerospace Sea Harrier, the McDonnell Douglas AV-8B Harrier II and the British Aerospace Harrier II. The Harrier GR5 was 46 feet 4 inches long, had a wingspan of 30 feet 4 inches and stood 11 feet 7 inches tall. The aircraft was fitted with a 23,800lbf Rolls-Royce F402-RR-408 vectored thrust turbofan engine, which gave the aircraft a maximum speed of 661 mph, a combat radius of 172 miles and an operational ceiling of 50,000 feet. The aircraft's vertical and short take-off capabilities meant that the RAF could deploy its Harriers in more strategic locations away from established aerodromes and where other fixed wing aircraft could not operate, which made them ideal for service in West Germany during the Cold War. The British Aerospace Sea Harrier was fitted with radar and was deployed by the Royal Navy on the aircraft carrier HMS *Invincible*. Both variants played an important role during the Falklands War in 1982.

With the acquisition of Blackburn Aircraft in 1960, Hawker Siddeley Group inherited the Buccaneer, a low-level strike aircraft that was equipped with nuclear weapons and which served with the Royal Navy, the RAF and the South African Air Force. Hawker Siddeley kept the Buccaneer in production following the merger and RAF 12 Squadron based at RAF Honington was the first to receive the aircraft in 1969. With the scaling back of the Royal Navy's aircraft carrier fleet during the 1970s, most of the Fleet Air Arm's Buccaneers were re-deployed with the RAF and were eventually retired from service in March 1994.

The Folland Gnat was another design that was inherited by Hawker Siddeley Group. The Gnat was a subsonic trainer and light fighter designed by William Petter, who was appointed chief engineer at Folland Aircraft in 1951. The Gnat first flew on 18 July 1955 and was developed from the Folland Midge lightweight fighter project. The T1 was introduced to the RAF in 1959 as a trainer and later joined the RAF's Red Arrows aerobatic team. The Gnat remained in service with RAF flying schools until 1978 when the aircraft was replaced by the British Aerospace Hawk.

In addition to aircraft production Hawker Siddeley Group worked extensively with missiles and rockets, including the nuclear stand-off missile Blue Steel, which was in service between 1963 and 1970. The company developed Blue Streak, an intermediate range ballistic missile that was originally designed in 1955 as a replacement for the V bombers, but the project was cancelled in 1960. The Sea Dart was more successful. Also known as the Guided Weapon System (GWS) 30, it was a surface-to-air and surface-to-surface missile developed by Hawker Siddeley Dynamics. More than 2,000 were manufactured by British Aerospace from 1977. It saw service in the Falklands War in 1982 and again in 1991 during the first Gulf War.

The Aircraft and Shipbuilding Industries Act 1977

On 30 April 1975 the British government under Labour Prime Minister Harold Wilson formally introduced to Parliament the Aircraft and Shipbuilding Industries Act that sought to nationalize the aircraft and shipbuilding industries in the UK. The government's plans for nationalization were first mooted during the general election in February 1974, when Wilson had defeated the incumbent Conservative Prime Minister Edward Heath. The Labour government's intention was to merge Hawker Siddeley Group, Hawker Siddeley Dynamics, British Aircraft Corporation and Scottish Aviation to create a new state corporation under the name of British Aerospace. The conglomeration of UK shipbuilding companies and interests became British Shipbuilders. By the time the Act received Royal Assent and passed into law in 1977 Wilson had resigned and had been replaced as Prime Minister by James Callaghan.

Scottish Aviation Limited was established in 1935 as a flying school and was based at Prestwick in South Ayrshire. In 1938 the company moved into aircraft maintenance and during the Second World War was involved with aircraft fitting, in particular with the Consolidated Liberator bomber. Scottish Aviation's factory was originally the Palace of Engineers at the Empire Exhibition in Glasgow in 1938. The Palace was painstakingly dismantled after the exhibition and was rebuilt at Prestwick.

After the Second World War Scottish Aviation developed a small number of short take-off and landing utility aircraft, which included the single-engined single-seater Pioneer that first flew on 5 November 1947. The aircraft was used by the RAF for a wide range of tasks, which included casualty evacuation during the Malayan Emergency. The Pioneer was 34 feet 9 inches long, had a wingspan of 49 feet 9 inches and stood 10 feet 3 inches tall. The aircraft could carry four passengers and was powered by a 520hp Alvis Leonides 501/4 radial engine that gave it a maximum speed of 121 mph, a range of 430 miles and a ceiling of 23,000 feet. The Pioneer had a remarkable rate of climb and could land on uneven airstrips as short as 600 feet in length. The aircraft was retired by the RAF in 1969. The Twin Pioneer was a twin-engined transport aircraft that entered service with RAF 78 Squadron in Aden in 1958. The Twin Pioneer had a crew of three and could carry sixteen passengers. It was 45 feet 3 inches long, had a wingspan of 76 feet 6 inches and stood 12 feet 3 inches tall. The aircraft was fitted with two 640hp Alvis Leonides 531 radial engines that gave it a maximum speed of 165mph at 2,000 feet, a range of 400 miles and an operational ceiling of 20,000 feet.

British Executive & General Aviation Limited, which was known as BEAGLE, was formed in 1960 as a joint venture between Pressed Steel and Auster Aircraft Company. The company became Beagle Aircraft Limited in 1962, but when Pressed Steel was absorbed into the British Motor Corporation the company sought government assistance to help keep Beagle in business. The British government bought Beagle Aircraft in 1966, but when further financial assistance was needed in 1969 the government put it into receivership and its assets were sold off. Scottish Aviation then acquired the Beagle Bulldog, a two-seater side-by-side trainer that first flew on 19 May 1969. The Bulldog Series 120 was 23 feet 3 inches in length and had a wingspan of 33 feet 2 inches. It was fitted with a 200hp Lycoming O-360 opposed piston engine that gave it a top speed of 148mph, a range of 620 miles and an operational ceiling of 16,000 feet. Scottish Aviation went on to build 320 of the aircraft. When Handley Page went into liquidation in 1970 Scottish Aviation acquired the Jetstream turboprop transport aircraft and continued the marque until the company was nationalized in 1977 and Jetstream was taken over by British Aerospace.

The Aircraft and Shipbuilding Industries Act was presented to the House of Commons by the Secretary of State for Industry, Tony Benn MP. The act was passed into law when it received Royal Assent on 17 March 1977. The Act states that its purpose was:

> ...to provide for the establishment of two bodies corporate to be called British Aerospace and British Shipbuilders, and to make provision with respect to their functions; to provide for the vesting in British Aerospace of the securities of certain companies engaged in manufacturing aircraft and guided weapons and the vesting in British Shipbuilders of the securities of certain companies engaged in shipbuilding and allied industries; to make provision for the vesting in those companies of certain property, rights and liabilities; to provide for payments to British Aerospace and its wholly owned subsidiaries, for the purpose of promoting the design, development and production of civil aircraft; and for connected purposes.

The shareholders and owners of the businesses that were nationalized were paid compensation in the form of government bonds as was laid out in Section 35 of the Aircraft and Shipbuilding Industries Act. The amount of compensation was based upon the average value of their shares over a six-month period up to the date of the general election on 28 February 1974. For owners who held non-listed shares in any of the nationalized businesses their compensation would be agreed by negotiation. The Act stated that the amount of compensation could be reduced if a company attempted to quickly redistribute their assets ahead of nationalization, such as by the payment of significant early dividends. The Aircraft and Shipbuilding Industries Arbitration Tribunal was established by the Act to handle any appeals regarding the value of compensation, although the Tribunal was not able to challenge the right of the government to take this action or the fairness of the method of calculating the compensation. The Lord Advocate for Scotland chaired the Tribunal in Scotland and the Lord Chancellor chaired the Tribunal in the remainder of the UK. The Court of Session in Scotland and the Court of Appeal in the remainder of the UK were able to hear appeals, which could then be referred to the House of Lords. If a shareholder still remained dissatisfied the Act did make provision for a judicial review. By the end of 1980 all compensation had been paid, which was followed by an application to the European Court of Human Rights by the companies Vosper, Vickers-Armstrongs and Yarrow, as well as a number of shareholders including English Electric, M&G Securities, Prudential and Sir William Lithgow. Their case centred around the claim that the compensation breached several of the articles of the European Convention on Human Rights, including the right to peaceful enjoyment of one's possessions, the right to a fair trial, the right to an effective remedy, the prohibition of discrimination, the prohibition of abuse of rights and the limitations on permitted restrictions of rights. The application was rejected by the European Court of Human Rights.

British Aerospace to BAE Systems
British Aerospace was formally created as a statutory corporation in the United Kingdom on 29 April 1977 and two years later bought 20 per cent of Airbus Industrie. The original Airbus 300 project was a three-way international development between Hawker Siddeley Group in the UK, Sud Aviation (which later became Aérospatiale) in France and Arbeitsgemeinschaft Airbus (later Deutsche Airbus) in Germany, which formally received funding approval from their respective governments on 25 July 1967. However, two years later on 10 April 1969 the British government pulled out, concerned that it would not be able to recoup its investment in the project. The Hawker Siddeley Group maintained an involvement as a preferred sub-contractor and developed the aircraft's wings. It invested £35 million in new tooling for its plants at Broughton and Filton for the purpose and also received a further £35 million by way of a loan from the German government. Airbus Industrie was established on 18 December 1970 with Aérospatiale and Deutsche Airbus holding 50 per cent of the share capital each. The following year the Spanish company CASA bought

4.2 per cent of the company and then in January 1979 British Aerospace formalized its relationship with Airbus by acquiring 20 per cent of the share capital.

The British Aerospace Act was introduced to Parliament in 1980 by Sir Keith Joseph, the Secretary of State for Industry. The Act stated that its purpose was:

> ...to provide for the vesting of all the property, rights, liabilities and obligations of British Aerospace in a company nominated by the Secretary of State and the subsequent dissolution of British Aerospace; and to make provision with respect to the finances of that company.

This Act amended the legislation laid down in the Aircraft and Shipbuilding Industries Act 1977 and enabled the new Conservative government under Prime Minister Margaret Thatcher to privatize British Aerospace. The Act passed into law when it received Royal Assent on 1 May 1980 and on 1 January 1981 British Aerospace changed from being a statutory corporation to a public limited company. The Conservative government then sold 51.75 per cent of the share capital a month later on 4 February 1981. Four years later in 1985 the British government sold its remaining shares in the company, except for a single £1 'golden' share, which enabled it to out vote all other shares in specific circumstances, which included if control of the company was likely to pass into foreign hands.

Competition from defence contractors in the United States of America grew markedly during the 1990s, which persuaded many European companies that consolidation was needed if they were to have a chance to compete. British Aerospace had been negotiating a merger with the German company DASA, which was owned by DaimlerChrysler, which until 1995 was known as Deutsche Aerospace. However, when it became known that Britain's General Electric Company (GEC) was planning to sell its defence division Marconi Electronic Systems, British Aerospace put the arrangements with DASA on hold and agreed a merger with GEC instead, in part to prevent any American company moving in and snapping up the local competition. The £7.7 billion merger between British Aerospace and Marconi Electronic Systems took place on 30 November 1999 and when it was completed the company changed its name to BAE Systems.

BAE Systems plc is based in Farnborough, Hampshire, and since its formation in 1999 has sold its interests in Airbus, EADS Astrium, AMS and Atlas Elektronik as it moved its focus away from Europe and towards markets in the United States of America, Australia, India and Saudi Arabia. The company is involved in numerous high-profile defence projects, including the Eurofighter Typhoon, the F-35 Lightning II, the Astute class submarine and the Queen Elizabeth class aircraft carriers. BAE Systems business activities are divided into three areas. The first is BAE Systems Incorporated, which includes the company's US-based businesses, Land & Armaments, Electronic Solutions, Intelligence & Security, Platform Solutions and Support Solutions. The second division is Programmes and Support, which includes the company's UK military, air and information business, maritime activities and the Detica security business. The third division is International, which includes the company's business operations in Saudi Arabia, Australia, India and Oman. It also includes a 37.5 per cent interest in MBDA, a joint venture missile developer and manufacturer that was formed by a merger of Aérospatiale–Matra Missiles, Finmeccanica and Matra BAe Dynamics in December 2001. The company also has a 10.2 per cent shareholding in Saab in Sweden and a 49 per cent shareholding in Air Astana. Today BAE Systems is one of the largest businesses in the UK. It is a global defence and security company that employs more than 100,000 people around the world. In 2010 the company reported sales of £22.4 billion and had customers in more than 100 countries. Despite its size and its undoubted business success BAE Systems recognizes that it owes a great deal to its heritage, to the pioneering heroes and their aviation landmarks that defended Britain in its hour of need and who opened up the skies and allowed business people and holidaymakers across the decades to pursue adventures of their own.

Appendix 1

Summary of the Main British Aviation, Mergers, Acquisitions and Nationalizations

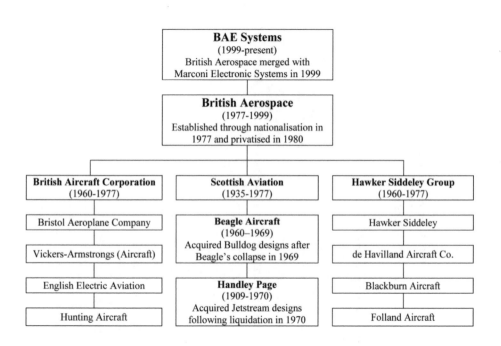

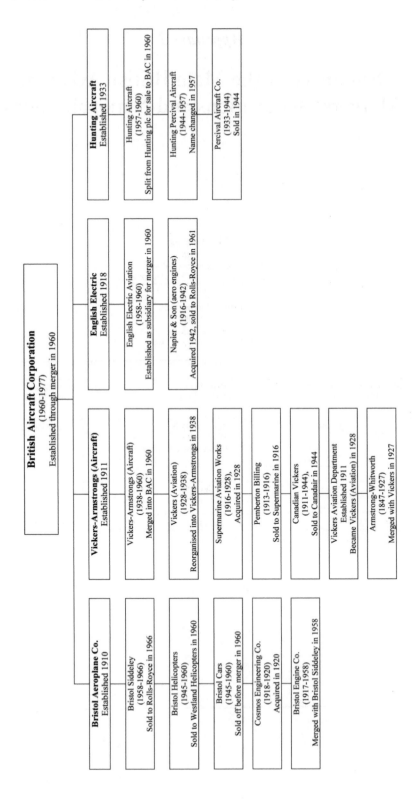

British Aircraft Corporation
(1960-1977)
Established through merger in 1960

Bristol Aeroplane Co.
Established 1910

Bristol Siddeley
(1958-1966)
Sold to Rolls-Royce in 1966

Bristol Helicopters
(1945-1960)
Sold to Westland Helicopters in 1960

Bristol Cars
(1945-1960)
Sold off before merger in 1960

Cosmos Engineering Co.
(1918-1920)
Acquired in 1920

Bristol Engine Co.
(1917-1958)
Merged with Bristol Siddeley in 1958

Vickers-Armstrongs (Aircraft)
Established 1911

Vickers-Armstrongs (Aircraft)
(1938-1960)
Merged into BAC in 1960

Vickers (Aviation)
(1928-1938)
Reorganised into Vickers-Armstrongs in 1938

Supermarine Aviation Works
(1916-1928),
Acquired in 1928

Pemberton Billing
(1913-1916)
Sold to Supermarine in 1916

Canadian Vickers
(1911-1944),
Sold to Canadair in 1944

Vickers Aviation Department
Established 1911
Became Vickers (Aviation) in 1928

Armstrong-Whitworth
(1847-1927)
Merged with Vickers in 1927

English Electric
Established 1918

English Electric Aviation
(1958-1960)
Established as subsidiary for merger in 1960

Napier & Son (aero engines)
(1916-1942)
Acquired 1942, sold to Rolls-Royce in 1961

Hunting Aircraft
Established 1933

Hunting Aircraft
(1957-1960)
Split from Hunting plc for sale to BAC in 1960

Hunting Percival Aircraft
(1944-1957)
Name changed in 1957

Percival Aircraft Co.
(1933-1944)
Sold in 1944

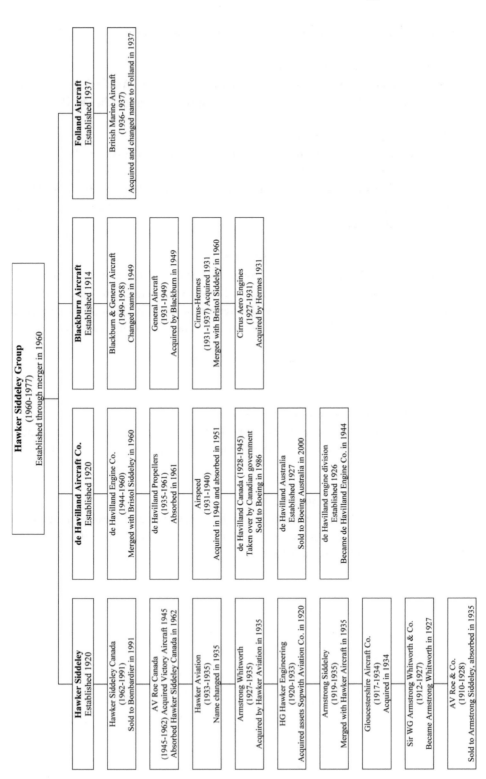

Hawker Siddeley Group
(1960-1977)
Established through merger in 1960

Hawker Siddeley Aircraft Co.
Established 1920

de Havilland Engine Co.
(1944-1960)
Merged with Bristol Siddeley in 1960

de Havilland Propellers
(1935-1961)
Absorbed in 1961

Airspeed
(1931-1940)
Acquired in 1940 and absorbed in 1951

de Havilland Canada (1928-1945)
Taken over by Canadian government
Sold to Boeing in 1986

de Havilland Australia
Established 1927
Sold to Boeing Australia in 2000

de Havilland engine division
Established 1926
Became de Havilland Engine Co. in 1944

Blackburn Aircraft
Established 1914

Blackburn & General Aircraft
(1949-1958)
Changed name in 1949

General Aircraft
(1931-1949)
Acquired by Blackburn in 1949

Cirrus-Hermes
(1931-1937) Acquired 1931
Merged with Bristol Siddeley in 1960

Cirrus Aero Engines
(1927-1931)
Acquired by Hermes 1931

Folland Aircraft
Established 1937

British Marine Aircraft
(1936-1937)
Acquired and changed name to Folland in 1937

Hawker Siddeley
Established 1920

Hawker Siddeley Canada
(1962-1991)
Sold to Bombardier in 1991

AV Roe Canada
(1945-1962) Acquired Victory Aircraft 1945
Absorbed Hawker Siddeley Canada in 1962

Hawker Aviation
(1933-1935)
Name changed in 1935

Armstrong Whitworth
(1927-1935)
Acquired by Hawker Aviation in 1935

HG Hawker Engineering
(1920-1933)
Acquired assets Sopwith Aviation Co. in 1920

Armstrong Siddeley
(1919-1935)
Merged with Hawker Aircraft in 1935

Gloucestershire Aircraft Co.
(1917-1934)
Acquired in 1934

Sir WG Armstrong Whitworth & Co.
(1912-1927)
Became Armstrong Whitworth in 1927

AV Roe & Co.
(1910-1928)
Sold to Armstrong Siddeley, absorbed in 1935

Other Companies not Associated with the 1960 Mergers

Short Brothers (1908 to present)
Airship assets at Cardington nationalized in 1919. Aircraft production nationalized in 1943. Privatized in 1984. Acquired by Bombardier in 1989.

Handley Page (1909–1970)
Went into voluntary liquidation in 1970. Handley Page Transport (1909–1924), assets merged with British Marine Air Navigation Company Ltd, Daimler Airway and Instone Air Line Ltd to create Imperial Airways in 1924. Miles Aircraft, acquired assets after the company went into receivership in 1947 and became Handley Page (Reading) Ltd

Sopwith Aviation Company (1912–1920)
Established in Kingston-upon-Thames by Thomas Sopwith in June 1912. Entered into voluntary liquidation in 1920 following demand for Excess Profits Duty. Thomas Sopwith and Harry Hawker established HG Hawker Engineering shortly afterwards and bought the Sopwith Aviation Company's assets.

Aircraft Manufacturing Company, Airco (1912–1920)
Bankrupt in 1920.

Fairey Aviation Company (1915–1960)
Aircraft production was taken over by Westland Aircraft, which subsequently merged with Saunders-Roe and the Bristol helicopter division in 1961 to form Westland Helicopters.

Power Jets Limited (1936–1945)
Nationalized in 1945 and became Power Jets (Research and Development) Ltd. Merged with Turbine Division of the Royal Aircraft Establishment to form the National Gas Turbine Establishment.

Selected UK Aviation Museums

This appendix contains a cross section of the many and varied aviation museums that can be visited around the UK. Details of their current range of exhibits and calendar of events can usually be found on their websites.

Brooklands Museum Trust Ltd
Brooklands Road
Weybridge
Surrey
KT13 0QN
Website: www.brooklandsmuseum.com

The de Havilland Aircraft Heritage Centre
Salisbury Hall
London Colney
Hertfordshire
AL2 1BU
Website: www.dehavillandmuseum.co.uk

Dumfries & Galloway Aviation Museum
Former Control Tower
Heathhall Industrial Estate
Dumfries
Scotland
DG1 3PH
Website: www.dumfriesaviationmuseum.com

Fleet Air Arm Museum
RNAS Yeovilton
Ilchester
Somerset
BA22 8HT
Website: www.fleetairarm.com

Imperial War Museum Duxford
Duxford Airfield
Duxford
Cambridgeshire
CB22 4QR
Website: http://duxford.iwm.org.uk

Midland Air Museum (Incorporating the Sir Frank Whittle Jet Heritage Centre)
Coventry Airport
Baginton
Warwickshire,
CV8 3AZ
Website: www.midlandairmuseum.co.uk

North East Aircraft Museum
Old Washington Road
Sunderland
SR5 3HZ
Website: www.neam.org.uk

RAF Museum Cosford
Shifnal
Shropshire
TF11 8UP
Website: www.rafmuseum.org.uk/cosford/

RAF Museum London
Grahame Park Way
Hendon
London
NW9 5LL
Website: www.rafmuseum.org.uk/london/

Science Museum, London
Exhibition Road
South Kensington
London
SW7 2DD
Website: www.sciencemuseum.org.uk

The Shuttleworth Collection
Shuttleworth (Old Warden) Aerodrome
Nr. Biggleswade,
Bedfordshire
SG18 9EP
Website: www.shuttleworth.org

Solway Aviation Society
Aviation House
Carlisle Airport
Crosby-On-Eden
Carlisle
Cumbria
CA6 4NW
Website: www.solway-aviation-museum.co.uk

Tangmere Military Aviation Museum
Tangmere
Nr Chichester
West Sussex
PO20 2ES
Website: www.tangmere-museum.org.uk

Yorkshire Air Museum
Elvington
York
YO41 4AU
Website: www.yorkshireairmuseum.org

Bibliography

Books

Adams, Jane, Chandler, D. and Robertson, F. (eds), *The World at War: 1939–1945* (CLB, 1991)

Barnes, CH, *Handley Page Aircraft since 1907* (Putnam, 1987)

Barnes, CH, *Shorts Aircraft since 1900* (US Naval Institute Press, 1989)

Bingham, Victor, *Halifax, Second to None* (Airlife, 1986)

Bowyer, C, *The Encyclopedia of British Military Aircraft* (Arms & Armour, 1982)

Broke-Smith, PWL, *History of Early British Military Aeronautics* (Chivers, 1968)

Bruce, JM, *British Aeroplanes 1914–1918* (Bodley Head, 1969)

Clarke, Basil, *The History of Airships* (Jenkins, 1961)

Conisbee, LR, *A Bedfordshire Bibliography* (Bedfordshire Historical Record Society, 1962)

Donald, David, *The Complete Encyclopaedia of World Aircraft* (Barnes Noble, 1998)

Edwards, Peter J, *The Rise and Fall of the Japanese Imperial Naval Air Service* (Pen and Sword Aviation Books, 2010)

Everett, Susanne and Young, Brigadier P, *The Two World Wars* (Bison Books, 1980)

Frederickson, John, *International Warbirds: An Illustrated Guide to World Military Aircraft, 1914–2000* (ABC CLIO, 2001)

Gillies, Midge, *Amy Johnson, Queen of the Air* (Phoenix, 2003)

Godber, Joyce, *History of Bedfordshire* (Bedfordshire County Council, 1999)

Gray, Charles, *A History of the Air Ministry* (Allen and Unwin, 1940)

Green, William, *War Planes of the Second World War: Volume 7 Bombers and Reconnaissance Aircraft* (Macdonald, 1967)

Green, William and Swanborough, G, compiled by, *An Illustrated Anatomy of the World's Fighters* (Salamander, 2001)

Green, William and Swanborough, Gordon, *The Complete Book of Fighters* (Salamander, 1980)

Green, William, *The Great Book of Fighters* (Zenith, 2001)

Green, William, *The Macdonald Aircraft Handbook* (Macdonald, 1964)

Green, William, *The Observer's Book of Aircraft* (Warne, 1955)

Gunston, Bill, *Jane's Fighting Aircraft of World War II* (Jane's Information Group, 2001)

Gunston, Bill, *Illustrated Encyclopaedia of Combat Aircraft of World War II* (Salamander, 1990)

Gunston, Bill, *The Illustrated Encyclopaedia of Combat Aircraft of World War II – A Technical Directory of The War Planes of 1939 to 1945* (Salamander, 1978)

Hearne, RP, *Airships in Peace and War, Being the Second Edition of Aerial Warfare* (Bodley Head, 1910)

Higham, Robin, *The British Rigid Airship 1908–1931* (GT Foulis, 1961)

Hood, Joseph F, *Story of Airships, When Monsters Roamed the Skies* (Arthur Barker, 1968)

Hough, Richard and Richards, Denis, *The Battle of Britain: The Jubilee History* (Guild, 1990)

Imrie, Alex, *Pictorial History of the German Army Air Service 1914–1918* (Ian Allan, 1971)

Jackson, Aubrey, *Avro Aircraft since 1908* (Putnam, 1965)

Jackson, Aubrey, *Blackburn Aircraft since 1909* (Putnam, 1989)

Jackson, Aubrey, *British Civil Aircraft since 1919*, Volume 1 (Putnam, 1973)

Jackson, Robert, *Strike from the Sea: A Survey of British Naval Air Operations, 1909– 1969* (Barber, 1970)

Jackson, Robert, *The Encyclopedia of Military Aircraft* (Parragon, 2002)

Jackson, Robert, *The Encyclopedia of Aircraft* (Amber Books, 2004)

Johnson, Brian, *The Secret War* (BBC, 1978)

Kemp, Lieutenant Commander P, *Fleet Air Arm* (Jenkins, 1954)

Lessor, James, *The Millionth Chance: The Story of the R101* (Hamish Hamilton, 1957)

Lewis, Peter, *Squadron Histories RFC, RNAS, RAF since 1912* (Putnam, 1959)

Lewis, Peter, *The British Bomber Since 1914* (Putnam, 2003)

Loftin, Laurence, *Quest for Performance* (United States Government Printing, 1985)

London, Peter, *British Flying Boats* (History Press, 2011)

Lysons, Rev. Dan and Lysons, Samuel, *Magna Britannia* (1806 T. Cadell and W. Davies, 1806)

March, Daniel (ed.) *British Warplanes of World War II* (Aerospace Publishing, 1998)

Mason, Francis, *The British Bomber Since 1914* (Putnam, 1994)

Mawer, A and Stenton, FM (eds.) *Place-names of Bedfordshire and Huntingdonshire*, Vol. 3 (English Place-Name Society, 1926)

McKinty, Alec, *Father of British Airships: Biography of ET Willows* (Kimber, 1972)

Meager AFC, Captain George, *My Airship Flights, 1915–1930* (Kimber, 1970)

Page FSA, William, *Victoria History of the County of Bedfordshire* (Constable & Company Limited, 1912)

Pevsner, Nickolaus, *Buildings of England (Beds, Hunts and Peterborough)* (Yale University Press, 1968)

Popham, Hugh, *Into Wind* (Hamish Hamilton, 1969)

Preston, Anthony, *History of the Royal Navy* (Bison, 1983)

Probert, HA, *The Rise and Fall of the German Air Force 1933 to 1945* (Arms & Armour Press, 1983)

Sanders, Hilary St. George, *Per Ardua – The Rise of British Air Power 1911–1939* (Ayer, 1971)

Sekigawa, Eiichiro, *Japanese Military Aviation* (Ian Allan, 1974)

Sinclair, Captain JA, *Airships in Peace and War* (Rich & Cowen, 1934)

Taylor, HA, *Fairey Aircraft Since 1915* (US Naval Institute Press, 1989)

Thetford, Owen, *Aircraft of the Fighting Powers* Vol. VII (Argus Books, 1946)

Thetford, Owen, *Aircraft of the Royal Air Force 1918–57* (Putnam, 1957)

Thetford, Owen, *Aircraft of the Royal Air Force* (Putnam, 2003)

Thetford, Owen, *British Naval Aircraft Since 1912* (US Naval Institute Press, 1991)

Toland, John, *Ships in the Sky* (Müller, 1957)

Winchester, Jim, *The World's Worst Aircraft: From Pioneering Failures to Multimillion Dollar Disasters* (Grange Books, 2007)

Winton, John, *Find, Fix and Strike – The FAA at War 1939–1945* (Batsford, 1980)

Wood, Derek and Dempter, Derek, *The Definitive Story of the Battle of Britain the Narrow Margin* (Arrow, 1969)

Grey, CC (ed.), *Jane's All the World's Aircraft, 1919* (David & Charles, 1969)
Taylor, John (ed.), *Jane's All the World's Aircraft, 1988–1989* (Jane's Information Group, 1988)
Taylor, John WR (ed.) *Jane's All the World's Aircraft, 1980–1981* (Jane's Information Group, 1988)
Taylor, Michael, *Jane's Encyclopaedia of Aviation* (Jane's Information Group, 1993)

Periodicals and Publications
Brewer, Griffith, 'The Short Brothers – A Personal Tribute' (*Flight*, 20/04/1939)
Bruce, JM, 'Sopwith Camel' (*Flight*, 22/04/1955)
Dafter, Ray, Article, title unknown (*Financial Times*, 05/11/1970)
Fedden, Sir Roy, 'Remembering Rex Pierson' (*Flight*, 21/11/1952)
Harper, Harry, 'The First Official Air-Mail' (*Flight*, 31/08/1951)
King George V, HM, 'The King's Message (R101)' (*Flight*, 10/10/1930)
King, HF, 'Mars to Javelin, Gloster Aircraft of Forty Years' (*Flight*, 27/05/1955)
Lockwood Marsh Lieutenant-Colonel W, 'Twenty One Years of Airship Progress' (*Flight*, 03/01/1930)
Macmillan, Wing Commander Norman, 'Who Designed the Famous Sopwith Types?' (*Flight*, 30/12/1960)
Peter Middleton, 'British Airways Looks Ahead' (*Flight International*, 08/03/1973)
Ramsden, JM, 'The Heroes, Flight's 70th Birthday' (*Flight*, 06/01/1979)
Simpson, John, 'Company Snapshot: Short Brothers plc' (*Belfast Telegraph*, 26/05/2009)

No author credited in the original publication
Aircraft and Shipbuilding Industries Act 1977, (HMSO, 1977)
Airship Manufacture by Short Bros. 1910-1921 Appendix B, (Short Brothers Limited, Publicity Department)
'Baron de Forest's £4,000 Prize' (*Flight*, 07/01/1911)
'East West Air Race' (*The Argus*, Melbourne, 23/09/1929)
'Fifteen Years Work by Imperial Airways' (*Flight*, 15/06/1939)
'Fifty Years to Paris' (*Flight International*, 21/08/1969)
Finance Act 1920 (HMSO, 1920)
'Imperial Airways Ltd' (*Flight*, 12/06/1924)
'London Terminal Aerodrome' (*Flight*, 16/08/1923)
'National Air Transport' (*Flight*, 30/08/1923)
Obituaries, Sir Frank Whittle (*The Daily Telegraph*, 10/08/1996)
'Profile: Sir Thomas Sopwith, The Hustler Who Always Keeps Calm' (*New Scientist*, 31/01/1957)
'*R101* Disaster' (*Flight*, 05/12/1930)
'Schneider Contest, 1931' (*Flight*, 14/08/1931)
'Some 1917 Type German Aeroplanes' (*Flight*, 12/07/1917)
'The British Aircraft Industry' (*Flight*, 29/05/1929)
'The Second *Daily Mail* £10,000 Prize' (*Flight*, 02/07/1910)
'The Story of a Yorkshireman's Pre-war Ventures and the Great Aircraft Business that was Born of Them' (*Flight*, 25/05/1939)
'Thirty Short Years' (*Flight*, 20/04/1939)
UK Shipping News (The Chamber of Shipping [Information Division] and the British Shipping Federation, December 1970/January 1971)
'Zeppelin Sheds Attacked by British' (*The New York Times* 21/07/1918)

Broadcasts

Battle of Britain: The Real Story (BBC, 2010)

Dam Busters, Building the Bouncing Bomb (Channel 4, 2011)

Spitfire Women (BBC, 2010)

Welcome to Sherwood: The Story of The Adventures of Robin Hood (Warner Bros. DVD, 2004)

Wellington Bomber (BBC, 2010)

Correspondence

British Aircraft Corporation

Buckley, Rear Admiral PN, Historical Records Section, Navy Department, Ministry of Defence

RAW Cardington employees Mr J Armstrong, Mr L Speed, Mr W Bowman, Mr L Ambler

Leader, Wing Commander, Station Commander, RAF Cardington 1950

Tibbutt, HG, Deputy Records Officer, Air Force Department, Ministry of Defence

Index